PLANTING THE GARDEN

Most women, until recently, were confined to the private sphere and an informal labour market. Only the women who operated outside this sphere as wage earners or reformers for social, economic and political causes attracted the attention of historians. The development of social history has widened the scope of historical research to include the majority of women who have until now been ignored by historical writing. This bibliography helps us to discover the daily lives, activities and beliefs of women who remained in the private sphere.

Mary Kinnear and Vera Fast have compiled and annotated a listing of over 1,400 archival records in Manitoba - oral, written and pictorial - providing both academics and general researchers with an invaluable tool for their inquiry into the historical situation of women.

This pioneering work will help historians to integrate the experience of women into a more comprehensive understanding of Manitoba history.

Mary Kinnear is an associate professor in the Department of History at the University of Manitoba.

Vera Fast is an archivist at the Provincial Archives of Manitoba.

MARY KINNEAR VERA FAST

PLANTING THE GARDEN

An Annotated Archival Bibliography
of the History of Women
in Manitoba

The University of Manitoba Press

© The University of Manitoba Press   1987
Winnipeg, Manitoba, R3T 2N2
Printed in Canada

Cover illustration: <u>Winnipeg</u> <u>Free</u> <u>Press</u> photograph,
Western Canada Pictorial Index, University of Winnipeg.

Cataloguing in Publication Data

Kinnear, Mary, 1942-
    Planting the garden : an annotated archival
bibliography of the history of women in Manitoba.

    Includes index.
    ISBN 0-88755-140-8

    1.Women--Manitoba--History--Bibliography.
2.Women--Manitoba--History--Sources--Bibliography.
I. Fast, Vera K., 1929- II. Title.
Z7964.C32M36 1987   016.3054'097127   C86-098053-7

When the baby is born and the garden's planted, spring has
arrived.

                              Alma Barkman in Mennonite Memories

C O N T E N T S

A C K N O W L E D G E M E N T S

This bibliography is the fruit of teamwork which operated over
several years. Vera Fast did the fieldwork and provided
invaluable advice concerning the neat pigeonholes into which we
placed the somewhat recalcitrant material. Richard Bennett was
the professional archival consultant. Debbie Norman created the
computer program and managed data entry. I thank Cathy Carlson,
Bev Suderman, Suzanne Grierson, Ronald Harpelle and Peter Nunoda
for help with data collection, and Michael Angel and Greg Mason
for general advice. Carol Adam and Lorenne Reimer typed the
manuscript. It was a pleasure to work with Patricia Dowdall,
Carol Dahlstrom and Richard Goulet of the University of Manitoba
Press. I retain overall responsibility for the project, and give
grateful acknowledgment to the University of Manitoba Research
Board, and the Social Sciences and Humanities Research Council of
Canada for research grants.

Mary Kinnear
St. John's College, University of Manitoba
August 1986

ABBREVIATIONS OF REPOSITORIES

A St-B Archdiocese of Saint-Boniface (Roman Catholic) Archives, 151 rue de la Cathédrale, Saint-Boniface, Manitoba, R2H 0H6.

AWC Archdiocese of Winnipeg (Roman Catholic) Chancery, 500 Stafford Street, Winnipeg, Manitoba, R3M 2V7.

AWCLH Archive of Western Canadian Legal History, Faculty of Law, University of Manitoba, Winnipeg, R3T 2N2.

BCA Boissevain Community Archives, 436 South Railway Street, Boissevain, Manitoba, R0K 0E0.

BGHA Brandon General Hospital Archives, 150 McTavish Avenue E., Brandon, R7A 2B3.

BMHCA Brandon Mental Health Centre Archives, Box 420, Brandon, Manitoba, R7A 5Z5.

BPL Brandon Public Library, 638 Princess Avenue, Brandon, R7H 0P3.

BUA Brandon University Archives, Umphrey Centre, Victoria at 20th Street, Manitoba, R7A 6A9.

CBWFT CSB Radio Canada CBWFT, programmes located in the archives of Collège Universitaire de Saint-Boniface, 200 ave de la Cathédrale, Saint-Boniface, R3H 0H7.

CCCJ Canadian Council of Christians and Jews, 110-388 Donald Street, Winnipeg, R3B 2J4.

CEFCO Centre d'Etudes Franco-Canadiennes de l'Ouest, 200 ave de la Cathédrale, Saint-Boniface, R2H 0H7.

CMBC Canadian Mennonite Bible College, 600 Shaftesbury Blvd., Winnipeg, R3P 0M4.

CMS Church Missionary Society. Provincial Archives of Manitoba, Winnipeg, R3C OV8.

CRIAW Canadian Research Institute for the Advancement of Women, 151 Slater Street, Suite 415, Ottawa, Ontario, K1P 6C4.

CSB Collège Universitaire de Saint-Boniface, 200 ave de la Cathédrale, Saint-Boniface, R3H 0H7.

CWA City of Winnipeg Archives, 380 William Avenue, Winnipeg, R3A 0J1.

DBA Diocese of Brandon Archives, 341-13th Street, Brandon, R7A 4P8.

DEL Manitoba Department of Education Library, 1181 Portage Avenue, Winnipeg, R3G 0T3.

DHM Daly House Museum, 122-18th Street, Brandon, R7A 5A4 (Assiniboine Historical Society).

DKA Diocese of Keewatin (Anglican) Archives, P.O. Box 118, Kenora, Ontario, P9N 3X1 (217A-6th First Avenue South, Kenora).

DMA J.A.V. David Museum Archives, 414 Williams Avenue, Box 584, Killarney, Manitoba, R0K 1G0.

ERL Evergreen Regional Library, 63 First Avenue, Box 1140, Gimli, Manitoba, R0C 1B0.

FFHS/FFPL Flin Flon Historical Society papers, deposited with the Flin Flon Public Library, 58 Main Street, Flin Flon, Manitoba, R8A 1J8.

GNPHA Grey Nuns Provincial House Archives (Soeurs de la Charité de Montreal ou Soeurs Grises de Montreal), 151 rue Despins, Saint-Boniface, R2H 0L7.

HBCA Hudson's Bay Company Archives, 200 Vaughan Street, Winnipeg, R3C 0V8.

HBHL Hudson's Bay House Library, 77 Main Street, Winnipeg, R3C 2R1.

HP DEP CW Historic Projects, Department of Environment Planning, City of Winnipeg, 395 Main Street, Winnipeg, R3B 1A6.

HRCCL Human Rights Commission of Canada Library, 200-323 Portage Avenue, Winnipeg, R3B 2C1.

HW MROL Health and Welfare Department, Manitoba Regional Office Library, 500-303 Main Street, Winnipeg, R3C 0H4.

IUS/U of W Institute of Urban Studies, University of Winnipeg, 515 Portage Avenue, Winnipeg, R3B 2E9.

JHSA Jewish Historical Society of Western Canada Archives, 402-365 Hargrave Street, Winnipeg, R3B 2K3.

JPL Jewish Public Library, 1725 Main Street, Winnipeg, R2V 1Z4.

LEG LIB Legislative Library, 200 Vaughan Street, Winnipeg, R3C
0V8.

MARNL Manitoba Association of Registered Nurses Library, 647
Broadway Avenue, Winnipeg, R3C 0X2.

MBA Mennonite Brethren Archives (Centre for Mennonite Brethren
Studies in Canada), 77 Henderson Highway, Winnipeg, R2L 1L1.

MHCA Mennonite Heritage Centre Archives, 600 Shaftesbury Blvd.,
Winnipeg, R3P 0M4.

MMN Manitoba Museum of Man and Nature Library, 190 Rupert
Avenue, Winnipeg, R3B 0N2.

MPC Musée Pointe-des-Chenes Villa Youville, Sainte-Anne,
Manitoba, R0A 1R0.

MSB Musée de Saint-Boniface, 494 Taché, Saint-Boniface Manitoba,
R2H 2B2.

MVMA Mennonite Village Museum Archives, Box 1136, Steinbach,
Manitoba, R0A 2A0.

NFB National Film Board, 245 Main Street, Winnipeg, R3C 1A7.

NFU National Farmers' Union, Manitoba Region, 2999-B Pembina
Highway, Winnipeg, R3T 3R1.

PABC Public Archives of British Columbia, 655 Belleville Street,
Victoria, B.C., V8V 1X4.

PAM Provincial Archives of Manitoba, 200 Vaughan Street,
Winnipeg, R3C 0V8.

PPPL Portage la Prairie Public Library, 170 Saskatchewan Avenue
W., Portage la Prairie, Manitoba, R1N 0M1.

RBC/UMA Rare Books Collection, University of Manitoba Archives,
Winnipeg, R3T 2N2.

RDRL Russell and District Regional Library, Russell, Manitoba,
R0J 1W0.

RLDA Rupert's Land Diocesan Archives, 935 Nesbitt Bay, Winnipeg,
R3T 1W5.

RWBA Royal Winnipeg Ballet Archives, 289 Portage Avenue,
Winnipeg, R3B 2B7.

SBHSA Saint-Boniface Historical Society Archives (La Société
Historique de Saint-Boniface), C.P. 125, Saint-Boniface, R2H
3B4.

SCRLM South Central Regional Library, Morden, Manitoba, R0G 1J0.

SMHCL   Selkirk Mental Health Centre Library, P.O. Box 9600, Selkirk, Manitoba, R1A 2B5.

St.JCA   St. John's College Archives, 400 Dysart Rd., Winnipeg, R3T 2M5.

TPL   Thompson Public Library, 81 Thompson Drive, Thompson, Manitoba, R8N 0C3.

TPPL   The Pas Public Library, 53 Edwards Avenue, Box 410, The Pas, Manitoba, R9A 1R2.

TRHM   Transcona Regional History Museum, 141 Regent Avenue W., Winnipeg, R2C 1R1.

UCA-W   United Church of Canada, Manitoba and Northwest Ontario Conference, Archives, University of Winnipeg, 515 Portage Avenue, Winnipeg, R3B 2E9.

UCECA   Ukrainian Cultural and Educational Centre Archives, 184 Alexander Avenue E., Winnipeg, R3B 0L6.

UMA   University of Manitoba Archives, Winnipeg, R3T 2N2.

UMMFA   University of Manitoba Medical Faculty Archives, 770 Bannatyne Avenue, Winnipeg, R3E 0W3.

WAGA   Winnipeg Art Gallery Archives, 300 Memorial Blvd., Winnipeg, R3C 1V1.

WCAM   Western Canada Aviation Museum, Hangar T2, Winnipeg International Airport, 958 Ferry Road, Winnipeg, R3H 0Y8.

WCPI/U of W   Western Canada Pictorial Index, Room 3G18, Media Services, University of Winnipeg, 515 Portage Avenue, Winnipeg, R3B 2E9.

WFPA Winnipeg Free Press Archives, 300 Carlton Street, Winnipeg, R3C 3C1.

WRL   Winkler Regional Library, Box 1030, Winkler, Manitoba, R0G 2Z0.

I N T R O D U C T I O N

This annotated archival bibliography is intended to aid both
academic and general researchers in their enquiry into the
historical situation of women in Manitoba. We define
"historical" as material relating to what happened before 1980;
"Manitoba" as the area covered by the boundaries established in
1912; and "archival" as relating to original documentary
material. We include pictures and tapes, but exclude most
other published printed material. We do not carry published
books or government reports but provide an appendix of
photographs. Other bibliographical guides are available which
include such entries, and we preferred to reduce duplication.[1]
   "Women" do not comprise a single homogeneous group.
Moreover, the population of Manitoba for a large part of the
last 150 years or so has rarely stayed still. Especially
during the generation before World War 1, many people migrated
to the province and soon moved further west. We have counted as
"women in Manitoba" those who lived a significant portion of
their lives here, acknowledging that this is an imprecise
measure. We have confined the bibliography to archival sources
available within the province.
   Categorization is a difficulty. The nineteenth-century
division of society by gender into public and private is an
understandable rift between male and female. One effect was to
banish women altogether from old-fashioned history, which was
conceived as the record and explanation of what went on in
public - male - life. In the twentieth century, social history
- meaning the history of an entire society, including the women
- has provided the vehicle for retrieval of material whose
relevance to political, diplomatic, constitutional, economic
and social events had not hitherto been apparent. The old
classifications and the old questions no longer suffice if we
wish to discover social structures and the experience of other
groups in society besides the male elites. New categories must
be offered, and new questions asked, realistically related to
the experience of newly examined groups.
   Most women until fairly recently were confined to the
private sphere and an informal labour market. Women of all
sorts were united in their reproductive activity, of
child-bearing, child-rearing and household management; but were
at the same time divided by class, religion and ethnic and
cultural background. The history of women is not to be
interpreted merely as an account of the few women who found
themselves outside the private sphere, at least occasionally,

as wage earners or reformers for social, economic and political
causes. Such women were exceptional and their activities were
important, as keys to their own biographies and also because of
the effect on other women of their own times and later. But
social history encourages us to study unexceptional people too.
This bibliography points the way to a discovery of the daily
lives, activities and beliefs of women who remained in the
private sphere. In one form or another they accepted the world
as it was, and tried to cope with life's opportunities and
problems as well as they could. These women include those who
frequently bore children, managed the farm accounts, worked the
vegetable garden and devised their own ways for accommodating
the stress of isolation; others who for a brief period of their
lives were the working poor, in Winnipeg candy factories,
earning a wage designed to bind them to their parental homes;
and women whose extra-domestic diversion was to discuss
missionary activity in China. We want to know who they were,
what they did and what they thought of the world around them.
Narrative history must be supplemented, if not supplanted, by
structural analysis of a society teeming with women's
activities which were rarely dignified by the term "work." We
need to add a further dimension. What were their perspectives?
How did their different viewpoints influence their behaviour
and beliefs? These are questions of prime importance when we
appreciate that the transmission of culture - standards,
values, attitudes and beliefs - was one of women's major
reproductive responsibilities. Answers are partly determined
by women's own testimony. Such witness, on paper or tape, is a
modern resource. Only in the last century has the spread of
literacy permitted ordinary women to record their own
articulate observations. As more social history is written, the
private sphere will disclose more of its secrets.

The bibliography is arranged in three general categories,
referring to identity, work and activities, and mentality. The
first is a consideration of identity. Who were the women? What
was their background? In this category are placed the large
number of biographical, autobiographical and local-history
collections, archives relating to early settlement, native life
and immigration.

The second category concerns their work and activities.
What did they do? What was their education or training? What
sort of renumerated labour did they perform, both in the formal
work force with its wages and fringe benefits and in the
informal economy, hidden from public record? What unpaid labour
did they do, both outside the home, on farms, for instance, and
within the home? Included in these considerations is the
reproductive work done by most women as their primary
occupation: their household work of rearing children and
homemaking. Here too is included the volunteer work which after
the nineteenth century became such a staple of women's way of
life. A substantial part of this section relates to social
welfare agencies whose dispensers and clients have been mainly
women.

The third general classification is mentality. How did women
interpret their environments? How did they define their fates?

PLANTING THE GARDEN

_____

BIOGRAPHICAL, AUTOBIOGRAPHICAL AND LOCAL HISTORY COLLECTIONS

1. ALLARD FAMILY
      Family file, 1946-69.
      1/4".   SBHSA (Box 7)

      Genealogical notes; marriage announcements; family
      tree.

2. ALLARY, RAPHAEL AND MME.
      Oral history, restricted (French). 1969.
      1 reel (7"), worksheet.   MMN (Tape 548-2)

      Métis beliefs, legends, customs and cooking recipes
      by these St. Eustache, Manitoba, pioneers.

3. ALTONA, MANITOBA
      Sawatsky, Louise.   "Index to 'Recalling Past Days' in
      Red River Valley Echo."
      Unpublished paper, 1979.   MHCA (Vertical file)

      Pioneer women in the Altona area.

4. ALTONA, MANITOBA
      "Pioneer Portraits: Mennonite Centennial Hymn Sing,
      Altona, 1974."
      Typed booklet, 1974.   WRL (MG2)

      Biographical sketches of Mrs. Maria Friesen of
      Gretna, Mrs. David Loewen of Altona, Catherine Schulz
      of Altona, and other area pioneers.

5. AMBROSE, JESSIE (1908-61)
      Papers, 1911-26.
      5".   PAM (MG14 C96)

      Family correspondence with parents, brother and
      sister who emigrated from England to live in Brandon,

Pioneer life at Selkirk and Berens River, Manitoba,
and southern Alberta; genealogical tables.

1 reel (7"), worksheet.   MMN (Tape 323)

12. BACON, VIOLA
    Reminiscences, 1888-1984.
    3 pp. Typescript.   PAM (MG8 A22)

    Reminiscences of Norway House, Manitoba, and
    Methodist Church.

13. BAERG, ANNA
    Papers.   MHCA (Personal Papers
                               XX Vol. 1720-1723)

    Life in Arnaud, Manitoba, during 1930s and 1940s with
    reflections.

14. BAIRD, AGNES
    Oral history, 1972.
    2 reels (7"), worksheet.   MMN (Tape 368 2)

    Her nursing career in World War I, overseas, and
    back in Canada.

15. BAKER, LUCY MARGARET
    Memoirs.   UCA-W

16. BALOUN, JERRY AND ANNA
    Family history.
    1 p. Typescript.   SCRLM

    History of this Polish family in Darlingford,
    Manitoba.

17. BALOUN, WALTER AND RUBY
    Family history.
    3 pp. Typescript.   SCRLM

    History of this Polish family now living in Morden,
    Manitoba.

18. BANNATYNE, ANNIE (1830-1908)
    Family history.
    9 pp. Photostats.   PAM (MG2 C7)

    Histories of Andrew McDermot and A.G.B. Bannatyne
    families.

5

19. BARBER, EDMUND LORENZO (1834-1909)
        Papers, 1849-1956. Finding aid.
        Correspondence, legal papers, business records.
                                PAM (MG14 C66)

        Papers relate primarily to Barber's business
        interests after his arrival in the Red River
        Settlement in 1860. Mrs. Lily Sparrow, his daughter,
        attended to real-estate matters.

20. BASKEN, MOLLY (d. 1970)
        Papers.
        3".   PAM (MG9 A77)

        Correspondence, clippings, notes, and photographs of
        this local author and historian.

21. BATTERSHILL, JOHN W.
        Papers, 1915-17.
        10".   PAM (MG6 D16)

        Frequent correspondence from three sons to their
        parents during World War I; other letters from
        relatives and friends.

22. BAZAY, MRS. M.
        Oral history, 1971.
        1 reel (7"), worksheet.   MMN (Tape 636)

        Ukrainian immigrant. Childhood; trip to Canada;
        marriage; life first in Winnipeg and then permanently
        in Dauphin, Manitoba; references to several Ukrainian
        friends and organizations.

23. BECKER, JOHANN
        Family history, 1837.
        Typescript (German).   MVMA (E673)

        Genealogy and family history of this Mennonite
        family.

24. BELL FAMILY
        Oral history, 1972. Restricted.
        1 reel (7"), worksheet   MMN (Tape 253)

        Jewish immigrant family from Odessa, World
        War I and the Russian Revolution; arrival in Canada
        in mid 1920s to settle in Winnipeg, Manitoba.

25. BELL, CHARLES NAPIER
        Papers.   PAM (MG14 C23)

        Included is a six-page article, "The First White
        Woman in the Canadian West," 1934.

26. BERGEN, ELIZABETH
        "The Bergen-Epp Family History."
        Unpublished paper, 1979.   MHCA (Vertical file)

        Data on both families.

27. BERGER, PAUL AND EVA
        Papers.   PAM (MG10 F3)

        Visa of Eva Berger, 1948; certificate of refugee
        status; marriage certificates; and other documents of
        this Jewish immigrant family.

28. BERNARD, RACHEL
        Booklet, 1901-02.   SBHSA (Box 3)

        Booklet of "Compositions et Exercise" (e.g., "the
        advantage of study"; "autumn"; "dialogue of a young
        girl").

29. BERNHARDT, MRS. A.E.
        Oral history, 1971.
        1 reel (7"), worksheet.   MMN (Tape 55)

        German immigrants. Arrival in Canada from Soratow in
        1910; seasonal celebrations, weddings, funerals and
        life in early Winnipeg; membership in Christ Lutheran
        Church.

30. BERNIER, MADELEINE
        Autobiography.   SBHSA (Box 3)

        Family information; clippings on family plans; and
        other data.

31. BERNSTEIN, EVELYN (1921-   )
        Oral history.   JHSA (Tape 335)

        Personal history and reflections on life on Burrows
        Avenue in Winnipeg's north end; family data.

32. BETKER, MRS. J.
        Oral history, 1971.
        1 reel (7"), worksheet.   MMN (Tape 44)

        A German immigrant. Arrival in Canada in 1897;
        land-clearing and farming in Friedensfeld, Manitoba;
        Winnipeg shopping trips; education.

33. BIRBECK, HENRY
        Family papers.   BCA CMG14 C15

        Ten-page manuscript on Birbeck family history by
        Laura Birbeck; newsclippings about the family;
        separate histories on the Birbeck and Burgess
        families; travel diary of Laura Birbeck, 1976.

34. BISSONIERE FAMILY
        Family history
        Typescript.   SBHSA (Box 3)

        Family life and size, description of grandparents,
        genealogical account of the Bissonière family.

35. BJORNSSON, AOUNN
        Family file.
        Various items.   ERL

        Several sheets of historical information on various
        branches of the family; family genealogy extending
        from 1202 to the present time.

36. BLAND, WINNIFRED E.
        Diaries.
        Original in private possession of Mrs. Ruth Grieve,
        39 McMaster Ave, Winnipeg, Manitoba, R3T 2Y2.

        Diaries of Mrs. Bland up until her marriage in 1913;
        and a biography (typescript) of her written by
        Charles Grieve, her grandson.

37. BLATZ FAMILY
        Blatz, Joan C. "Blatz Family Tree."
        Unpublished paper, 1980.   MHCA (Vertical file)

38. BLATZ, ANDREW
        List, 1875.   MVMA (E891-892)

        List of Mennonite immigrants and the amount of money
        they brought with them.

8

39. BOHONOS, JOHN (IWAN) AND ANNA
    Family history.   ERL

    The 1898 immigration of this Galacian family to the
    Foley district just west of Sandy Hook, Manitoba;
    their farm home; family and Church life; change in
    family fortunes.

40. BOISSEVAIN, MANITOBA
    Biographical collection, 1930s.
    Loose-leaf book of typescripts ("Old Timer's Book").
                                       BCA

    Amassed by W.V. Udall, former publisher of the
    Boissevain Recorder. Individual entries written by
    the individuals themselves, including many women.

41. BOISSEVAIN, MANITOBA
    Carter, Susan. "A Study of Boissevain, Manitoba."

    Unpublished essay, 1977.   BCA (GM9 D3)

42. BOISSEVAIN, MANITOBA
    Genealogy file.   Finding aid.   Restricted.
    Separate entries.   BCA

    Information on over 250 area families.

43. BOISSEVAIN, MANITOBA
    Lists.   BCA (MG9 A2)

    Lists of early settlers in township 5, range 185, and
    townships 5 and 6, range 20. Prepared by Margaret
    McKee in the 1950s.

44. BOISSEVAIN, MANITOBA
    Scrapbook, 1977-78.   BCA (MG10 C18)

    Clippings on the Boissevain Community Centre.

45. BOISSEVAIN, ADOLPHE (1843-1921)
    Correspondence, 1963-73.
    Originals and copies.   BCA (MG14 C9)

    Correspondence between Boissevain family members and
    the town of Boissevain and the Boissevain Community
    Archives; 3 pp.; Boissevain family tree.

46. BONNYCASTLE, MRS. R.
        Oral history, 1972.
        1 reel (7"), worksheet.   MMN (Tape 323)

        Removal from Ottawa to Winnipeg in 1905; and farm
        life in Russell, Manitoba, after her marriage.

47. BOSWELL, CLARENCE MONTAGUE (1876-1965)
        Papers, 1899-1963.   Finding aid.
        20'.   PAM (MG14 C4)

        Personal and family correspondence; professional
        concerns of Mr. Boswell while a barrister at law in
        Souris and later in Winnipeg, Manitoba; scrapbook
        kept by Mrs. Boswell of her school days at St.
        Mary's Academy; courting letters; clippings and
        letters concerning her work with the Federation of
        French Canadian Women, 1927-36.

48. BOUCHER, ETIENNE FAMILY
        Family file.
        Various items.   SBHSA (Box 3)

        Short biographies of Francoise Boucher, 1798-78,
        who accompanied her husband to posts in the
        North-west as wife and interpreter; short history of
        Madelene (Menette) Boucher, 1810-99;
        marriage/baptismal records of Marie Bouchier.

49. BOULTON FAMILY
        Mann, Jessie Boulton. "Pioneering in Western
        Canada." Unpublished paper,
        1970.   PAM (MG10 F2 Box K-M)

        Reminiscences of a pioneer English family in
        south-western Manitoba.

50. BOULTON, CHARLES ARKALL FAMILY
        Papers, 1855-1961.   Finding aid.
        20".   PAM (MG14 B20)

        Early Red River surveyor; settler and farmer in
        Shellmouth area of Manitoba. Correspondence with
        Mrs. C.A. Boulton and children, 1872-1917; Boulton
        family genealogies; Augusta Boulton's speeches and
        reminiscences; other family items.

51. BOURNS, BEULAH
        Letter, 1945.
        1 p. Original and typescript.   UCA-W (Biographical
                                        file)

References to her work as a missionary in Korea and
to her Home Missions work.

52. BOUTAL, PAULINE (1894-1978)
    Oral history, 1972.
    1 reel (7"), worksheet.   MMN (Tape 84)

    Artist. Emigration from France to Canada in 1907 and
    settlement in St. Laurent, Manitoba; father's
    hardships as an unemployed artist; husband's post-war
    printing business; her work as an artist for
    Brigden's (Fashion Art) Ltd.; her co-founding of the
    "Cercle Molière."

53. BOUTAL, PAULINE (1894-1978)
    Resource file.   SBHSA (Box 4)

    Pamphlets; clippings; copies of articles; honours;
    awards.

54. BOWLES, FRANCES (1870-1970)
    Papers.   Finding aid.
    5".   PAM (MG9 A49)

    Chatelaine of Government House, 1965-70.
    Specifications and plans for government House, 1881
    and 1883.

55. BOWSFIELD, MRS.
    Oral history, 1972.
    1 reel (7"), worksheet.   MMN (Tape 369)

    Service as a nurse in Britain in World War I;
    marriage to a Canadian; immigration to Toronto and
    later to Winnipeg, Manitoba, in 1933; family matters.

56. BRADSHAW, LAURA ELIZABETH (1875-1956)
    Reminiscences, 1906 ("Prairie Dreams and Realities")
    74 pp. Typescript.   PAM (MG9 A120)

    Recollections of her childhood in Guelph, Ontario;
    the family move to Fairview Farm near Morden,
    Manitoba.

57. BRAKE, MRS. WILFRED
    Family file.
    Various items.   BCA (MG 14 C59)

Clippings, 1942-76, on Brake family; recipe booklet; music programs; Mrs. Brake's 1977 visit to Africa.

58. BRANCONNIER, ISABELLE (b. 1856)
    Two autobiographies. Handwritten (6 pp);
    typewritten (4 pp).   SBHSA (Box 4)

    Account of the Riel Rebellion; her two marriages; other concerns.

59. BRANDON, MANITOBA
    Biographical clipping files.   BUA

    Numerous files on Brandon-area women.

60. BRAUN, MR. AND MRS. ABRAHAM
    Oral history, 1971.
    1 reel (7"), worksheet.   MMN (Tape 49)

    Mennonite farmers. Settlement; wedding ceremony; Russian dancing.

61. BRELAND, M. JOSUE
    Oral history, 1969.
    1 reel (7").   MMN (Tape 554)

    St. François-Xavier, Manitoba, settler. Sings folk songs.

62. BRIGDEN, BEATRICE (1888-1977)
    Oral history, n.d.
    2 reels (7"), worksheet.   MMN (Tape 584-2)

    Women's suffrage; rights of women; Winnipeg General Strike of 1919; On-to-Ottawa Trek; Political Equality League; Women's Labour League; other of her efforts as a pioneer leader in the women's rights movements.

63. BRIGDEN, BEATRICE (1888-1977)
    Papers, 1904-75. Finding aid.
    6'9". Originals and copies.   PAM (MG14 C19)

    Women's rights activist, reformer, suffrage activist.

    Correspondence with the Department of Social Sciences and Evangelism of the Methodist Church, 1913-20; papers regarding Indian and Métis conferences, 1954-69 and the Indian and Métis Friendship Centre; Voice of Women, 1961-70; Council of Women, 1942-65;

Civil Service Federation of Canada, 1942-66;
International Association of Public Employment
Services, 1948-66; papers of the Voice of Women
including minutes, newsletters, reports, and
financial statements; publications, correspondence,
and minutes of the Winnipeg branch of the Religious
Society and Friends (Quakers) in Canada;
correspondence with T. Albert Moore, General
Secretary of the Department of Social Science and
Evangelism of the Methodist Church, 1912-20.

64. BRISTOW, MRS M.
       Oral history, 1972.
       1 reel (7"), worksheet.   MMN (Tape 437)

       Removal with parents from Ontario to Balmoral,
       Manitoba; life as a teacher; building bees;
       harvesting; and the Depression.

65. BROWN, ALEXANDER (1842-1922)
       Papers, 1872-84.
       1 1/2". Originals and copies.   PAM (MG8 B92)

       Correspondence relating to the family's immigration
       to Winnipeg, Manitoba, in 1872; letters from Margaret
       Alexander Brown; family letters.

66. BROWN, ANNE W.
       Letter, 1885.
       9 pp. Typescript.   PAM (MG1 B32)

       Trip from Montreal, Quebec, to Regina.

67. BROWN, CAROLINE VERE
       Canadian Red Cross
       Invitation, 1915.   PAM (MG14 B45)

       President of the Women's Executive of the Canadian
       Red Cross (Manitoba) inviting Valentine Winkler to
       visit headquarters.

68. BROWN, MARY
       Reminiscences.
       8 3/4". Typescript.   PAM (MG9 A81)

       Reminiscence of Portage Plains, Manitoba, in the
       1870s.

69. BROWNSTONE, CHARLES AND MAGGIE
   Oral history, 1971. Restricted.
   1 reel (7"), worksheet.   MMN (Tape 18)

   Immigration to Canada in 1883 because of anti-Jewish
   persecution in Europe; Jewish family life on a
   Manitoba homestead and in early Winnipeg.

70. BROWNSTONE, GOLDS LAYA
   Oral history, 1972. Restricted.
   1 reel (7"), worksheet.   MMN (Tape 131)

   Jewish immigrant to Winnipeg in 1896; difficulties of
   living on a farm with no previous farming experience;
   her work for Israel.

71. BRUDY, NINA (1924-   )
   Oral history.   JHSA (Tape 328)

   Personal history.

72. BULLOCK, MRS. J.D.
   Reminiscences, 1902-41.
   Typescript.   BCA (MG14 C13)

   Her life in Ninga, Manitoba.

73. CAMPBELL, LT. BEVERLEY
   Biographical sketch.
   1 p. Typescript.   LEG LIB

74. CAMPBELL, MINNIE JULIA BEATRICE (1862-1952)
   Papers, 1865-1944. Finding aid.
   7'.   PAM (MG14 C6)

   Philanthropist, volunteer worker, wife of the
   Honorable Colin H. Campbell. Personal
   correspondence, 1878-1943; correspondence and notes
   of the Fort Garry (Winnipeg) Chapter of the IODE,
   1910-33; correspondence with Canadian Child Welfare
   Bureau, 1918-21; papers of her father, Anson Buck;
   clippings and articles.

75. CARLSON, NELS FAMILY
   Family file, 1888-1932.
   Originals and clippings.   BCA (MG14 C50)

   Two-page manuscript history of the family; 50th
   anniversary; various clippings.

14

76. CARNAHAN, ARTHUR P. AND FLORENCE DOROTHE (1889-1982)
    Papers.
    In private possession of Bill and Helen Schroeder,
    Box 1718, Altona, Manitoba, R0G 0B0.

    Courtship letters; husband-wife correspondence;
    wills; business contracts; postcards; much other
    material regarding these British immigrants, their
    home in Winnipeg, Manitoba, his career as a salesman
    and hers as a contractor.

77. CASSON, MARY
    Autobiography.
    7 pp.   LEG LIB (Biographical
                                   file)

    Manitoba pioneer.

78. CASWELL, MISS C.
    Oral history, 1972.
    1 reel (7"), worksheet.   MMN (Tape 436)

    Removal with parents from Ontario to Rathwell,
    Manitoba; early life in the community; references to
    the Riel Rebellion.

79. CEMETERIES AND FUNERAL HOMES
    Histories.   FFHS/FFPL

    Flin Flon Temporary Cemetery; Ross Lake Cemetery;
    Hillside Cemetery; Channing Cemetery.

80. CHAFE, JAMES
    Oral history, 1971.
    1 reel (7"), worksheet.   MMN (Tape 36)

    Life in father's farm (now corner of Portage and
    Main); early Winnipeg education, recreation,
    transportation; women's franchise.

81. CHAPMAN, R.F. FAMILY
    Memoirs.
    Written by daughter Marge Mrs. Elbern Hawking.
                                   BCA (MG 14 C45)

    History of this Boissevain, Manitoba, family.

82. CHERNIAK, DOMINIC FAMILY
    Reminiscence.
    1 p. Typescript.   ERL

    15

Ukrainian immigrant. Emigration from western Ukraine
to the Teulon, Manitoba, area in 1897.

83. CHILDS, GERTRUDE
          Biographical sheet.
          1 p.   LEG LIB
          (Biographical file)

          Active in formative years of Winnipeg Social Welfare.

84. CHOCHINOV, SARAH (1904-)
          Oral history. Restricted.   JHSA (Tape 340)

          Russian Jewish immigrant in 1923.

85. CHOWN, BRUCE (1893)
          Resource file, 1907-27. Finding aid.
          3".   PAM (MG14 C95)

          Concert programmes; minutes, 1907, of Winnipeg Boys
          Club Ladies Auxiliary; syllabus.

86. CLARKE, FRANK AND FRANCES J.
          Biographical sketches.   LEG LIB (Biographical
                                         file)

          Four-page biographical sketch of Mr. Frank Clark;
          two-page biography of Mrs. Clarke; a 1931 letter
          (typescript).

87. CLIFFE, WILLIAM FAMILY
          Family histories, 1982.   BCA (MG 14 C99)

          Histories of William, Winfred and Austin Cliffe of
          Boissevain, Manitoba; genealogical data compiled by
          Thelma Cole.

88. CLINGEN, IDA
          Correspondence, around 1952.   LEG LIB (Biographical
                                         file)

          To and from this Virden, Manitoba, resident.

89. COATES, ANNIE MAY
          Oral history, 1972.
          1 reel (7"), worksheet.   MMN (Tape 309)

          Homesteading near Portage la Prairie, Manitoba.

90. COATES, PEARL (b. 1898)
        Oral history, 1972.
        1 reel (7"), worksheet.   MMN (Tape 397)

        Sod houses; school days; social life in the Melita,
        Manitoba, area.

91. COBBLEDICK, MR. AND MRS. ELLIS
        Oral history, 1972.
        1 reel (7"), worksheet.   MMN (Tape 476)

        Early life; advent of automobiles; bootlegging; flu
        epidemics; prairie fires; Depression times in
        Cartwright, Manitoba.

92. COLCLEUGH, MURRAY C.
        Papers, 1897-1923.   PAM (MG14 C69 Box 2)

        Correspondence with wife and daughter; a biographical
        sketch, 1974, written by Dorothy Colcleugh Garbutt.

93. COLDWELL, WILLIAM (1834-1907)
        Papers, 1856-1904.
        28".   PAM (MG14 C73)

        Pioneer Red River settler, 1859, journalist, and
        co-founder of the Nor'Wester and Red River Pioneer in
        1869. Personal and legal correspondence pertaining
        to the Roderick McKenzie, Jr., estates; accounts of
        visitors; family news.

94. COOPER, JOHNSTON E. FAMILY
        Family file.
        2".   PAM (MG8 B5)

        Clippings of the Cooper family of Emerson, Manitoba;
        activities of the local Loyal Orange Lodge.

95. COULTER, INA ELIZABETH
        Oral history, 1972.
        1 reel (7"), worksheet.   MMN (Tape 366)

        Resident of Clearwater, Manitoba. Teaching; clothing
        styles; social life at the turn of the century.

96. CRAIG, MRS.
        Oral history, 1972.
        1 reel (7"), worksheet.   MMN (Tape 415)

Removal from Ontario to Portage la Prairie around
1862; schooling; farm life; inclement weather;
prairie fires in the Portage la Prairie area.

97. CRAN HEATHER (1946-)
Oral history. Restricted.   JHSA (Tape 329)

Personal history. Landscape architect.

98. CRIDDLE, NORMAN AND ALICE
Biographical sketch.
4 pp.   LEG LIB (Biographical
                                  file)

Upper middle-class immigrants who settled at Aweme,
Manitoba.

99. CUNNINGHAM, ROBERT AND ANNIE
Papers, 1872-1938.
4'. Originals, copies and microfilms.
                                  PAM (M914 B16 and
M156)

Correspondence between Mr. and Mrs. Cunningham
(Scottish immigrants); correspondence between them
and other family members and friends; materials
concerning Cunninghams's founding of the Manitoban
and his election in 1872 as a Member of Parliament
for the riding of Marquette.

100. CURRIE, GEORGE
Family file.   BCA (MG 14 C102)

Family history; letters; land deed; genealogies of
this Boissevain, Manitoba, pioneer family.

101. CURTIS, MRS.
Oral history, 1972.
1 reel (7"), worksheet.   MMN (Tape 382)

Family life in Springbrook, Ontario, before moving
to Winnipeg, Manitoba, after World War I.

102. DAFOE, JOHN WESLEY (1866-1944)
Papers, 1888-1943. Finding aid.
23".
Originals and typescript.   PAM (MG14 C38)

Author, editor and politician. Correspondence and reports.

103. DALY, HELENA (1894-   )
     Oral history, 1972.
     1 reel (7"), worksheet.   MMN (Tape 461)

     Homesteading near Cartwright, Manitoba; the coming
     of the railway; World War I; her teaching career.

104. DALY, MANITOBA
     Local history by a Mr. Cousins.
     Unpublished manuscript.   BUA

     Histories of both Daly and Rivers, Manitoba;
     photographs; lists of teachers; numerous
     biographical sketches of local residents.

105. DAMBLY, AIME
     Autobiography, 1929 (French).
     6 pp. Handwritten.   SBHSA (Box 6)

106. DARLINGTON, VICTORIA (b. 1895)
     Oral history, 1972.
     1 reel (7"), worksheet.   MMN (Tape 346)

     Family and community life in and near Rosser,
     Manitoba, during early 20th century.

107. D'ASSIT, MME.
     Historical notes (French).
     4 folders, 1905-07.   A St-B (BG0619-0768)

108. DAVIS, HELEN
     Oral history, 1973.
     1 reel (7"), worksheet.   MMN (Tape 595)

     Card reader and fortune teller. Life's experience;
     childhood; move from Saskatchewan to Winnipeg.

109. DAWSON, GEORGE, AND COPELAND, HANNAH DAWSON
     Correspondence, 1892-96.
     In private possession of M. Jean Louis Perron, P.R.
     201, St. Joseph, Manitoba, R0G 2C0.

     Family letters; printed religious material.

110. D'ESCHAMBAULT, MARY AND SUZANNE
          Historical notes.   A St-B

111. DEMOISSAC, SISTER ELIZABETH
          Oral history, 1977.
          1 reel (7"), worksheet.   MMN (Tape 86)

          Grey Nun. Early history of the Grey Nuns, schools
          and hospitals.

112. DESROSIERS FATHER, AND THERESE, MERE
          Oral history, 1950.
          1 reel (7").   MMN (Tape 577)

          Family farm operation; history of Oblate Sisters;
          local activities in and near Otterburne, Manitoba.

113. D'ESCHAMBAULT FAMILY
          Family file.
          3 items.   SBHSA (Box 7)

          Eight-page biographical account of Soeur
          D'Eschambault, 1925; newsclippings; various family
          notes.

114. DEWAR, MISS M.
          Oral history, 1972.
          1 reel (7"), worksheet.   MMN (Tape 325)

          Homesteading in Rapid City, Manitoba, and later in
          Newdale, Manitoba; quilting; making lye and yeast;
          preserving and disposing of milk.

115. DIAKOW, MRS. A.
          Oral history, 1974.
          1 reel (7"), worksheet.   MMN (Tape 641)

          Ukrainian immigrant to Canada since 1914; youthful
          widowhood; religious commitment; life in early
          Winnipeg.

116. DIAMOND, MIRIAM (1932-   )
          Oral history. Restricted.   JHSA (Tape 339)

          Personal history; one-time resident of Chicago,
          Illinois, pre-1970.

117. DICKS, MRS.
        Oral history, 1972.
        1 reel (7"), worksheet.   MMN (Tape 304-2)

        Sewing; schooling; church and social gatherings in
        Teulon, Manitoba.

118. DICKSON FAMILY
        Family history, 1982
        Handwritten.   BCA (MG 14 C33)

        Account of the Benjamin Dickson family in
        Boissevain, Manitoba, 1863-1977.

119. DEIBERT, MR. AND MRS. CONRAD
        Oral history, 1971.
        1 reel (7") worksheet.   MMN (Tape 51)

        German immigrants from Russia who arrived in Canada
        in 1900. Immigration; early life in Winnipeg;
        special celebrations among German immigrants.

120. DIEHL, LES
        Family life.
        Various items.   BCA (MG 14 C62)

        Auctions bills; estate sale matters; and various
        family correspondence.

121. DILLISTONE, MRS. (b. 1902)
        Oral history, 1972.
        1 reel (7"), worksheet.   MMN (Tape 358)

        Morden Sunday school teacher. Winnipeg social life
        (theatre, opera) during World War I.

122. DOERN, PHILIP AND KATERINA
        Family history.
        6 pp. Typewritten.   SCRLM

        Austrian immigrants. Settlement near Morden,
        Manitoba; Doern family reunion.

123. DONNELLY, J.H. FAMILY
        Family history, 1961.
        Typescript.   DHM ("Brandon People
                                         File")

Ontario residents who eventually moved west to homestead near Hartney, Manitoba.

124. DORAN FAMILY
3 volumes on microfilm (2 reels).
                                    PAM (MG14 C109
                                    M328,329)
Family file.
Various items.   BCA (MG 14 C63)

Eight-page genealogy/history of the Doran family; copies of certificates and obituaries about the family; a manuscript history, 1892.

125. DORFMAN, SARAH (b. 1888)
Oral history, 1972. Restricted.
1 reel (7"), worksheet.   MMN (Tape 188)

Ukrainian Jewish immigrant who came to Canada in 1904; active in Jewish orphanage.

126. DOUPE FAMILY
Family papers and genealogies, 1829-1982. Finding aid.
1.5'.   PAM

An early Irish immigrant family that settled in Upper Canada (Ontario), a branch of which later relocated in Manitoba shortly after the Riel Rebellion.

Correspondence of early family progenitors such as Samuel Doupe, 1768-1848, and of later descendants in Manitoba such as Jacob Lonsdale Doupe and Sarah (Sadie) Cranston; materials documenting J.L. Doupe's career with the Canadian Pacific Railway; various legal papers of successive generations; newspaper clippings on the Doupe family history.

127. DRAGUSHIN, DORA (b. 1910)
Oral history, 1972. Restricted.
1 reel (7"), worksheet.   MMN (Tape 302)

Teacher. Jewish life in Winnipeg.

128. DRESSLER, TONY AND ANNIE
Reminiscences.
1 p. Typescript.   SCRLM

Immigration to Morden, Manitoba, from Poland.

22

129. DREWRY, C.E.
      Family movies, 1928-37.
      11 b/w silent films, 30+
      minutes.   MMN

      Winnipeg scenes; ballet recitals; picnics; aerial
      view of Winnipeg; woman sewing; family life.

130. DRING, GEORGEA
      Family history, by Gwen Dring, 1977.
      Copy.   BCA (MG9 E3)

      Life in the Boissevain, Manitoba, area.

131. DRING, MYRNA (b. 1944)
      Oral history, 1983.   BCA (Oral History)

      Social life in Boissevain, Manitoba, in the 1980s.

132. DUBUC, EUGENIE
      Resource file.
      4 articles/lectures.   SBHSA (Box 7)

      Life in early Winnipeg, 1816-68.

133. DUBOIS, MARIANNE
      Oral history, n.d.
      1 reel, 30".   MSB

      Recollections by Marianne Dubois, Marie-Louise Boily
      and others, of life in St. Malo, La Broquerie,
      Richer, and St. Pierre, Manitoba.

134. DUCH, MR. AND MRS. J.
      Oral history, 1971.
      1 reel (7"), worksheet.   MMN (Tape 643)

      Ukrainian immigrants to Dauphin and Keld, Manitoba.
      Views on Ukrainian life in western Manitoba; views
      on the future.

135. DUGAS, AMELIE
      Historical notes, 1901-05.
      1 folder.   A St-B

136. DYCK, ANNA REIMER
      Papers (German).
      1 box.   MHCA (XX Vol. 1679)

Autobiography of life in Niverville, Manitoba; World
War II; family life.

137. EDGE HILL DISTRICT, MANITOBA
     Local histories, 1900, 1929.
     Photocopy, 18 pp.; Typescript, 12 pp.
                                       PAM (MG 9 A59)

     Historical sketch; pioneer life; church and school;
     prairie fires.

138. ELKIN, ROSE
     Papers.   PAM (MG10 F3)

     Correspondence; will; testimonials; obituaries
     (Yiddish).

139. ELLIOT, MARGARET
     Oral history, 1972.
     1 reel (7"), worksheet.   MMN (Tape 376)

     Pioneer life in Melita, Manitoba; changes in rural
     living; patrolling the American/Canadian border.

140. ELLIOT, MAUD
     1 reel (7"), worksheet.   MMN (Tape 394)

     Early life on a homestead near Melita, Manitoba;
     women's work and activities in rural Manitoba.

141. ENGBRECHT, MARGARET ALBRECHT
     Life history, by Elsie Klassen Neufeld (1974).
     15 pp. Typescript.   BCA (MG14 C78)

     History of Margaret Engbrecht of Boissevain,
     Manitoba; local Mennonite customs and local economic
     conditions, especially during the Depression.

142. ENGBRECHT, MRS. NICK
     Family history, 1978.
     3 pp.   BCA (MG14 C78)

     Early life in Whitewater, Manitoba; Mennonite life
     and customs; hardships during the Depression.

143. ENGBRECHT, MARGARET
     Elsie Klassen, "Biography of Margaret Albrecht
     Engbrecht," (1975).
     Unpublished paper, 1975.   MHCA (Vertical file)

Prize-winning biography.

144. EVASIUK, NATALIA
       Autobiography, 1981,   "Sunrise Years in Manitoba"
       24 pp. Typescript.   PAM (MG9 A122)

       Childhood in Ethelbert, Manitoba; father's career as
       a local teacher; their involvement in Ukrainian
       cultural and educational activities.

145. EWANCHUK, WASYL AND PARASKA
       Family history.
       6 pp. Typescript.   ERL

       Ukrainian immigrants. First Ukrainian family in
       Gimli, Manitoba; construction (1903) of their
       four-room log home.

146. FACEY, ALFRED J. FAMILY
       Family history, 1857-1937, by Mabel Clarke.
       Original copy.   BCA (MG 14 C74 and
                                     C166)

147. FAINSTEIN, CLARA
       (a) Papers, 1932-66. Finding aid.
       4 1/4".   PAM (MG14 C63 and
                                     C63-1)

       Information on the D.A. Skaletar, M.A. Gray, and
       Hoffer families; biographical notes on early pioneer
       Jewish families of Manitoba and Saskatchewan;
       reminiscences of Clara Fainstein; various family-
       related reminiscences.

       (b) Miscellany.

       Mt. Carmel Clinic publicity and invitations,
       1940-68; Marcus Hyman obituaries; Sarah Pukoff
       obituary, n.d.; issue of _Manitoba_ with article on
       Ernest Sirluck, 1970; stock-exchange membership
       certificate, 1916; tribute to Arnold Hoffer, n.d.

148. FALCONER, MRS. STUART
       Letters, 1980.
       4 items and photographs.   BCA (BG14 C112)

       Early life in Boissevain, Manitoba; descriptions and
       photographs of the Morrison home (i.e., "Miller
       House" or "Zeller House").

149. FANNYSTELLE, MANITOBA
        Letterbook, 1889-90.
        108 pp.   PAM (MG8 A3)

        Information on the origins of the village in 1889
        provided by the philanthropist Countess of Albutera
        who named the settlement in memory of Fanny Rivers.

150. FARROW, CHARLES FAMILY
        Family history, 1851-1975, by Marge Riddell and
        Mildred Hammond.
        Manuscript.   BCA (MG14 C58)

        History of this Boissevain, Manitoba, family.

151. FETHERSTONHAUGH, MARGARET ADELE (d. 1975)
        Papers, 1918-74.
        2'.   PAM (MG14 C78)

        Musician, teacher. Family and personal
        correspondence, 1918-71; programmes, clippings, and
        correspondence relating to the Women's Musical Club,
        1926-69, Eva Clare Studio Club, 1923-29; Wednesday
        Morning Musicales, 1937-73; relevant documentation
        of her career and marriage to Edward P.
        Fetherstonhaugh.

152. FINKELSTEIN, MRS. MOSES
        Biographical sketch.   JPL (Vertical file)

        Short biography of a community leader in Jewish
        philanthropic work.

153. FINKLEMAN, EDA (1889-   )
        Oral history.   JHSA (Tape 346)

        Reminiscences; emigration from Russia at age 16; two
        marriages.

154. FISHER, MISS E.M.
        Memoirs, 1887-1967.
        Handwritten.   DBA

155. FISHER, MARY
        Oral history, 1972.
        1 reel (7"), worksheet.   MSB

        School teacher. Personal life and family
        experiences in Kelwood, Manitoba.

156. FJELDSTED, GUDMUNDUR AND JAKOBINA
Family history, "Gudmundur and Jakobina Fjeldsted"
(English).
9 pp. Typescript   ERL

Family life in the Gimli, Manitoba, area.

157. FLIN FLON, MANITOBA
Letter, n.d.
1 item.   FFHS/FFPL

Written to Linda McDowell about early Flin Flon
women.

158. FORSYTH, JANE
Oral history, 1972.
1 reel (7"), worksheet.   MMN (Tape 443)

Grasshopper plagues; droughts; social life; lack of
medical services in the Melita, Manitoba, area.

159. FORTIER FAMILY
Family history, 1972.
1 p.   SBHSA (Box 9)

Marriage contract; family history.

160. FOULDS, MAZIE
Oral history, 1964.
1 reel (7"), worksheet.   MMN (Tape 349-2)

Vaudeville entertainer in British Columbia. Life in
the entertainment world and her days with Gypsy Rose
Lee's family.

161. FOURNIER, ADELARD AND MME.
Oral history, 1969. Restricted.
1 reel (7").   MMN (Tape 558)

Songs and reminiscences of residents of La
Broquerie.

162. FRAME, EDNA
Oral history, 1972.
1 reel (7"), worksheet.   MMN (Tape 440)

Farming; schooling and community life; childhood in
the Hamiota, Manitoba, area.

163. FRANCIS, SARAH MARGARET (1856-1937)
      Papers, 1906-19.
      1'.   PAM (P302-303)

      Correspondence with husband (Frederick Francis),
      children and relations.

164. FRASER, JAMES AND SUSAN
      Family history, 1856-1931.
      15 pp.   PAM (M68 C11)

      Historical notes on this Pilot Mound, Manitoba,
      couple.

165. FRIEDGUT, ANNA
      Biography by Mrs. H.M.
      Becherman.   PAM (MG10 F3)

166. FRIESEN, DAVID AND SARA
      Friesen, Ted. "My Parents: David Wiens Friesen,
      1879-1951, Sara Klippenstein Friesen, 1882-1963."
      Unpublished family history. MHCA (Vertical file)

      A prominent Altona, Manitoba, family involved in the
      publishing business.

167. FRIESEN, JOHANN (1768-1835) AND HELENA (1773-1845)
      "Stamm Register."   MHCA (Vertical file)

      Genealogical data; farm records; memoirs.

168. FRIESEN, PETER AND KATHARINA
      Friesen, J. R. F., "The Family Register of Peter and
      Katherina Friesen, Reinfeld, Manitoba, 1859-1974."
      Unpublished family
      history/register   WRL

      Biographical sketches; photographs; family accounts.

169. FUGA, OLGA
      Oral history, 1971.
      1 reel (7"), worksheet.   MMN (Tape 580)

      Childhood, schooling; involvement in the Winnipeg's
      Ukrainian community; activities as chair of Greater
      Winnipeg School Board.

170. FUNK, PETER (1899-1974)
Family file.   WRL

Various biographical sketches of this and other
Winkler, Manitoba residents.

171. FURTNEY, MRS. K.
Oral history, 1972.
1 reel (7"), worksheet.   MMN (Tape 438)

Family, social and church life; weather in Melita,
Manitoba, through the years.

172. GABOURY FAMILY
Family file, 1944.
1/2". Typescript.   SBHSA (Box 10)

Includes marriage contracts.

173. GABOURY, MARIE-ANNE AND SARA RIEL
Video history, 1983 (colour).
1 cassette (3/4"), 60 minutes. CBWFT CSB

Life stories.

174. GAGNON, MRS. B.
Oral history, 1971.
1 reel (7"), worksheet.   MMN (Tape 47)

Economy (Depression); government and policies; early
life of Winnipeg, Manitoba.

175. GAMBLE, ANNIE
Oral history, 1972.
1 reel (7"), worksheet.   MMN (Tape 338)

Removal to Manitoba from Ontario in 1910; farming
until 1944; family life.

176. GARBUTT, DOROTHY
Papers, 1911-71. Restricted. Finding aid.
9 '.   PAM (MG9 A63)

Freelance writer. Correspondence; diaries;
articles, stories, poems; radio talks; scrapbook of
published articles.

177. GARBUTT, DOROTHY
Reminiscences. ("I Remember Winnipeg")
Unpublished paper.   PAM (MG10 F2 Box F-J)

Winnipeg at the turn of the 20th century.

178. GARLAND, AILEEN (b. 1892)
Oral history, 1972-1973.
1 reel (7"), worksheet.   MMN (TAPE 583)

Author and teacher. School teaching; historical
research; her interests in the status of women, in
the teaching profession and of children in public
schools.

179. GARLAND, AILEEN (b. 1892)
Papers, 1922-68.
10".   PAM (MG10 G2)

Assorted materials on her life and career.

180. GAYLOR, MRS. N.
Oral history, 1971.
1 reel (7"), worksheet.   MMN (Tape 647)

Ukrainian immigrant. Life in Garland, Manitoba;
homesteading; church life; Ukrainian customs in the
community.

181. GERIN, ALIDA AND EUGENE
Historical notes, 1901-14.
1 folder.   A St-B

182. GLASS, MRS. B.
1 reel (7"), worksheet.   MMN (Tape 190)

Russian Jewish immigrant. Life before and after her
arrival in Canada in 1896; early days in Winnipeg.

183. GOLDIE, MRS.
Oral history, 1971
1 reel (7"), worksheet.   MMN (Tape 329)

Work as a domestic near Boissevain, Manitoba, after
moving from Ontario; marriage in 1900; subsequent
homesteading at Birch River, Manitoba.

30

184. GOLDSTINE, FAN (b. 1894)
       Oral history, 1972. Restricted.
       1 reel (7"), worksheet.   MMN (Tape 299)

       Move from Stratford, Ontario, to Winnipeg, Manitoba,
       in 1903; schooling at Havergal College (later
       re-named Rupert's Land Ladies' College); the
       Winnipeg General Strike of 1919 and its effects.

185. GOODWIN, MRS. ROBERT
       Oral history, 1964.
       2 reels (7"), worksheet.   MMN (Tape 359-2)

       Wife of early country doctor; rural Manitoba in the
       1880s and 1890s; their interesting motorings around
       the province in the early 20th century.

186. GORDON, ANNIE COPP (1840-1931)
       Biography, by her daughter (1953).
       Typescript and carbons.   UCA-W

       English immigrant. Lay preacher of the Bible
       Christian (Methodist) Church in Devon, England;
       immigration to Canada in 1857; marriage to Rev.
       Andrew Gordon in 1859 and settlement in St. Thomas,
       Ontario; involvement in Temperance and women's
       suffrage movements; move to Pembina Hills, Manitoba,
       in 1880s and later to Manitou, Portage la Prairie,
       Carmen, and Wawanesa, Manitoba.

187. GOSSELIN, MLLE
       Oral history.   MSB

       Interview with a long-time La Broquerie, Manitoba,
       resident.

188. GOW, MRS. MARGARET
       Oral history, 1973.
       1 reel (7"), worksheet.   MMN (Tape 597)

       Teacher. Early University of Manitoba graduate
       (Science). Teacher of immigrant children; events
       surrounding World War I; life during the Depression.

189. GRAHAM, MRS. (b. 1904)
       Oral history, 1972.
       1 reel (7"), worksheet.   MMN (Tape 341)

       Teacher. Birth at Salt Creek, Manitoba; childhood
       in Dauphin, Manitoba; farm life; rural Manitoba
       schooling.

190. GRAHAM, ROBERT BLACKWOOD WHIDDON (1870-1951)
Biography.
3 Volumes on microfilm (2 reels).
PAM (MG14 C109
M328,329)

Accountant and police magistrate. Family ancestry;
personal reminiscences; daily journal entries from
May 1934 on describing work, family matters, social
life and related activities in Winnipeg, Manitoba.

191. GRANGER FAMILY
Assorted papers (French).
In the personal possession of M. Jean Granger, La
Broquerie, Manitoba.

Biography of M. Joseph Granger, 1859-1949, of La
Broquerie, Manitoba; correspondence between Louis
Granger and wife Emma, 1891-1908, of the Rev. Sister
Marie Martin, 1903-23, and of other Granger family
members.

192. GREEN, ELIZABETH (b. 1875)
Oral history, n.d.   MMN (Tape 351 3)

Birth and early life in East Kildonan, Manitoba;
experiences as a teacher; description of Old
Kildonan church and cemetery; history of her early
Selkirk settlement grandparents.

193. GREEN, WALDRON ALVORD
Papers.   FFHS/FFPL

Personal history; biography of Irene Green of Flin
Flon, Manitoba; correspondence.

194. GREENBERG, JACOB AND BERTHA
Family history.   ERL

Merchants. Jewish family life in Gimli, Manitoba,
after 1914; operation of their general store.

195. GRIFFIS, EDITH
Journal, 1913.   PAM (MG1 B36)

Account of her canoe trip from Norway House to York
Factory, Manitoba.

196. GUILD, ANNIE
        Oral history, 1972.
        1 reel (7"), worksheet.   MMN (Tape 334)

        Early resident, 1889, of Deleau, Manitoba. Life as
        a teacher and involvement in local-level politics.

197. GUINESS, MRS.
        Oral history, 1972.
        1 reel (7"), worksheet.   MMN (Tape 345)

        Life in Starbuck, Manitoba.

198. HALL, S.A.
        Letter, 1977.
        1 item.   BCA (MG14 C24)

        Description of the S.A. Hall family of Brownlea,
        Manitoba.

199. HALLETT, EDWIN FAMILY
        Family history, by Perry and Phyllis Hallett.
                                         BCA (MG14 C10)

        History and ancestry of the Hallett family of
        Boissevain, Manitoba.

200. HALTER, MRS. LIONEL
        Oral history, 1970. Restricted.
        1 reel (7"), worksheet.   MMN (Tape 105)

        Jewish immigrant. Immigration to Canada in 1882 to
        escape anti-Jewish persecution; establishment of
        family business (Weidman Bros. Wholesale Grocers);
        education and customs of the Winnipeg Jewish
        community; anti-semitism; the Winnipeg General
        Strike of 1919.

201. HAMILTON, JEAN V.
        Oral history, 1972.
        1 reel (7"), worksheet.   MMN (Tape 541)

        School teacher. Education and teaching
        opportunities in Winnipeg, Manitoba, in the 1910s;
        immigrant children in the public school system; the
        role of teachers in education.

202. HAMMOND, MRS.
        Oral history, 1972.
        1 reel (7"), worksheet.   MMN (Tape 430)

        33

School teacher. Marriage and family at La Rivière,
Manitoba; family history of the Fargey family.

203. HAMMOND, GARDNER FAMILY
         Family histories.
         2 items.   BCA (MG14 C56)

         Biography of Hammond Gardner of Boissevain,
         Manitoba; autobiography of Frances Hicks; assorted
         clippings.

204. HANSEN, ANN
         Oral history, 1972.
         1 reel (7"), worksheet.   MMN (Tape 340)

         Childhood and farm life near Deloraine, Manitoba.

205. HARDER, ABRAM AND ANNA
         Harder, Sarah. "Sarah Harder Recalls Events in the
         Life of her Parents' Family, Abram and Anna Harder."
         Family history, unpublished.
         43 pp.   MHCA (Vertical file)

         History of this Mennonite family.

206. HARRIS, NEIL
         Interviews, 1974.
         10 videotape recordings.   PAM (AV D1)

         Interviews of Maureen Walker, Mary Field, Ruby
         Freygood, Victoria Wallace, and others.

207. HARRISON, JAMES
         Reminiscences, 1882-1961.
         4 pp.   BCA (MG 14 C39)

         History of this Boissevain, Manitoba, resident.

208. HAYNES, SHIRLEY
         Diaries (1946-) and family history.
         Diaries restricted.   PPPL

         Daily personal account of life in The Pas, Manitoba;
         family history entitled "Kerr Family History."

209. HAYWARD, MARGARET GRACE (b. 1897)
         Oral history, 1972.
         1 reel (7"), worksheet.   MMN (Tape 362)

34

Career training as a nurse at Winnipeg Children's
Hospital and involvement in nursing profession,
1913-20; active in the Children's Hospital Alumni.

210. HEFT FAMILY
       "My Family Tree," by Sybil Heft.
       Family history.   PAM (MG10 F3)

       Family background and ancestry.

211. HENDERSON, CLAIR FAMILY
       Family file, 1900-66.
       Originals and copies.   BCA (MG14 C28)

       Storey family record and marriage certificates of
       these residents of Boissevain, Manitoba.

212. HENDERSON, JOHN FAMILY
       Papers, 1832-1962.
       25".   PAM (MG10 F3) and
                                     (MG14 C62)

       Correspondence, 1877-1920; financial records,
       1871-1959; legal documents, 1832-1940; papers
       relating to the Municipality of East Kildonan,
       1890-1940; Ladies Aid Minute Book, 1888-1901;
       miscellaneous items.

213. HENRY, MRS. W.A.
       Letter, 1929.
       2 pp.   UCA

       Letter of sympathy written at the death of Reverend
       W.M. Henry.

214. HERSHFIELD, ROSE AND AARON
       Family file.   PAM (MG6 F18)

       Two World War II ration books; dance programs;
       assorted materials.

215. HICKS, ELEANOR
       Papers.   BCA (MG14 C25)

       Autobiography; poems; family history of Joseph
       Hicks; letters and speeches written and collected by
       this Boissevain, Manitoba, resident.

216. HIEBERT, HELEN (b. 1874)
     "Granny Stories as Written c. 1959 by Helen Hiebert
     (1874-) of Manitoba."
     Biography, 108 pp.   MHCA (XXV 13 Vol.
                                   1074 Fd. 53)

     Childhood days with her Mennonite parents, Erdmann
     and Maria Penner.

217. HILL, THOMAS FAMILY
     Family history, by Tony Hill, 1956.
     1 p.   BCA (MG14 C64)

     Early pioneer days in Boissevain, Manitoba.

218. HOEPPNER, ISAAC AND ELIZABETH
     Family history.
     4 pp. Typescript.   SCRLM

     Short historical sketch of this Mennonite family;
     photographs.

219. HOEPPNER, ISAAC AND ELIZABETH
     Family history. "The Heritage of Isaac and
     Elizabeth Hoeppner," by Katherine Loewen.
     Typescript.   WRL

     Family history; biographical sketches; genealogies.

220. HOGG, HELEN (b. 1897)
     Oral history, 1972.
     1 reel (7"), worksheet.   MMN (Tape 92)

     Scottish immigrant. Work in La Salle, Manitoba, as
     a domestic and later at Eaton's in Winnipeg,
     Manitoba; references to criticisms of some
     Presbyterians of the formation of the United Church
     in 1925 and of the construction of the First
     Presbyterian Church on Canora St., Winnipeg; life as
     a single person.

221. HOLDITCH, MABEL
     Personal history.
     4 pp.   BCA (MG14 C40)

     Pioneer times in Boissevain, Manitoba.

222. HOLENSKI, KOLA AND MARY
     Family history.
     1 p. Typescript.   SCRLM

Polish immigrants in the Morden, Manitoba, area.

223. HOLLAND, MRS. L.J.
     Papers, 1924-77; photographs.
     Photostats, 11 pp.   PAM (MG10 C60)

     Information on Agnes K. Thomson and her daughter,
     L.J. (Nancy) Holland.

224. HORN, ELIZABETH
     Essay, 1956, "Farming Conditions in Manitoba from
     1885."
     Handwritten.   PAM (MG10 F2 Box F-J)

     Pioneer farming as experienced by the author.

225. HOSKINS, MS. M.
     Oral history, 1972.
     1 reel (7"), worksheet.   MMN (Tape 355)

     Family life; early development of Winnipeg,
     Manitoba; activities in the Girl Guides including
     her service as Provincial Secretary.

226. INKSTER, COLIN
     Papers. Finding aid.
     Multiple family files.   PAM (MG14 B30)

     Colin family estate administrator. Files relating
     to the estates of William Inkster, John Inkster,
     James Inkster, Mary Isabella Inkster Hughes,
     1877-1920, Mary White, 1909-10, Colin Robertson
     Inkster, and other family members.

227. ISFELD FAMILY
     Resource file.
     4 pp. Typescript.   ERL

     "Copy of Statistics and Data on the Isfeld and
     Narfason Families."

228. JACKSON, MRS.
     Oral history, 1972.
     1 reel (7"), worksheet.   MMN (Tape 107)

     Cree Indian artisan known for her knowledge of
     Indian crafts and making of bannock. Childhood;
     schooling; family and beliefs; Indian lifestyle.

37

229. JANZ, MARY
        Oral history, 1981.   Interviewed by Winnifred
        Ransom.
        1 reel.   BCA (Oral History)

        Mennonite immigrant. Mennonite life in Russia and
        Canada; immigration in 1930; farm life near
        Boissevain, Manitoba.

230. JANZEN, LINDA
        Notebooks (German).
        Faded, yellow pages.   MVMA (E691 and E697)

        Family register; poems; songs; "historical stories."

231. JENTSCH, MR. AND MRS. E.
        Oral history, 1971.
        1 reel (7"), worksheet.   MMN (Tape 43)

        Marriage celebrations; rural parties; farming at
        Cree Bay (Beausejour), Manitoba.

232. JESSIMAN, WILLIAM
        Oral history, interviewed by Don Schroeder.
        1 reel (90 m).   SCRLM (Oral History)

        Women in the Jessiman family; pioneer life.

233. JOHANNESON, MRS.
        Oral history, 1977.
        2 reels (7"), worksheet.   MMN (Tape 8-2)

        Hecla Island housewife. Life on Hecla Island,
        Manitoba; lake fishing; food and diet; recreation;
        country doctoring on the Island.

234. JOHNSON, ETHEL (b. 1888)
        Oral history, 1972.
        2 reels (7"), worksheet.   MMN (Tape 308-2)

        Move from Ontario in 1888; life in Holland and
        Cypress River, Manitoba; school teaching in
        Saskatchewan in one-room schools; small town, rural
        life.

235. JOHNSON, KATE
        "Cameos of Pioneer Life in Western Canada."
        (a) Historical essay and autobiography.
        Typescript, 59 pp.   PAM (MG8 B42)

Western Canada history; Danish emigrant 1888; early
homesteading in south-eastern Saskatchewan.

236. JOHNSON, MRS. W.L.
     Papers, 1825-1916.
     Multiple items. In the private possession of Mrs.
     W.L. Johnson, 171 Canora St., Winnipeg, Manitoba.

     Last Will and Testament; ledger of expenditures;
     birth and death cards; photographs of and about
     Caroline Railton.

237. JOHNSTONE, MRS. R.
     Oral history, 1971.
     1 reel (7"), worksheet.   MMN (Tape 3)

     Pre World War I Winnipeg; childhood, schooling and
     religious training; household management; the place
     of women and children on the frontier; pioneer
     burials.

238. JONSSON, MRS. BALDOIN
     Papers.   PAM (MG8 A6-6)

     Poem and funeral sermon written on the death of her
     three sons.

239. JONSSON, MARTEIN
     Genealogies.
     30 pp. Typescript.   ERL

     Some biographical notes.

240. JOHNSTON, C.
     Unpublished article.
     Photocopy, 2 pp.   PAM (MG1 A18)

     Account of naming a lake in honour of Miss Johnston
     who nursed on the Way-Way-See-Cappo Reserve from
     1906 to 1909.

241. JOSEPHSON, ADA
     Oral history, 1972.
     1 reel (7"), worksheet.   MMN (Tape 390)

     Birth and childhood in the Waskada region of
     Manitoba; career as an elementary school teacher.

39

242. JOSEPHSON, OLI PETUR
        Genealogy, 1969.   ERL

        Short biographical sketches of the various members
        of this Gimli, Manitoba, family.

243. KANE, MRS. WALTER
        Oral history, 1981.
        1 reel (7"), worksheet.   MMN (Tape 718)

        Life on an Idaho Blackfoot Indian reserve;
        pioneering in Alberta; life on the rodeo circuits as
        wife of a rodeo rider; eventual move to Winnipeg,
        Manitoba, where the family established Kane
        Equipment.

244. KARLINSKY, SONYA (b. 1887)
        Oral history, 1972.
        1 reel (7"), worksheet.   MMN (Tape 194)

        Russian-born Jewish immigrant who came to Winnipeg,
        Manitoba, in 1912; work as a textile worker in a
        knitting factory; finances.

245. KEHLER, DAVID
        Family file, 1880-1912.
        Originals (German and Gothic script).
                                       MHCA (XXV B Vol. 1073
        Fd. 63)

        Greetings; announcements; poems; related materials.

246. KEMPTHORNE FAMILY
        Family history and genealogy, 1978, compiled by
        Doreen Noble.
        46 pp.   BCA (MG14 C89)

        History of the Kempthorne and Noble families of
        Desford, Manitoba.

247. KENNEDY, ALEXANDER D. FAMILY
        Papers, 1903-64. Finding aid.
        15".   PAM (MG14 C104)

        Correspondence and assortments of other papers on
        the married life of Alexander and Jessie Clark;
        marriage in Ontario in 1911; removal to Eden,
        Manitoba; her involvement in the WCTU, the United
        Church and the Eden Branch of the Women's Institute;
        his experience with the Neepawa Consumers Co-op and
        the Manitoba Federation of Agriculture.

        40

248. KENNEDY, MARY LOUISA (1861-1945)
        Papers, 1875-1938.   PAM (MG14 C1)

        Correspondence, notebooks and diaries. Daughter of
        William and Eleanor Kennedy. Correspondence,
        notebooks and diaries. Education in England; return
        to St. Andrews, Manitoba; work in a law office;
        later court reporter in Virden, Manitoba.

249. KENNEDY, WILLIAM (1813-90)
        Correspondence.   PAM (MG2 C1)

        Education in the Orkney Islands; employment in the
        Hudson's Bay company in 1830s; marriage to Eleanor
        E. Cripps; settlement at Red River in 1861; letters
        from Sophia Cracroft and Lady (John) Franklin.

250. KENT, GERTRUDE
        Oral history, 1972.
        1 reel (7"), worksheet.   MMN (Tape 356)

        A teacher in a Winnipeg, Manitoba, school for the
        deaf.

251. KILTON, M. FAMILY
        Family history.
        Handwritten.   ERL

        History of a Camp Morton, Manitoba, pioneer family.

252. KITSON, MRS. TOM
        Journal, 1906-15.
        220 pp. Handwritten.   PAM (MG8 B96)

        Daily activities of the Kitson family.

253. KLAPOUSCHUK, MR. AND MRS. H.
        Oral history, 1971.
        1 reel (7"), worksheet.   MMN (Tape 500)

        Early life and immigration of these Ukrainian
        immigrants and problems caused by the gradual loss
        of their language and culture.

254. KLASSEN, ANNA
        Diary (German).   MHCA (XXV B Vol.
                                     1073)

41

255. KLYM, WASYL AND MARIA
      Historical sketch.   ERL

      Short review of the lives of an Austrian family that
      immigrated to the Gimli, Manitoba, area in 1899.

256. KNAPP, MARTHA (1892-1972)
      Papers.
      2".   PAM (MG9 A51-1)

      Correspondence of her father, Klaas de Jong; travels
      of Richard Knapp.

257. KOBZEY, THOMAS AND OLENA
      Papers (Ukrainian).
      Unprocessed.   UCECA

      Winnipeg socialist and community activist during
      1920s-1970s.

258. KOZLOWSKI, JOHN AND MARY
      Family history.   ERL

      Short history of a family that immigrated to the
      Gimli, Manitoba, region about 1914.

259. KREZANSKI, PAUL AND KATERINA
      Family history.   ERL

      History of this Austrian family living in the Gimli,
      Manitoba region since 1902.

260. KULBABA, MRS. M. (b. 1891)
      Oral history, 1971.
      1 reel (7"), worksheet.   MMN (Tape 653)

      Emigration from the Ukraine in 1909; details of
      journey; early life, marriage and ethnic customs;
      family farm in Selkirk, Manitoba; references to
      German immigrants in Canada.

261. KURNARSKY, FREDA (1891-   )
      Oral history.   JHSA (Tape 325)

      Russian Jewish immigrant. Life as a seamstress in
      Russia; immigration 1912.

262. LA BROQUERIE, MANITOBA
        Assorted town records mostly French.
        Contact: Janine Dubé, La Broquerie, Manitoba.

        Lists of early pioneer families and new family
        arrivals since 1960; dates of arrivals of families
        from 1878 to 1977; place of origin of immigrants
        arriving between 1878 and 1889; local history.

263. LAFOURNAISE FAMILY
        Family file.
        Photocopies.   SBHSA (Box 14)

        Scattered data on selected family members such as
        Marie McGillis (married 1823), Marie Rose
        Lafournaise, and others.

264. LAND, RUTH
        Oral history, 1972.
        1 reel (7"), worksheet.   MMN (Tape 419)

        Rural school teaching and farm life near Portage la
        Prairie, Manitoba.

265. LARIVIERE FAMILY
        Recording 1969 (French).
        1 reel.   MMN (Tape 554)

        Family immigration to the St. François-Xavier and
        St. Pierre, Manitoba, area; early farming
        experiences; present-day gardening; French
        folksongs.

266. LARIVIERE, JOSEPH MME.
        Oral history, 1969 (French). Restricted.
        1 reel (7").   MMN (Tape 555)

        Life in St. Pierre, Manitoba, since the 1920s;
        games, customs, and amusements (dancing, card
        playing, taffy pulls); holiday times such as
        Christmas and New Year's.

267. LARIVIERE, MME. JOSEPH; AND LAMOUREUX, IRENE
        Recording, 1969 (French). Restricted.
        1 reel (7").   MMN (Tape 559)

        Residents of St. Pierre, Manitoba; legends; dance
        music.

268. LARIVIERE, MME. LOUIS
        Biographical sketch, 1940.
        1 p.   SBHSA (Box 15)

269. LARRIVEE, LOUIS AND ALIZA
        Family history, 1972.
        4 pp. Typescript.   SBHSA (Box 15)

        Short history.

270. LATIMER, ROBERT SR., FAMILY
        Family history, by Doreen Dingwall.
        Manuscript.   BCA (MG14 C219)

        History of the Latimer brothers of Boissevain,
        Manitoba, and of their families.

271. LAVITT, CLARA (b. 1889)
        Oral history, 1972. Restricted.
        1 reel (7"), worksheet.   MMN (Tape 263)

        Birth and childhood in Winnipeg, Manitoba; summer
        activities at Bender Hamlet; activities in various
        Jewish organizations; the Depression and its
        economic effects.

272. LAWSON, MYRTLE ALTHERA
        Reminiscences, 1980.
        5 pp. Handwritten.   UCA-W (Biography
                                          file)

        Early 20th-century church life and work in rural
        Manitoba; temperance groups; Women's Missionary
        Society; Women's Institute.

273. LAZONBY, EDITH G. (b. 1882)
        Reminiscences ("Happy Days").
        Typescript, 48 pp.   PAM (MG8 B48)

        Reflections on life in Ireland, England and western
        Canada.

274. LEMAIRE, MARIE-ANTOINETTE
        Oral history, 1971.
        1 reel (7"), worksheet.   MMN (Tape 69)

        French-Canadian school teacher and school trustee
        well informed on early schools in Manitoba.

44

275. LENNARD, MANITOBA
        Family histories.
        6 pp.   PAM (MG9 A113)

        Romanian immigrant. Sketch of the Elie Burla and
        Gregorie Gaber families and their immigration from
        Romania to Lennard, Manitoba.

276. LEWIS, MRS. GEORGE T. (b. 1894)
        Oral history, 1973.
        1 reel (7"), worksheet.   MMN (Tape 703)

        Birth in High Bluff, Manitoba; early life in
        Winnipeg; effects of the Depression in Saskatchewan.

277. LIPSETT, FLORENCE
        Oral history, 1973.
        1 reel (7"), worksheet.   MMN (Tape 581)

        Teacher in Winnipeg, Manitoba, in early 1900s;
        service on the executive committee of the Manitoba
        Teachers' Society.

278. LIVESAY, FLORENCE HAMILTON RANDAL (1874-1953)
        Papers, 1902-76.
        8".   PAM (P59-62)

        Journals; articles for newspaper publication; album
        of clippings re: Songs of Ukraina, 1914-18 stories
        poems; translations; correspondence with Dorothy
        Livesay and other family members; some papers of
        Dorothy Livesay.

279. LLOYD, RUBI
        Oral history, 1972.
        1 reel (7"), worksheet.   MMN (Tape 507)

        English immigrant. Work as a photographer; farming
        in Mather, Manitoba; references to farm equipment
        during the 1920s and 1930s.

280. LOEWEN, MARY J.
        Papers, 1910-60 (in German and English).
        1 box.   MHCA (XX 104 Vol.
                                      1154)

        House-keeping records; school notebooks; teaching
        contract from the Mary J. and Anna Loewen
        households.

    45

281. LOG CABIN INN, BERENS RIVER, MANITOBA
        Business records and personal papers, 1929-71.
        5".   PAM (MG11 D5)

        Log Cabin Inn of Berens River, Manitoba, built
        around 1931 by George and Ruth ("Ma") Kemp. Guest
        records; notebook; journal of George Kemp relating
        to the Inn; operating records and articles on "Ma"
        Kemp who, after her husband's death, operated the
        Inn with her two sons until her death in 1977.

282. LONGMAN, A.D.
        Papers, 1935-69.
        Several items.   PAM (MG10 C48)

        Poetry Society of Winnipeg programmes, 1944-47;
        Overseas Education League circulars, 1935; Indian
        Handicrafts of Manitoba papers; concert programmes
        of the Young Women's Musical Club Choir, 1950-68;
        papers of the Co-operative Women's Guild, 1952-68.

283. LOWES, ELLEN (1865-1925)
        Reminiscences, 1882-1900.
        94 pp. Photocopy.   PAM (MG8 B50)

        Homesteading in Elliott Settlement, near Brandon,
        Manitoba.

284. MCALLISTER, MRS. JOHN
        Oral history, 1950.
        1 phonograph (78 rpm)   PAM (AV C1)

        Recitation of "Bungi Stories" (a Cree Indian
        dialect) learned in her childhood.

285. MCAULAY, ELIZABETH (b. 1881)
        Oral history.
        1 reel (7"), worksheet.   MMN (Tape 433)

        Life experiences in the Lake Winnipegosis area of
        Manitoba; reflections on changes in Winnipeg during
        the 20th century.

286. MCBETH, ISABEL AND JANET
        Oral history, 1972.
        1 reel (7"), worksheet.   MMN (Tape 418)

        Stories of early settlement along the Red River;
        Winnipeg business; recreational activities; everyday
        life in Selkirk, Manitoba.

287. MCCOLL, EBENEZER (1835-1902)
McColl family papers, 1861-1945. Finding aid.
3". PAM (MG14 C29)

Notes on the McColl family, 1791-1860;
correspondence with his children, Mary and John,
1905-40; diary of Flora and Mary McColl (1942-45).

288. MCCOLL, HARRIET
Oral history, 1983. BCA (Oral History)

Early days in Boissevain, Manitoba; church life as a
United Church minister's wife.

289. MCDERMOT, MS.
Oral history, 1972.
1 reel (7"), worksheet. MMN (Tape 339)

Hardships of pioneer life in Portage la Prairie,
Manitoba, since 1891; information on clothing styles
from the 1890s to the 1910s.

290. MCDIARMID FAMILY
Family movies and photographs.
2 b/w and 2 colour films (16 mm).
MMN

Home-movie footage of Lt. Governor McDiarmid and his
wife and family.

291. MCDONALD GEORGE W.
Historical sketch, 1875-1956.
1 item. BCA (MG14 C32)

Booklet on the history of this former mayor of
Boissevain, Manitoba, and of his wife, Jennie Myrtle
Taylor.

292. MACDONALD, MISS K.
Oral history, 1971.
1 reel (7"), worksheet. MMN (Tape 57)

World War I and its effect on Winnipeg, Manitoba;
the Winnipeg General Strike of 1919; and horse
racing.

293. MCDOUGALL, MATHILDE
Letter, 1902.
1 p. PAM (MG8 B51)

47

Written to Virginia McDougall.

294. MCEWEN, MRS. A.E. (1875-1950)
Memoirs ("Those Days of Long Ago").
55 pp. Photocopy.   PAM (MG8 B52)

Histories of the Thomas Lusted family of Winnipeg
and Stonewall, Manitoba, and of the Douglass McEwen
family of Stonewall, Berens River, and Winnipeg,
1865-1950.

295. MCGOWAN, MRS.
Oral history, 1972.
1 reel (7"), worksheet.   MMN (Tape 502)

Childhood; schooling; farm life in and near
Cartwright, Manitoba.

296. MCINTYRE, DEBORAH
Oral history, 1972.
1 reel (7"), worksheet.   MMN (Tape 357)

Childhood in Oak Bluff, Manitoba, school life and
married life in Roblin, Manitoba.

297. MACIVER, MR. AND MRS. ANGUS
Oral history, 1971.
1 reel (7").   MMN (Tape 319)

Mrs. MacIver's life as a trapper before her
marriage; married life in Emerson and Churchill,
Manitoba.

298. MACKINNON FAMILY
Papers, 1797-1927.
In private possession of Mrs. Beverly Lamb, 318
Crescent Road, Winnipeg, Manitoba, R1N 0Y7.

Account books, ledgers, and journals, 1797-1821;
correspondence relating to war and the MacKinnons'
law practice; World War I ration books; personal
family correspondence, 1825-1917; photographs; other
family records.

299. MCKECHNIE, MR. AND MRS.
Oral history, 1972.
1 reel (7"), worksheet.   MMN (Tape 347)

Farm life near Carberry, Manitoba, since the 1880s.

300. MCKENZIE, MRS. CHARLES H.
Reminiscences, 1960 ("The Story of Deepdale
District, Roblin, Manitoba").
10 pp. Typescript.   PAM (MG10 F2)

Pioneer life in the Deepdale region of Manitoba.

301. MCKNIGHT, ETHEL M. (1883-1970)
Papers, 1903-70. Finding aid.
15".   PAM (MG14 C50; also
                           MG16 B3)

Religious and historical newspaper clippings;
various programmes; menus and cookbooks; materials
on the Commercial Girl's Club; other scattered
materials by this life-long employee of Bulman Bros.
Ltd. of Winnipeg.

302. MACLEAN, JEAN
Oral history, 1972.
1 reel (7"), worksheet.   MMN (Tape 98)

Singer and wife of a former mayor of St. Boniface,
Manitoba. Founding of the Canadian Legion in
Manitoba; various Red Cross activities; christening
of a mine sweeper in St. Boniface.

303. MCMILLAN, JESSIE (b. 1882)
Oral history, 1972.
1 reel (7"), worksheet.   MMN (Tape 352)

Family life; farming; bee keeping in Marquette,
Manitoba.

304. MCPHAIL FAMILY
McPhail, Effie. "The McPhails of Elton Municipality,
Manitoba." Family history.
                           DHM ("Brandon People
file")

A family history from 1878 to 1970. Genealogy;
detailed information of farm life; daily routine;
interior decorations.

305. MCRAE, GEORGE AND HELEN AND FAMILY
Holst, M. "Red River to Blairich."
Family history, c. 1964.
68 pp.   PAM (MG8 C15)

The history and genealogy of the McRae family.

49

306. MACRAE, MELVIN AND MARION
          Oral history, 1972.
          1 reel (7"), worksheet.   MMN (Tape 447)

          Childhood; schooling and farm life; eventual
          residence in Winnipeg, Manitoba.

307. MCRUER FAMILY
          Family histories.   BCA (MG14 C233)

          Histories of the James McRuer, John McRuer, and
          James Gilbert McRuer families of Boissevain,
          Manitoba.

308. MCVICAR, MRS. DOUGLAS
          Reminiscences. ("Reminiscences of Early Brandon").
          22 pp. Typescript.   Brandon Public
                                        Library (Vault)

          1879 settlers in Grand Valley (later Brandon,
          Manitoba) and life as homesteaders.

309. MACVICAR, GEORGE D.
          Papers, 1869-70. Finding aid.
          27 pp. Typescript.   PAM (MG3 B9)

          Letters to his fiancée, Josephine Larwill, who came
          with him to Manitoba in 1871. Siege of Fort Garry;
          capture by Louis Riel; other related topics.

310. MACVICAR, HELENA
          Papers, interviews, 1880-1949. PAM (MG9 A62)
          Originals and typescripts.

          Transcripts of interviews, 1946-47, with numerous
          Manitoba women including the following: Mrs. J.W.
          Gillies of Portage Plains; Mrs. Hay of Portage
          Plains; Mrs Erskine Hoskin of Portage la Prairie;
          Sybil L.M. Macmorine; Mrs. Edwin H. Muir; Mrs. Colin
          Setter; Lynn Sissons; Mrs. Bert St. John; Mrs.
          Stidston; Margaret Stewart; and her sister, Mrs. R.
          McCarthy; some others. Included also are interviews
          and documents relating to Millford, Manitoba,
          settlers, 1880-1946.

311. MAGNACCA, STEVE FAMILY
          Papers, mostly unprocessed.   DHM ("Brandon People
                                        File")

Mayor of Brandon, 1961-69. Correspondence;
clippings; other materials relating to both his
private and public life.

312. MAINS, JEAN (b. 1907)
        Oral history.   BCA

        Rural school teacher. Social life in Boissevain,
        Manitoba, in the early 1900s; the place of the
        church in rural life; the effects of World War I on
        the area.

313. MAIR, HOLMES R. AND ELIZABETH
        Family file, 1955-1941. Unprocessed.
        0.5'.   PAM (MG8 B54)

        Early settlers from Ontario in Westbourne, Manitoba.
        Diaries of H.R. Mair; genealogical information;
        newspaper clippings; scattered photographs.

314. MALMAEUS, MARY ELIZABETH
        Family history, 1810-1976, compiled by Mary E.M.
        Malmaeus.
        3 1/2".   PAM (MG8 C27)

        Biographical and genealogical sketches of the
        McIntyre family, 1810-1976, and the Clark family, c.
        1920-76.

315. MAMAKEESIK, MAGGIE
        Oral history, 1966.
        1 reel.   MMN (Tape 696)

        Interview with a 101-year-old Cree Indian.

316. MARTIN FAMILY
        Genealogy ("Descendents of Gunnlauger Martin and
        Sigridur Finnson").
                        ERL

        Gimli, Manitoba, area Icelandic settlers.

317. MAY, GERALD AND LAURIENE
        Reminiscences.
        11 pp.   BCA (BG14 C88)

        Lauriene May's life in Michigan in the 1850s; six
        pages of May family ancestry.

318. MAYBANK, RALPH (1890-1954)
        Papers. finding aid.
        23."   PAM (MG14 B35)

        Correspondence; speeches; clippings; an assortment
        of other materials, including personal and family
        papers.

319. MEDOVY, MOLLY
        Oral history. Restricted.
        1 reel (7"), worksheet.   MMN (Tape 206)

        Early life in Russia; reasons for immigrating to
        Canada in 1906; Jewish life in Winnipeg, Manitoba,
        including customs, schools and organizations.

320. MERCIER, SISTER PAULINE
        Oral history.
        1 reel (7"), worksheet.   MMN (Tape 391)

        Teacher; sister of the Franciscan Mission of St.
        Mary. Teaching among various Indian and Métis
        settlements; Métis efforts to upgrade their standard
        of living; history of St. Laurent, Manitoba;
        activities of the Franciscan Mission of St. Mary.

321. MICHENER, NOAH WILLIS
        Papers, 1922-74.   BCA (MG14 C30)

        Biographical sketch, booklets, letters (including
        one from Mrs. Roland Michener); photos of this
        Boissevain, Manitoba, resident.

322. MIKOLASEK, TONI AND BESSIE
        Family history.
        1 p. Typescript.   SCRLM

        Settlement of a Polish family in Morden, Manitoba.

323. MILLER, JAMES
        Family history.   BCA (MG14 C65)

        Marriage certificate, 1891; short history of this
        Boissevain, Manitoba, family.

324. MILLER, MRS. K.
        Oral history.
        1 reel (7"), worksheet.   MMN (Tape 48)

Emigration from Germany to Canada in 1911; harsh
economic conditions until 1921; family sickness;
fear of deportation to Europe.

325. MILLER, LAURA (b. 1890)
    Oral history, 1972.
    1 reel (7"), worksheet.   MMN (Tape 315)

    Teacher in one-room Boissevain and Morden, Manitoba,
    schools; description of Morden churches.

326. MILLIKEN FAMILY (1759-1972)
    Family file.
    41 pp.   PAM (MG8 C13)

    Genealogy and notes on the Milliken family reunion
    at Reston, Manitoba, 1973.

327. MINNEDOSA, MANITOBA
    Personal history, 1880-81.
    77 pp. Typescript.   PAM (P267)

    Anonymous account by a "Mrs. E.L.A." of a trip from
    Liverpool, England, to Manitoba; experiences in
    establishing a homestead near Minnedosa.

328. MONCUR, WILLIAM
    Papers, 1884-1981.
    Various items.   BCA (MG14 C164)

    Sketch of Gould Mound (Indian Burial Ground)
    excavated in 1953; a brief history of this
    Boissevain, Manitoba, family, 1900-1981; a book of
    pioneer biographies; manuscript on family history
    written for Beckoning Hills Revisited.

329. MORDEN, ALBERT MARVIN
    Family file.   SCRLM (Vertical file)

    Four-page biographical sketch and clippings of this
    Morden, Manitoba, family.

330. MORDEN, MANITOBA
    History.
    4 pp. Typescript.   SCRLM

    Icelanders pioneering in the Brown Settlement near
    Morden; brief mention of the women involved.

331. MORDEN, MANITOBA
     Oral history, 1981.   SCRLM (Oral History)

     Interviews of Mary Currie, Gail Krieger, and Jacob
     H. Janzen (all Morden area early settlers) by Don
     Schroeder.

332. MORTON, GEORGE LEWIS
     Family file.
     Copies.   BCA (MG14 C109)

     Two-page history of the Morton family farm (by Anna
     G. Diehl) near Boissevain, Manitoba; various
     articles on the G. Lewis Morton family.

333. MORTON RURAL MUNICIPALITY
     Local history.   BCA (MG15 C1)

     Early area history on the municipality and the role
     of the pioneer housewife.

334. MULAIRE, CATHERINE (b. 1843)
     Biographical sketch.
     1 p. Typescript.   SBHSA (Box 19)

335. MUSGROVE, MILDRED
     Papers. Finding aid.   BCA (MG14 C17)

     Boissevain, Manitoba, resident. Family history;
     articles of her international travels;
     correspondence; photographs; miscellaneous
     certificates; newspaper clippings.

336. NANTON, AUGUSTUS MEREDITH (1860-1925)
     Papers, 1915-72.
     49 pp.   PAM (MG14 C85)

     Lawyer. Founding partner of the Osler, Hammond and
     Nanton Law firm, 1884.

337. NAPINKA, MANITOBA
     Local history, 1881-1938.   PAM (MG8 A25)
     30 pp. Typescript.

     Pioneer days, plus addendum by Agnes Yeomans
     Cosgrove.

54

338. NELL FAMILY
          Family history, 1966, ("75 Years of Nell," by Mrs.
          Louis Leipsic).
          4 pp.   PAM (MG10 F3) and
                                         (MG6 F3)

          ("75 Years of Nell," by Mrs. Louis Leipsic.)

339. NELSON, MR. AND MRS. H.A.
          Oral history, 1972.
          1 reel (7"), worksheet.   MMN (Tape 361)

          Farming and sports activity in Carberry, Manitoba,
          in the early 20th century.

340. NELSON RIVER, MANITOBA
          Oral history.
          1 reel (7"), worksheet.   MMN (Tape 694)

          Norman and Dora Macleod and other Cree Indians sing
          songs and relate stories and personal experiences of
          the Nelson River and Jack River areas of northern
          Manitoba.

341. NEUFELD, PETER L.
          Family file.   BCA (MG 14 C68)

          Family history and personal memoirs; clippings;
          history of the Boissevain district area.

342. NEUFELD, MRS. WERNER
          Articles.
          Handwritten and typescript.   BCA (MG14-C20)

          "The School Bus," by Mrs. George Neufeld; several
          other topics.

343. NEWTON, MRS. T.D.
          Oral history, 1980.
          1 reel (7"), worksheet.   MMN (Tape 715)

          Family background; comments on her grandfather and
          prominent Winnipeg financier, Sir Augustus Nanton;
          life in London, England, during World War I; various
          frequent travels.

344. NICKEL FAMILY
          Family file ("The Nickel Story").
                                         WRL

Several biographical sketches and genealogies, since
1821, of this Mennonite family which moved from
Holland to Russia, and eventually to the Winkler,
Manitoba, area.

345. NICKEL FAMILY
Family history, 1977. Nickel, and Grace. "The
Nickel Family Tree: Rooted in Experience and
Memories."
Unpublished paper.   MHCA (Vertical file)

A history of this Altona, Manitoba, Mennonite family
since immigration.

346. NOBLE, AGNES M.
Family file.   BCA (MG14 C104)

Family photos and letters of this Boissevain,
Manitoba, resident.

347. NOBLE, ERNEST AND LUELLA
Family file.   BCA (MG14 C85)

Short history of this Richview, Manitoba, family;
social events in the Richview School District;
discussion of the Richview Beef Ring.

348. NORTHCOTT, MRS.
Oral history, 1972.
1 reel (7"), worksheet.   MMN (Tape 435)

Childhood in Morris, Manitoba; community life;
nursing career at the St. Boniface Hospital;
Winnipeg General Strike of 1919; World War II; and
family life.

349. NORTH KNIFE LAKE, MANITOBA
Oral history, 1973 (Chipewyan). Restricted.
1 reel (7"), worksheet.   MMN (Tape 496)

Ronnie Bussidor, Joe Ellis, Adam Solomon, Tom Celia
and Baptiste Thorassie (all Chipewyan Indians at
North Knife Lake) reciting, sending messages and
singing.

350. NORTON, GEORGE FAMILY
Family file.   BCA (MG14 C3)

History of this Boissevain, Manitoba, family by
Douglas Norton; clippings and picture.

351. NORWAY HOUSE, MANITOBA
         Oral history, 1971.
         1 reel (7"), worksheet.   MMN (Tape 686)

         James Clyne, Jessie Yorke, Flora Balfour, Sophie
         McDonald and Frederick Moore (all Cree Indians at
         Norway House). Food; native clothing from animal
         hides and utensils from clay; trapping and fishing;
         recreational activities; worship; other comments on
         the Cree Indian lifestyle at the turn of the
         century.

352. NORWAY HOUSE, MANITOBA
         Oral history, 1971.
         1 reel (7"), worksheet.   MMN (Tape 685)

         Interviews with Alpheus Wilson, Jemina Folster and
         James and Ellen Apetagon, all Cree Indians, on life
         in the Norway House area. Schooling, upbringing,
         changing values of modern youth.

353. NOWAK, MR. AND MRS.
         Oral history, 1971.
         1 reel (7"), worksheet.   MMN (Tape 660)

         Oppression and religious persecution in the Ukraine;
         immigration to Winnipeg and then to Pine River,
         Manitoba, in the early 1900s; community life in Pulp
         River, Manitoba.

354. OBERLIN, MRS. T.
         Oral history, 1972.
         1 reel (7"), worksheet.   MMN (Tape 378)

         Pioneer days in Melita, Manitoba; rural life; the
         great prairie fires of 1888 and 1890.

355. OGLETREE FAMILY
         History, 1955. ("The Ogletrees of Portage," by O.
         Moss).
         85 pp. Handwritten.   PAM (MG10 F2 Box K-M)

         Louis Riel uprising and the Portage interference;
         education; breaking prairie sod; family life in
         Portage la Prairie, Manitoba.

356. OLAFSON FAMILY
        Family and local history,
        1941.   ERL

        "The Pioneer History, Akra Township, Pembina County,
        North Dakota," compiled by S.T. Olafson and Anna
        Samson Olafson. Documents the Olafson family move
        from Gimli, Manitoba, to North Dakota.

357. OLIVE, G.
        Papers.   TRHM (MG14 B2 Box2)

        Transcona, Manitoba; list of electors, 1953,
        including women and their occupations.

358. OLIVER, MRS. (b. 1894)
        Oral history, 1973.
        1 reel (7"), worksheet.   MMN (Tape 619)

        Immigration to Canada from Iceland in 1900; textile
        worker in Winnipeg; detailed descriptions of
        spinning materials and methods of the weaving craft.

359. O'NEILL, MRS. E.D.
        Oral history, 1972.
        1 reel (7"), worksheet.   MMN (Tape 365)

        Move from Ontario to Winnipeg, Manitoba in 1910;
        education; social and religious life in the city.

360. O'REILLY, MRS. A.M.
        Reminiscences, 1969.
        14 pp. Typescript.   PAM (MG8 B47)

        Historical details of the Larose family and of The
        Pas, Manitoba, 1902-30.

361. ORLIKOW, LIONEL
        Oral histories, 1961.
        (Transcriptions available.)   PAM (MG10 F2 Box 11)

        Interviews conducted by Lionel Orlikow with Mrs.
        James Aiken, Mrs. Stewart and several other Manitoba
        residents.

362. ORR, MRS. J. (b. 1904)
        Oral history, 1972.
        1 reel (7"), worksheet.   MMN (Tape 517)

Childhood and youth in the Mylor district of
Manitoba; farm life and school teaching; effects of
World War I and the Depression on the Pilot Mound,
Manitoba area.

363. ORRISS FAMILIES
     Family histories.   BCA (MG14 C69; C248;
                                               C249)

     Histories of the Arthur Orriss, David and Gabriel
     Orriss, and John Orriss families of Boissevain,
     Manitoba.

364. OSTERWICK, MANITOBA
     Church and village records.
     Microfilm.   MHCA (Microfilm 16)

     One set of genealogical data on the generations of
     persons born between 1800 and 1860 and of another
     generation born between 1820 and 1899.

365. OTTERBURNE, MANITOBA
     Interviews, 1978 (French).   MSB

     Interviews with Antoinette Canaigne, M. and Mme.
     William Clément and Charles Lambert of Otterburne,
     Manitoba.

366. PALMASON, BJARNI AND ANNA
     Family file.   ERL

     A genealogy ("The Palmasons of Vidirasi");
     immigration certificate; homestead patents; other
     materials of this Icelandic family living in the
     Gimli, Manitoba, area.

367. PANTING, GERALD
     Interviews, 1953.   PAM (MG8 B62)

     Several interviews by Gerald Panting with early
     settlers of Morden-Killarney, Manitoba, area
     including the following women: Bella Blackburn,
     Pilot Mound; Mrs. John Broadbent, Thornhill; Mrs.
     F.A. Cowie, Morden; Mrs. Isabella Fargey, La
     Rivière; Mrs. Eleanor High, Killarney; Mrs. Sarah
     Keir, Morden; Mrs Fred Oke, Darlingford; Mrs.
     Stephenson, Morden; Mrs. Austin Watts, Cartwright;
     and several others.

368. PARKINSON, MRS. H.
        Oral history, 1971 (tape faulty).
        1 reel (7"), worksheet.   MMN (Tape 314)

        Author and teacher. Manitoba history and six years
        in Quebec.

369. PATTERSON, ALBERT FAMILY
        Family file, 1847-1979.   BCA (MG14 C1)

        Several histories of the Albert and James A.
        Patterson families of Boissevain, Manitoba; family
        genealogies and descriptions of barn raising and
        pioneering experience.

370. PATTERSON, R. ALVIN FAMILY
        Family file, 1834-1962.   BCA (MG14 B5)

        History of Morden, Manitoba, 1940-64; family
        history, 1982; newsclippings; photograph; and
        descriptions of pioneer life.

371. PATRICK, STEVE AND ANN
        Oral history.
        1 reel (7"), worksheet.   MMN (Tape 711)

        Ukrainian immigrants. Wedding ceremonies; other
        social and cultural activities; folksong.

372. PAUL, IDA (b. 1888)
        Oral history, 1972. Restricted.
        1 reel (7"), worksheet.   MMN (Tape 250)

        Jewish immigrant. Birth in Odessa and immigration
        to Canada in 1905; father's abduction into the
        Russian (Czar's) army; life in Morden, Manitoba, and
        later relocation to Winnipeg; raising chickens for
        extra needed income.

373. PEACOCK, MR. AND MRS. JOHN
        Family history, 1982.   BCA (MG14 C82)

374. PEARLMAN, BERYL RITA
        Family history.   PAM (MG10 F3) and
                                     (MG6 F27)

        "History of the Family Background."

375. PENNER, KATHERINA
        Notebook (Gothic script).   MVMA (E 1184)

        "Schoenschreibsheft der Schuelerin Katerina Penner
        den 25 Januar 1881."

376. PENSONNEAULT, MR. AND MRS. WILHELM
        Video history.
        1 video cassette (3/4"), colour.
                                        CBWFT CSB

        Family history.

377. PETERS, MRS.
        Oral history, 1971.
        1 reel (7"), worksheet.   MMN (Tape 52)

        Family life, seasonal celebrations, and war-time
        hardships in Austria; immigration to Canada and
        consequent hardships; church life (Lutheran); and
        preparation of ethnic foods.

378. PETERSON FAMILY
        Family history.
        8 pp. Typescript.   ERL

        History and genealogy of this Gimli, Manitoba,
        family.

379. PICKERING-THOMSON, MARIE LOUISE
        Diary, about 1960.   PPPL

        Diary and photographs of this Portage la Prairie,
        Manitoba, family.

380. PICKMAN, ROSE (b. 1916)
        Oral history, 1972. Restricted.
        1 reel (7"), worksheet.   MMN (Tape 262)

        Polish Jewish immigrant. Life and marriage in
        Poland; German invasion and occupation during World
        War II; efforts to mask ethnic identity by
        pretending to be Ukrainian; gruesome details of
        anti-Semitism in Poland.

381. PLOTKIN, BERTHA (b. 1889)
        Oral history, 1972.
        1 reel (7"), worksheet.   MMN (Tape 244)

Russian Jewish immigrant. Birth and childhood in
Gomol, White Russia; immigration to Canada in 1905;
move to Winnipeg, Manitoba in 1925; Jewish cultural
life.

382. POCOCK, GEORGE
     Papers, 1884-1905   PAM (MG11 C5)

     Papers include the diary, 1892-93 and 1886-97, of
     Mrs. George Pocock of West Lynne, Manitoba.

383. PRAIRIE ROSE, MANITOBA
     Local history, 1874-1976, ("Love God and Your
     Neighbor Too").
     Typescript.   MVMA (E119)

     History of pioneers in the Prairie Rose district,
     especially of Heinrich R. and Helena Reimer.

384. PRIMROSE, SOUTH DAKOTA
     Minutes, 1950-1972
     10 vols. Handwritten.   BCA (MG10 C2)

     Minutes of the "Primrose Homemakers" and a pamphlet,
     "Pages from Primrose."

385. PROMISLOW, MRS. SHAINDLE
     Oral history, 1972. Restricted.
     1 reel (7"), worksheet.   MMN (Tape 208)

     Jewish immigrant who arrived in Winnipeg as a widow
     shortly after World War I.

386. RABINOVITCH, VERA
     Passports.   PAM (MG10 F3) and
                                    (MG6 F38)

     Russian immigrants. Russian, 1910, and Canadian,
     1957, passports.

387. RANSOM, FAWCETT, FAMILY
     Family history, 1982.   BCA (MG14 C259)

388. RAPID CITY, MANITOBA
     Journal, 1880.   PAM (MG1 B28)

     Extracts from the journal of an anonymous lady on a
     trip from Liverpool, England, to Rapid City.

389. RAYMAN, PEARL (b. 1900)
        Oral history, 1972. Restricted.
        1 reel (7"), worksheet.   MMN (Tape 271)

        Well-educated Austrian Jewish immigrant who
        emigrated with her three children after her husband
        was killed during World War II.

390. REED, MRS. (b. 1897)
        Oral history, 1972.
        1 reel (7"), worksheet.   MMN (Tape 336)

        Early teacher in the Valley River District of
        Manitoba; descriptions of her father; the Winnipeg
        General Strike of 1919.

391. REIFSCHNEIDER, OLGA
        Family file. Finding aid.
        Several items.   PAM (MG9 A97)

        "Memoirs of John Reifschneider re: Manitoba Glass
        Factory"; journals of a 1954 trip from Reno to
        Norway House and Churchill, Manitoba; a 1954
        Churchill Ladies Club Plan of Churchill.

392. REMPEL FAMILY
        Family history, 1980. ("The Rempel Family").
        Unpublished paper, 42 pp.   MHCA (Vertical file)

        Illustrations, maps, tables, accounts.

393. REMPEL, FRANZ FAMILY
        Family file.   SCRLM

        Family history (3 pp.) of a pioneer Morden,
        Manitoba, Mennonite family; a genealogy, 1836-1965.

394. REMPEL, OLGA
        Papers.   MHCA (XX 59 V. 1026,
                                1666, and 1667)

        Mennonite immigrant who moved to Winnipeg, Manitoba,
        in 1947. Brief biographical sketch of the Rempel
        family; Rempel family correspondence (German); one
        notebook (German) of clippings, poetry, and
        correspondence; another mainly of Mennonite women
        who fled Russia first to Germany and ultimately to
        Canada.

395. REMPLE, SUSE
          Family history, 1979. ("The Story of Mrs. Suse
          Remple and her Family" by Debbie Kirkpatrick).
          65 pp. Typescript.   MHCA (Vertical file)

          Story and illustrations.

396. RICE, JESSIE ADELE (b. 1883)
          Oral history, 1972.
          1 reel (7"), worksheet.   MMN (Tape 384)

          Life in Treherne, Manitoba, and later in Toronto,
          Ontario, as an occupational therapist.

397. RICHARDS, HAZEL (b. 1903)
          Oral history, 1972.
          1 reel (7"), worksheet.   MMN (Tape 465)

          Birth and childhood near Cartwright, Manitoba; farm
          life; the effects of World War I, the Depression,
          and the coming of hydro electric power to
          Cartwright.

398. RICHER, MANITOBA
          Oral history, 1972 (French).   MSB (CS)

          Interview with Mme. Elzire Vermette and other Richer
          area residents.

          Biographical Sketch.
          2 pp. Typescript.   SCRLM

399. RIEDIGER, JACOB P. FAMILY
          Biographical sketch.
          2 pp. Typescript.   SCRLM

400. RIEL, SARA
          Papers.   SBHSA (Box 23)

          Photocopies of several 1871 letters; an account of
          her journey to Fort Garry (June 19 to August 25,
          1871); a letter about Sara (Sister) Riel; and a
          typed, 32-page article, "Sara Riel, Témoin de son
          Temps," dealing with her journeys to Red River and
          her relationship with Louis Riel.

401. ROBERTSON, EDWARD AND MATILDA, ET AL
          Oral history, 1971.
          1 reel (7"), worksheet.   MMN (Tape 687)

     64

Cree Indians of northern Manitoba. Schooling in
Norway House, Manitoba; life and survival in the
bush; trading and trapping; snowmobiling;
recreational and religious activities among the
Indians in northern Manitoba.

402. ROBINSON, BETTY
Oral history, 1971.
1 reel (7"), worksheet.   MMN (Tape 663)

Development of the first hospital and a boys' home
in Teulon, Manitoba; reading of her father's (Dr.
Hunter) article, "Educational Experiences at
Teulon"; problems of racial relations with the
Ukrainian teachers in Teulon.

403. ROBINSON, MOLLY
Research and resource file. Restricted. In
personal possession of Ms. Molly Robinson, 39 Nickel
Road, Thompson, Manitoba, R8N OY5.

An unpublished essay, "The Y and I," by a former
director of the YWCA and member of the City Council
in Thompson, Manitoba; other biographical research
material on local women available but restricted.

404. ROBLIN, FINLEY PORTE
Letters, 1874-80.
1".   PAM (MG14 B84)

Winnipeg alderman, 1876. Letters from his wife
describing Winnipeg events.

405. ROBLIN, JOHN AND ELIZABETH MOORE
Family history, 1775-1942.
4 pp. Typescript.   PAM (MG8 C9)

Historical notes on this United Empire Loyalist
family.

406. ROSE, ARTHUR
Papers, 1904-20.   PAM (MG10 F3) and
                          (MG6 D12)

Certificates of naturalization; affidavits of Esther
Rose; marriage licences; memberships; teaching
certificates; other documentary material.

407. ROSS, "GRANNY"
        Biographical sketch.   FFHS/FFPL

        Brief biography of Granny Ross of Flin Flon,
        Manitoba.

408. RUCCIUS, JANET W.
        Oral history, 1971.
        1 reel (7"), worksheet.   MMN (Tape 56)

        Austrian immigrant and wife of an early minister of
        Trinity Lutheran Church in Winnipeg. Immigrations;
        sod hut building; seeding and harvesting; infant
        mortality; anti-German sentiment during World War
        II.

409. ST. BONIFACE, MANITOBA
        Oral history, 1971 (French). Restricted.
        1 reel (7").   MMN (Tape 565)

        M. and Mme. A. Beaudin, Mary Desjardins, Mlle.
        Gosselin, Mme. A. Carrière, Mme. Létourneau and
        several other St. Boniface pioneers sing
        French-Canadian folksongs.

410. ST. BONIFACE, MANITOBA
        Oral history, 1970-71 (French).
        1 reel (7").   MMN (Tape 568)

        Napoleon Lussier, Achille and Mme. Plamondon, and
        other St. Boniface and St. Eustache, Manitoba,
        residents sing French-Canadian folksongs.

411. ST. BONIFACE, MANITOBA
        Oral history 1976 (French).   MSB (CS)

        Interviews with Mme. Helene Kreitz and Mme. Amanda
        Le Bleu, early residents of St. Boniface. Folksongs
        and recollections.

412. ST. BONIFACE, MANITOBA
        Oral history, 1971 (French).   MSB (CL)

        Interview with M. and Mme. Achille Plamondon.

413. ST. BONIFACE, MANITOBA
        Oral history, 1976 (French).   MSB (CL)

Interviews with Mme. L. Vaudry, Mme. Rosanne Chartier, and Mlle. Anna Deschambault of St. Boniface and St. Lazare, Manitoba.

414. ST. CHARLES, MANITOBA   MSB (CL)
     Oral history, 1979 (French).

     Interview with Mme. Maquet.

415. ST. EUSTACHE, MANITOBA
     Oral histories, 1969 (French).
     1 reel.   MSB

     Interviews with Mme. Mackay and M. and Mme. J. Lussier.

416. ST. EUSTACHE, MANITOBA   MSB(CS)
     Oral histories, 1975 (French).

     Interviews with Mme. Théophile Rivard and M. and Mme. Alphonse Sénégal.

417. ST. GEORGES, MANITOBA
     Oral histories, 1977 (French). MSB (CL)

     Interviews with Mme. Fréboine and Mme. Raoul Vincent.

418. ST. JOSEPH, MANITOBA
     Oral history, 1976 (French).   MSB (CL)

     Interviews with M. and Mme. Pelletier and others.

419. ST. LABRE, MANITOBA
     Oral histories, 1950.
     1 reel (7").   MMN (Tape 574)

     Interviews with Mme. René Landry, Mme. Ross and other local residents about hardships in the early years of the community.

420. ST. LAZARE, MANITOBA
     Oral histories, 1976 (French). MSB (CL)

     Interviews with M. and Mme. Boucher, Mme Pauline Pelletier, Mme. Alex Hayden, and other elderly area residents.

421. ST. MALO, MANITOBA
     Oral histories, 1969 (French). Restricted.
     1 reel.   MMN (Tape 552)

     Interviews with and folksongs by M. and Mme.
     Gosselin, Mme. V. Charette and other local
     residents.

422. ST. MALO, MANITOBA
     Oral histories, 1969 (French). Restricted.
     1 reel (7").   MMN (Tape 550)

     Interviews with and songs by Amedée Lambert, Mme.
     Ulysse Lambert, Henri Létourneau and others. Songs,
     fairytales, and reminiscences of pioneer community
     life in St. Malo and in St. Boniface, Manitoba.

423. ST. MALO, MANITOBA
     Oral histories, 1969 (French). Restricted.
     1 reel.   MMN (Tape 551)

     A story by Amedée Lambert entitled "Le Bonnet
     Rouge"; reminiscences of early farm life by Mme.
     Lambert.

424. ST. MALO, MANITOBA
     Oral histories (French).   MSB

     Interviews with Mme. U. Lambert, M.A. Lambert and M.
     Létourneau.

425. ST. PIERRE, MANITOBA
     Oral histories, 1950 (French).
     1 reel.   MMN (Tape 576)

     Mme. Lambert recounts her arrival in St. Pierre,
     describes early village life, and sings folksongs;
     M. and Mme. Lamoureux recall early pioneer days in
     the village.

426. ST. PIERRE, MANITOBA
     Oral history, 1969 (French). Restricted.
     1 reel.   MMN (Tape 560)

     Joseph and Arthur Larivière and Irène Lamoureaux
     sing and play folksongs of the area.

427. SABEL, WILLIAM TURNER
     Papers, 1875-82.
     12 pp.   PAM (MG8 B66)

Diary, 1875; correspondence with his wife and other
family members, 1875-82.

428. SACRE-COEUR PARISH, MANITOBA
Oral histories, 1950 (French).
1 reel (7").   MMN (Tape 575)

Mme. L'Heureux recounts her arrival in Winnipeg,
Manitoba, in 1886; Mme. Enard tells of early times
in St. Charles, Manitoba; several others reminisce.

429. SAIDMAN, MANYA (b. 1888)
Oral history, 1972. Restricted.
1 reel (7"), worksheet.   MMN (Tape 210)

Jewish immigrant. Life in Russia before her
immigration to Canada in 1914; husband's sunflower
seed business; Jewish community life in Winnipeg.

430. SANDISON FAMILY
Family history,("Sandison, the Wheat King" by John
T. McGregor).
Typescript.   DHM ("Brandon People
                                File")

Scottish immigrants. Emigration of family from
Scotland in 1884; early pioneering in Brandon,
Manitoba; fluctuations in family fortunes; eventual
economic ruin and disappearance.

431. SAWSCZYN, Mrs. O.
Oral history, 1971.
1 reel (7"), worksheet.   MMN (Tape 664)

Birth and childhood near Sifton, Manitoba; Ukrainian
religious celebrations and ethnic holidays; later
schooling in southern Saskatchewan; descriptions of
life in Sifton.

432. SCHACTER, MRS. J.C.
Family file (Romanian).
6 pp.   PAM (MG10 F3) and
                                (MG6 D21)

433. SCHAF, MRS. G.A. (b. 1890)
Oral history, 1971.
1 reel (7"), worksheet.   MMN (Tape 33)

Arrival in Canada as an Austro-German immigrant in 1905; market gardening in Brandon, Manitoba; life among the local Austro-German community.

434. SCHIFFERS, MRS.
Oral history, 1971.
1 reel (7"), worksheet.   MMN (Tape 46)

German immigrant. Immigration to Canada from Germany in 1904; her mother's Winnipeg boarding house for rural Mennonite farmers and their wives visiting the city; anti-German prejudice during World War I; her excommunication; desire for assimilation and eventual membership in the First Baptist Church.

435. SCHLIOM, DORA
Oral history, 1971. Restricted.
1 reel (7"), worksheet.   MMN (Tape 272)

Jewish immigrant. Education in the Cheder; father's participation as a co-founder of the Beth Yaacov Shul; its role as a quasi clearing house for immigrants.

436. SCHOM, GITEL (b. c. 1880)
Oral history, 1972. Restricted.
1 reel (7"), worksheet.   MMN (Tape 290)

Jewish immigrant from Russia to Canada in 1906. Difficulties in Russia before emigration; operating her own furniture store in Winnipeg without knowing English; family education.

437. SCHROEDER HILDEGARD AND WILHELM
Ancestral papers.
Diary and Memoirs.   MHCA (XXV B Vol. 1681
                            FD. 67)

1874 diary (5 pp.) of Gertrude Pankratz (b. 1862), Mennonite immigrant, recounting her experiences in Russia before immigrating to Canada; memoirs of Gertrude Enns covering her Russian and Canadian experiences (7 pp.).

438. SCHULTZ, ELIZABETH (1866-1943)
Autobiography. "What A Heritage: Autobiography of Elizabeth Schultz, née Unruh."
147 pp. Typescript.   MHCA (Vertical file)

Translated into English by Mrs. Harry Keyes.

439. SEARLE, MRS. FRED
         Oral history, 1972.
         1 reel (7"), worksheet.   MNN (Tape 316)

         Birth in Treherne, Manitoba; marriage in 1928 at
         Sherritt-Gordon mines; matron of the United Church
         School for Boys at Norway House, Manitoba.

440. SEEBACH FAMILY
         Diaries, 1898-1900; 1929-30.
         1/2".   PAM (MG8 B100)

         Farm diaries of a Mr. and Mrs. Seebach of the
         Seeburn-Angusville district of Manitoba.

441. SELCHEN, NACHMAN
         Oral history, 1969. Restricted.
         1 reel (7"), worksheet.   MNN (Tape 211)

         Jewish Russian immigrant. Immigration to Canada in
         1912; teacher in Ashern, Manitoba; and activities in
         the I.L. Peretz Folk School.

442. SHACK, PAULINE (1891-)
         Oral history.   JHSA (Tape 183)

         A Russian Jewish immigrant from the Ukraine who
         first went to the United States and then to Winnipeg
         at age 13.

443. SHEPPARD, RUBY (b. 1896)
         Oral history, 1972.
         1 reel (7"), worksheet.   MNN (Tape 354)

         Birth and childhood near Binscarth, Manitoba;
         homesteading; illness; prairie fires; grasshopper
         plagues; and her church associations.

444. SIDENBERG, ZELDA (b. c.1894)
         Oral history, 1972. Restricted.
         1 reel (7"), worksheet.   MNN (Tape 294)

         Jewish immigrant. Immigration to Canada in 1913 to
         escape anti-semitism; work in Winnipeg as a servant
         for $2.50/week; efforts to further education;
         marriage and family life.

445. SIGMUNDSON FAMILY

Family history, ("The History of the Sigmundson
Family, compiled by Mrs. June Valgardson, 1977-78
including some material on the Martin Family and the
Valgardson Family").
12 pp. Typescript.   ERL

History and genealogy of this Gimli, Manitoba, area
Icelandic pioneer family.

446. SIGURDSON F.E.
        Reminiscence ("My Childhood on a Bush Farm").
        19 pp.   PAM (MG10 F2)

        An Icelandic woman's childhood on a Manitoba farm.

447. SIGURDSSON, JON FAMILY
        Family file ("Jon Sigurdsson of Gautlönd").
                                       ERL

        An annotated genealogy containing biographical
        sketches, copies of articles and other backgrounds
        material, much of it on the women of this Gimli,
        Manitoba, area Icelandic family.

448. SILVER, PEARL
        Oral history, 1968. Restricted.
        1 reel (7"), worksheet.   MMN (Tape 292)

        Jewish immigrant. Activities in the Jewish
        Orphanage and other Jewish organizations, both as a
        volunteer and staff member.

449. SIMPSON, MRS. A.A.
        Oral history, 1971.
        1 reel (7"), worksheet.   MMN (Tape 12)

        Comparatively recent Danish immigrant. Problems in
        adjusting to modern Canadian society; comparison of
        Canadian and Danish funerals.

450. SINGER, FANNY
        Papers.   PAM (MG10 F3) and
                                       (MG6 D16)

        School diplomas; marriage agreements; resource
        material on the Russian Czars.

451. SISLER, WILLIAM J.
        Interviews, 1949-62.
        Transcripts and photographs.   PAM (MG14 C28 Box2)

Several interviews (some with women). Mr. Sisler
conducted with pioneers and early settlers of the
Rockwood and Woodlands, Manitoba, region.

452. SISSONS, LYNN
Oral history, 1972.
1 reel (7"), worksheet.   MMN (Tape 94)

Winnipeg artist and co-founder of the Winnipeg
Sketch Club. Art techniques; art environment in
Manitoba, 1910-40; pottery painting in the 1920s.

453. SKAPTASON, GUDRUN AND JOSEPH
Family history ("The Genealogy of Gudrun and Joseph
Skaptason taken from the letters they wrote...until
they married," translated by Margaret Stevens.)
54 pp. Typescript.   ERL

Icelandic immigrants. Excerpts of Gudrun
Skaptason's courtship letters describing her work as
a maid after immigrating; her switch from the
Lutheran to the Unitarian church; other of her
life's activities.

454. SLOBINSKY, JACOB AND SARAH (b. 1894)
Oral History. Restricted.
1 reel (7"), worksheet.   MMN (Tape 214)

Jewish immigrant to Canada in 1904. Farm life in
Bird's Hill, Manitoba; reflections on the
grocery-store business from their first general
store in Dominion City, Manitoba, to operating
wholesale and retail grocery concerns in Winnipeg;
data on various Jewish organizations.

455. SMITH, FLORA
Oral history, 1972.
1 reel (7"), worksheet.   MMN (Tape 106)

Birth in Westbourne, Manitoba, of Métis background;
native medicines and midwifery; Red River carts and
pioneer life; experiences as a housekeeper on a
dairy farm with several boarders.

456. SNIKERIS, ELIZA
Oral history, 1974.
1 reel (7"), worksheet.   MMN (Tape 113)

Latvian immigrant. Immigration to Canada in 1948;
academic studies; multiculturalism.

457. SOKOLOV, MR. AND MRS. HYMAN
        Oral history, 1961. Restricted.
        1 reel (7"), worksheet.   MMN (Tape 224)

        His work as former editor of The Jewish Post, their
        activities in local Jewish organizations.

458. SOLTZMAN, ESTHER
        Family history. ("Personal Historical Background").
        1 item.   PAM (MG10 F3) and
                                              (MG6 F25)

        Includes family genealogy.

459. SPARLING, MRS. G.
        Oral history, 1972.
        1 reel (7"), worksheet.   MMN (Tape 97)

        English immigrant of 1902; marriage and subsequent
        domestic farm life at Oak River, Manitoba; Women's
        Institute in Oak River; and boarding German POW's
        during World War I.

460. SPEECHLY, H.M.
        Papers, 1925-71. Unprocessed.
        2 cu. ft.   UMA

        Over 1,300 letters between H.M. Speechly, M.D., and
        his married daughter, Margaret Stansfield detailing,
        his work as a public health official and his fight
        to control mosquito infestations; observation on
        Winnipeg society; comments on Manitoba nature.

461. SPEECHLY, MARY (1873-1968)
        Papers.
        1 folder   UMA (MSS SC 35)

        Bibliography of her papers; various biographical
        materials including a chronology of her life;
        tributes, honours and awards; speeches; one
        photograph; assorted miscellany.

462. SPIGELMAN, SARAH
        Oral history, 1972. Restricted.
        1 reel (7"), worksheet.   MMN (Tape 264)

        Russian Jewish immigrant. Arrival in Canada in
        1907; detailed description of early Winnipeg,
        Manitoba.

74

463. SPIVAK, ANNA (b. 1898)
        Oral history, 1971.
        1 reel (7"), worksheet.   MMN (Tape 668)

        Ukrainian immigrant. Birth and childhood in the
        Ukraine; immigration to Canada in 1923, and
        difficulties adjusting to a new society and being
        accepted; life in Selkirk, Manitoba, during the
        Depression and World War II; her experience in the
        Selkirk Day Care Centre for Senior Citizens.

464. SPIVAK, MIRA
        Personal file.   PAM (MG10 F3) and
                                    (MG6 B7)

        Brochure and circular letter supporting her
        successful candidacy as a school trustee for the
        Winnipeg School Board.

465. SPRINGMAN, ANN
        Oral history, 1972. Restricted.
        1 reel (7"), worksheet.   MMN (Tape 215)

        Lithuanian immigrant. Move to London, England, in
        her early teenage years and her marriage there at
        age 16; immigration to Edenbridge, Saskatchewan,
        before World War I; family life and social events.

466. STACEY, FLORENCE
        Oral history, 1972.
        1 reel (7"), worksheet.   MMN (Tape 479)

        Life and entertainment in Cartwright, Manitoba, and
        surrounding areas; effect of World War I on the
        area.

467. STANKOVIC, MRS.
        Oral history, 1973.
        1 reel (7"), worksheet.   MMN (Tape 317)

        Winnipeg-born, of Polish ancestry; school teaching
        and social work; 1933 appointment as registrar of
        the women's section of the Unemployment Relief (now
        Public Welfare Department); case histories and data
        on relief services during the Depression.

468. STEWART, MRS.
        Oral history, 1961. Interview by Lionel Orlikow.
        Transcription.   PAM (MG10 F2 Tape 3)

Irish immigrant. Arrival in Manitoba in 1881;
Indian trouble in Saskatchewan in 1885; routine
interaction with the native community; Methodist
revivals; farm life; and other incidents.

469. STEWART, GRACE
Oral history, 1972.
1 reel (7"), worksheet.   MMN (Tape 431)

Native of Lancaster, Ontario; youth and marriage in
Oak Lake, Manitoba; descriptions of social and
sports activities in the community.

470. STOCKS FAMILY
Reminiscences, 1870-90 ("The Stocks Family Tree").
12 pp. Photocopy.   PAM (MG8 B43)

In the Lizzie Johnson collection.

471. STOESZ, DAVID
Sermon-books, 1875-1931.   MHCA (XX136, Vol.
1559-1563)

Mennonite minister in the Hanover, Manitoba, area.
Sermon-books full of notes of marriages and burials
giving names, ages at time of wedding, and other
vital-statistics data.

472. STOUGHTON, ARTHUR A. (-1955)
Papers.   UMA (MSS SC16)

Founder of the Department of Architecture at the
University of Manitoba. Letters between him and his
wife, Florence E. Stoughton; three family
photographs; Dr. Elinor Black's 108 pp. unpublished
manuscript, "The Professor and His Wife: The
Stoughton Story: A Memoir."

473. SWAIN-BELL, CAROLYN
Family history, ("A Lamp Was Lit").
48 pp.   PAM (MG8 C33)

History of the Swain and related families.

474. SWAN RIVER, MANITOBA
Local histories.
9 items. Regional Library, Box 999, Swan River,
Manitoba, R0L 1Z0.

The different versions of the history of the Swan
"River Valley," "Swan River Vignettes," the Swan
River Valley "Old Timers Recall Trails" and other
titles.

475. SYKES, MARY
Oral history, 1973.
1 reel (7"), worksheet.   MMN (Tape 99)

Reminiscences of her father, R.B. Russell, a
Winnipeg labour leader; the Winnipeg General Strike
of 1919; her father's imprisonment and involvement
in the OBU (One Big Union).

476. SWARTZMAN, ANNIE
Reminiscence, 1969.   PAM (MG6 F49)

Written by her daughter, Mrs. Eva Durnin.

477. TADOULE LAKE, MANITOBA
Oral history, 1973 (Chipewyan), Restricted.
1 reel (7"), worksheet.   MMN (Tape 488)

Annie and Sandy Clipping and Baptiste Thorassie, all
Chipewyan Indians, encourage relatives to move, as
they did, from Churchill to Tadoule Lake, Manitoba,
where life is perceived as easier and more peaceful.

478. TADOULE LAKE, MANITOBA
Oral history, 1973. Restricted.
1 reel (7"), worksheet.   MMN (Tape 487)

Baptiste Thorassie, Simon and Mary Duck, Sammy
Yassie, and Mary Ton (all Chipewyan Indians in
Tadoule Lake) send messages by way of folksongs,
stories, and drum music to relatives at Churchill,
Manitoba.

479. TADOULE LAKE, MANITOBA
Bussidor, Ronnie, et al.
Oral history, 1973 (Chipewyan and English).
Restricted.
1 reel (7"), worksheet.   MMN (Tape 495)

Ronnie Bussidor, Mr. and Mrs. Adam Solomon, Alfred
Sandberry, Baptiste Thorassie and other Chipewyan
Indians of Tadoule Lake, Manitoba, send messages,
songs and games to relatives in Churchill, Manitoba.

480. TAIT, MARY I. (b. 1914)
        Oral history, 1972.
        1 reel (7"), worksheet.   MMN (Tape 400)

        Life-long resident of Brandon. Reminiscences of life
        in this western Manitoba community.

481. TALBOT, MRS. P.A.
        Oral history, 1971.
        1 reel (7"), worksheet.   MMN (Tape 60)

        Wife of a former speaker of the Manitoba
        legislature. Political life in Manitoba, viewpoints
        on the Winnipeg General Strike of 1919; and Craft
        Guild operations in Winnipeg.

482. TAYLOR, ELIZABETH (b. 1885)
        Oral history, 1972.
        1 reel (7"), worksheet.   MMN (Tape 311)

        Early Quebec childhood before moving west to
        Tyndall, Manitoba, in 1903; family involvement in
        the stone-mason business; domestic work; one-room
        school education; medical services in Tyndall and in
        Selkirk; early dental services in Winnipeg.

483. THEXTON FAMILY
        Family history, 1783-1968.
        In private possession of Mrs. Doris Binding,
        1004-1305 Taylor Ave., Winnipeg, Manitoba, R3W 2K5.

        Unpublished history of a Winnipeg family.

484. THIESSEN, ANNA
        Oral history, 1971.
        1 reel (7"), worksheet.   MMN (Tape 45)

        Mennonite missionary. Church life; education;
        homesteading.

485. THOMAS, LILLIAN BEYNON (1874-1961)
        Letter, 1939.
        2 pp. Photocopy of
        typescript.   PAM

        Written to her cousin, Jennie Macham, with
        references to her scribblings, family genealogy, and
        personal activities.

486. THOMAS, MRS. S.
        Oral history, 1972.
        1 reel (7"), worksheet.   MMN (Tape 478)

        Schooling in West Derby, Manitoba; prairie fires and
        storms; the effects of the Depression on the
        Cartwight, Manitoba, area; events pertaining to both
        world wars.

487. THOMPSON, MRS. E.
        Oral history, 1972.
        1 reel (7"), worksheet.   MMN (Tape 367)

        Schooling; social life; family experiences in
        Hartney, Manitoba.

488. THORSTEINSSON, EFTIR GUDNA
        Personal history (Icelandic).
        14 pp. Typescript.   ERL

        Icelandic settler. "Saya Gimli-boejar fro 1875 ti
        1940": The story of one of Gimli's first
        postmistresses.

489. THORSTEINSSON, GUDNI
        Family genealogy.
        12 pp. Typescript.   ERL

        Annotated genealogy of this Gimli, Manitoba, area
        Icelandic family.

490. THORSTEINSSON, THORSTEIN
        Local history ("History of New Iceland").
        Translation in the possession of Prof. David
        Arnason, St. John's College, Winnipeg, Manitoba.

        Contains passages by Margaret Sveinsson who came to
        Gimli in 1908 from the homestead where she was born
        (p. 27); some anecdotal material; many facts about
        the pioneer settlement and its development into a
        20th-century town.

491. TILLENIUS, MRS. CARL L.
        Oral history, 1964.
        1 reel (7"), worksheet.   MMN (Tape 137-2)

        Norwegian immigrant and mother of artist, Clarence
        Tillenius. Pioneering life in the interlake area of
        Manitoba.

492. TIPPING, FRED.
          Oral history, 1971.
          3 reels (7"), worksheet.   MMN (Tape 88-3)

          Winnipeg labour leader. Manitoba trade unions and
          the Winnipeg General Strike of 1919; socialism;
          women's rights.

493. TRANSCONA, MANITOBA
          Oral histories, 1950 (French).
          2 reels (7").   MMN (Tape 579-2)

          Interviews with Sister St. Odile (of the Oblate
          Sisters), Mme. Comeau, Mme. Béatrice St. Amant, Mme.
          Omer and other Transcona residents providing details
          on Catholic school education, community life and
          work with retarded children.

494. TRUDEL, MRS. J.J.
          Oral history, 1971.
          1 reel (7"), worksheet.   MMN (Tape 32)

          Early life in St. Boniface, Manitoba; house
          descriptions; personalities; recreation in early
          20th-century Winnipeg.

495. TUCK, MRS. (b. 1885)
          Oral history, 1972.
          1 reel (7"), worksheet.   MMN (Tape 442)

          Home and farm life in Brandon, Manitoba.

496. TURNPENNY, MARGARET
          Biographies.
          5". Typed and printed.   PAM (MG9 A58)

          Compilation of biographies of early residents of
          Ste-Anne des Chênes, Giroux, Ridgewood, Clear
          Springs and Steinbach, Manitoba.

497. URIE, MR. AND MRS. ALBERT EDWARD (1903-67)
          Diaries, 1903-67.
          57 vols.   PAM (MG8 B32)

          Mr. Albert Urie's diaries, 1903-62; Mrs. Urie's
          diaries, 1962-67.

498. VARE, ETHEL (b. 1898)
        Oral history.
        Transcript available.   TRHM

        Move from Ontario to Transcona, Manitoba, with
        family in 1909; career work as a millinery;
        involvement in the Winnipeg General Strike of 1919;
        religious and social experiences.

499. VAUGHAN FAMILY
        Papers, 1786-1875.
        1".   PAM (MG8 D24)

        "Historical Traditions of the Vaughan Family" by
        A.H. Vaughan; various commissions and appointments.

500. VICTOR, DR. B.A. AND ROSE
        Correspondence, 1931-42.   PAM (MG10 F3) and
                                    (MG5 A11)

        Includes a 1919 medical registration certificate.

501. VICTOR, ROSE (b. 1897)
        Oral history, 1972. Restricted.
        1 reel (7"), worksheet.   MMN (Tape 429 2)

        Lithuanian Jewish immigrant. Teacher of
        underprivileged children and immigrants; husband's
        medical practice in Winnipeg, Manitoba; their visit
        to Russia in 1936; World War II and her efforts on
        the home front.

502. VINCENT, THE REVEREND W.R.
        Papers.
        In his personal possession, 871 Autumnwood Dr.,
        Winnipeg, R2J 1C2.

        Letters, 1880-1902; diaries, 1888-1902 of Archdeacon
        Vincent of the Rupert's Land Diocese; family
        photographs, 1850-1900.

503. VISCHER, MR. AND MRS. FRANS S.
        Oral history, 1972. Restricted.
        1 reel (7"), worksheet.   MMN (Tape 225)

        Painters. Post-war Dutch immigrants. Life in
        Holland during World War II; problems of Canadian
        artists and painters; views on Jews.

504. VOLGA, MANITOBA
        Local history, 1898-1957 ("The History of Volga
        (1878-1957)," prepared by the Junior Historians of
        Don School, 1963).
        Handwritten; illustrated.   PAM (MG10 F2 Box P-Z)

        Extensive accounts and pictures of early pioneering
        life in Volga, Manitoba.

505. WACH, ANNE
        Oral history, 1972.
        1 reel (7"), worksheet.   MMN (Tape 540)

        Ukrainian immigrant. Secretary Ukrainian Canadian
        Committee. Immigration to settlement in
        Saskatchewan, 1934; schooling; removal to Winnipeg,
        Manitoba, in 1944; substantial information on the
        Ukrainian National Federation, the Ukrainian Youth
        Organization, and several other Ukrainian societies
        and organizations.

506. WALDHEIM CEMETERY
        History.   SCRLM

        Listing of those interred.

507. WALDMAN, IDA (b. 1895)
        Oral history, 1972. Restricted.
        1 reel (7"), worksheet.   MMN (Tape 254)

        Russian Jewish immigrant. Birth, youth and marriage
        in Russia; immigration to Canada in 1921 to join her
        husband; difficulties in learning English; husband's
        death and eventual remarriage; family finances.

508. WALLACE, MARY
        Oral history, 1973.
        1 reel (7"), worksheet.   MMN (Tape 599)

        Family and community life in Addington, Manitoba;
        teacher in both rural and urban settings and once as
        an exchange teacher to England; comments on the
        Manitoba Teacher's Society.

509. WALLACE, MRS. W.D. (b. 1895)
        Oral history, 1972.
        1 reel (7"), worksheet.   MMN (TAPE 477)

        Railroading in Manitoba in the early 1900s (father
        was a railroad contractor); tent living;

entertaining; World War I; various highlights in the
history of Cartwright, Manitoba.

510. WATT, MRS. G. (b. 1891)
     Oral history, 1972.
     1 reel (7"), worksheet.   MMN (Tape 448)

     Turn of the century Winnipeg society, schools and
     downtown area; recreation; local events pertaining
     to World War I.

511. WAUGH, RICHARD DEANS (c. 1868-1938)
     Papers, 1910-38.
     1".   PAM (MG14 B4)

     Mayor of Winnipeg, Manitoba, 1912, 1915-16. Family
     papers; scrapbook of newspaper clippings.

512. WAWRYKOW, GEORGE AND MARTHA
     Family file.   ERL

     Genealogy and brief sketches of various members of
     this Gimli, Manitoba, family.

513. WEINSTEIN, ROSE
     Oral history, 1972. Restricted.
     1 reel (7"), worksheet.   MMN (Tape 218)

     Jewish immigrant. Youth spent in Bender Hamlet
     Colony before her marriage; Jewish life in
     Winnipeg, Manitoba.

514. WEISMAN, MRS. JACK (b. 1896)
     Oral history, 1972.
     1 reel (7"), worksheet.   MMN (Tape 219)

     Romanian Jewish immigrant. Immigration to Winnipeg,
     Manitoba, in 1909; detailed description of Jewish
     life in Winnipeg as well as pertinent information
     regarding her education and early years in Romania.

515. WESTBOURNE, MANITOBA
     Historical collection.

     Papers and oral histories. In the personal custody
     of Mr. and Mrs. Gamble, Box 113, Westbourne,
     Manitoba, R0H 1P0.

Interviews with such early settlers of Westbourne as
Kate Lynch, Edna Davey and Verna Garrioch. Much
other material.

516. WESTOVER, LUCINDA AND ADA
        Letter, n.d.   PAM (MG8 A16)

        This letter to Rev. and Mrs. James Davidson
        regarding life at Lowe Farm, Manitoba.

517. WHITESIDE, MISS R.
        Oral history, 1972.
        1 reel (7"), worksheet.   MMN (Tape 542)

        Career as a history teacher in Winnipeg High
        Schools; her work with immigrant children; the role
        of the teacher in the education process.

518. WIEBE, DR. AND MRS. C.W.
        Biographical sketch, 1972.
        3 pp. Typescript.   WRL

        Specially designed historical flashback to highlight
        the contributions of the Wiebe family to Winkler,
        Manitoba, area.

519. WIEDEMAN, AGATHA PETERS
        Biographical sketch, 1977 ("Early Days: An Interview
        with Mrs. Agatha Wiedeman, Plum Coulee, Manitoba").
        1 item.   MHCA (Vertical file
                                       biography)

        An unpublished paper of a Manitoba Mennonite family.

520. WIENS, JOHANN J. (b. 1891)
        Autobiography.   SCRLM

        Daily life of a devout Mennonite family from the
        vexing times of the 1917 Russian Revolution to
        immigration and settlement in the Morden, Manitoba,
        area.

521. WILDER, MRS. H.E.
        Biographical sketch.   JPL (Vertical file)

        Leader in community and philanthropic ventures.

522. WILLIAMS, MR. AND MRS. J.N.E.
        Oral history, 1972.
        1 reel (7"), worksheet.   MMN (Tape 370)

        School days at St. John's College, Winnipeg,
        Manitoba.

523. WILLIAMSON, THELMA (b. 1916)
        Oral history.
        Transcription available.   TRHM

        Childhood and education in Transcona, Manitoba;
        financial and social aspects of the Depression in
        this railroad, blue-collar community.

524. WILLMS, ANNA WARKENTIN (1824-1910)
        Biographical sketch, 1975 ("Taunty Wellmschy" by
        Mary Regehr Dueck).
        1 item.   MHCA (Vertical file)

        A Mennonite family.

525. WILSON, HELEN
        Oral history, 1971.
        1 reel (7"), worksheet.   MMN (Tape 78)

        Scottish immigrant. Anglican Church; Depression;
        Winnipeg General Strike of 1919; World War II and
        its effect on Winnipeg.

526. WINKLER, HOWARD W.
        Papers and family file, 1859-1970. Restricted.
        10'.   PAM (MG14 B44)

        Member of Parliament for Lisgar, 1935-63.
        Correspondence relating primarily to the Winkler
        family, 1859-1970.

527. WINKLER, VALENTINE
        Papers. Finding aid.
                                       PAM (MG14 B45)

        Manitoba politician. The collection includes many
        letters of the World War I era with many other
        Manitoba women such as E. Cora Hind, Jane J.
        Pulsford, Maude E. Pearson, Kate Hemming, and Adèle
        S. Shragge.

528. WOODRIDGE, MANITOBA
          Oral history, 1971 (French).   MSB (CL)

          Interviews with Ovila Vandal, M. and Mme. Poitras,
          M. and Mme. Henri Grenier, and Mme. Rémi André,
          residents of Woodridge and St. Labre, Manitoba.
          Singing and instrumental music included.

529. YOUNG, MRS. M.
          Oral history, 1972.
          1 reel (7"), worksheet.   MMN (Tape 364)

          School teaching in the Holland, Manitoba, area;
          relations between various nationalities in that
          region.

530. ZEAL, MRS. CHARLES
          Correspondence, 1921-22.
          2 items.   PAM (MG10 F3) and
          (MG6 F20)

          Includes a letter on immigration matters of the
          Zelezniok family.

531. ZEILIG, ESTHER
          Oral history. Restricted.
          1 reel (7"), worksheet.   MMN (Tape 221)

          Jewish immigrant from Romania. Immigration to
          Canada as a youth; farm life at Fort Qu'Appelle;
          marriage in Winnipeg; activities in several Jewish
          organizations; life during the Depression.

532. ZUK, MR. AND MRS.
          Oral history, 1971.
          1 reel (7"), worksheet.   MMN (Tape 451)

          Ukrainian immigrants. Life in the Ukraine;
          immigration to Canada; social life.

PRE-1867.   FUR TRADE AND THE RED RIVER SETTLEMENT

533. ASSINIBOIA, COUNCIL OF
          Papers, 1811-70. Finding aid.
          7 boxes; several reels of microfilm (35 mm)
                                    PAM (MG2)

The Council of Assiniboia dates from the appointment of Andrew Bulger to govern the Red River settlement in 1822. The community was then composed of Selkirk settlers; Hudson's Bay and former North-West Company officers, men, and their country-born families; the Des Meurons soldiers who settled along the banks of the Seine River; a fairly large contingent of Swiss immigrants for a relatively brief period; and the French Canadians.

Although the Council was appointed, it "became representative and usually reflected the sense of the community"; it was also "proprietary government by the House of Douglas until 1834 when it was returned to the Hudson's Bay Company."

The papers of the Council are divided into three categories:
(a) Selkirk Period, 1811-35;
(b) Council of Assiniboia, 1835-69;
(c) Individuals and Settlement (5 women are specifically listed).

Minutes of the Council, 1832-69 and of the Executive Relief Committee (including statistical summaries of each Roman Catholic parish of 1868); financial records of the Council, 1838-69; census enumerations and tabulations, 1831-70; settlement papers, 1845-47; court records; and military correspondence, 1845-70.

534. BEGG, ALEXANDER
Questionnaires, mid 1880s.
1 volume.   Public Archives of
                                  British Columbia

Historian. Questionnaires devised, disseminated, and retrieved by Alexander Begg among western Canadian settlements and which gave respondents' birthplaces, nationalities and places of residence, many of which were in Manitoba. For a printed study of this questionnaire see Susan Jackel, ed., A Flannel Shirt and Liberty: British Emigrant Gentlewomen in the Canadian West, 1880-1914 (Vancouver and London: The University of British Columbia, 1982).

535. BELANGER, HORACE
Family file.   SBHSA (Box 1)

Marriages; age at marriage; number of children in 1880s.

536. DUBUC, JOSEPH (1840-1914)
        Papers.   PAM (MG14 B26)

        Letters from Louis Riel, 1870s; his sister Sara
        Riel, 1871-78; Archbishop A.A. Taché, 1871-91;
        clippings, autobiography and memoirs.

537. GABOURY, MARIE ANNE
        Papers.
        3".   SBHSA (Box #10)

        Biography; articles and newsclippings on early
        French Canadians in the Canadian Northwest; several
        articles on Jean-Baptiste Lagimodière.

538. GARRY, NICHOLAS
        Diary, 1822-35.
        1 item.   HBCA

        Deputy-Governor of the Hudson's Bay Company,
        1822-35. Life in the fur trade-era.

539. GENERAL QUARTERLY COURT. DISTRICT OF ASSINIBOIA
        Minutes, 1844-92.
        2".   PAM (MG2 B4-1)

540. "A GLIMPSE OF YESTERDAY"
        Film, 1974. Located at Brandon Historical Society,
        62 Clement Drive, Brandon.
        15 minutes, 16 mm., sound.

        Series of old stills of early pioneer days.
        Produced by Mrs. Effie McPhail.

541. GUNN, GEORGE H.
        Papers and compilations.   PAM (MG9 A78.2)

        Historian. Original licences and permits to men and
        women to trade in the Red River Settlement;
        collected essays including "Old Julia," by Leonora
        K. Hoff; "Sketch of the Tully Tragedy," by Mrs.
        A.J. Goodall; "History of the Scotch Settlement from
        Pioneer Days," by Mrs. John Sutherland; and "The
        Pembina Country," by Mrs. Alice G. Hager; other
        papers.

542. HARBRIDGE, MRS. GEORGE
        References, 1822.   PAM (C.1/M.1 CMS)

Schoolmistress in the Red River Settlement. A
controversial figure during the tenure of James West
and David Jones.

543. HUDSON'S BAY COMPANY
     Corporate Archives,
     1670-present.   HBCA

Constitutes a separate division of the Provincial
Archives of Manitoba. A gift to Manitoba from Great
Britain documenting over 300 years of the
involvement of the Hudson's Bay Company in North
America. The voluminous holdings have been
subdivided into at least 8 categories:

(a) London main office records (1670-1960's):
correspondence; minute books; ledgers; account
books; personnel records;

(b) Post records, 1715-1950s: trading post and fort
records of all North American Hudson's Bay Company
installations, past and present; minute books;
journals; correspondence; account books; post files;

(c) Ships logs, 1750s to mid 1900s: passenger lists;
accounts; crew lists;

(d) Governor/Commissioner papers: papers of
highest-ranking Company officials in Canada
including, but not confined to, Governor George
Simpson. Correspondence; accounts; staff records.

(e) Private manuscripts: papers by or about
individuals or events not employed by or directly
pertaining to the Bay. Journals; correspondence;
some census returns, 1830s; scattered baptism and
marriage certificate records.

(f) Subsidiaries of the Bay: some papers of the
North-West Company, Puget Sound Agricultural
Society, the Russian American Company, the XY
Company and other fur-trading companies.

(g) Maps.

(h) Western department land records.

(i) Twentieth-century corporate files.

Of particular value for their references to
frontier/fur-trading women are at least the
following: the Winnipeg Post Journals (B 235/a/3);
Governor George Simpson's Journal, 1821-22 (D 3/3);
Frances Simpson's Journal, 1830 (D 6/4); Red River

89

Census (E 5/1); Red River Settlement Papers relating
to the Disturbances, 1814-90 (E 8/8); Journal
ascribed to Paul Reynberger (Swiss settler), 1821-22
(E 8/9); diaries of Colin Robertson (6 Vols),
1814-17 (E 10/1).

Hundreds of women referred to by name in the
archives including Anne Thomas Christie
(B59/2/1:86), Mrs. William Cochran (C1/M1), Mrs.
George Harbridge, teacher (C1 M1), and Mrs. David T.
Jones.

544. INKSTER, JOHN AND MARY
     Papers, 1850-1916. Finding aid.
     1 1/2".   PAM (MG2 C22)

     Mainly correspondence, including letters from two of
     their daughters married to employees of the Hudson's
     Bay Company, which provides details and insights
     into fur-trade life.

545. KENNEDY, ELEANOR E. (1825-1908)
     Papers, 1854-1905   PAM (MG2 C2)

     Painter, musician and teacher. Red River Settlement
     women and social events; comparisons of English and
     American women; 1861 trip from London to the Red
     River; women's role in assisting departing Union
     soldiers from St. Paul, Minnesota during the U.S.
     Civil War; attitudes towards Louis Riel; teacher at
     Miss Davis Academy; settlement in St. Andrews,
     Manitoba, with husband Captain William Kennedy.
     (St. Andrews homestead is now a museum.)

546. LAGIMODIERE, JEAN BAPTISTE
     Biographies.
     2 items.   PAM (MG 8 C1)

     Biography of his wife, Marie-Anne Gaboury and of
     himself.

547. LOGAN, ROBERT (c. 1775-1866)
     Family papers, 1819-92.   PAM (MG2 C23)

     Employee of the North West Company and later of the
     Hudson's Bay Company. Correspondence; last will and
     testament; legacies; biographies; related papers.

548. MCDERMOT, ANDREW (c. 1790-1881)
     Letters.
     11 pp.   PAM (MG 8 C26)

Include letters from Felicity McDermot, from
Ireland, to an Elizabeth Pace.

549. MACFARLANE, RODERICK
        Papers, 1841-1929.
        121 pp.   PAM (MG1 D16)

        Geographers. Chief Factor of the Hudson's Bay
        Company who previously served the Company at
        Pembina, Fort Good Hope and Athabasca.

550. MCLEOD, JOHN (1788-1849)
        Journal, 1811-14.   PAM (MG1 D5)

        Hudson's Bay Company post master at the Red River
        Settlement.

551. MACLEOD, MARGARET (1877-1966)
        Papers.
        7 boxes.   UMA (MSS 15)

        Voluminous research notes produced by the author for
        her publication, Letters of Letitia Hargrave. Much
        data given on Letitia Hargrave, her husband James
        Hargrave, and several other employees of the
        Hudson's Bay Company between 1837 and 1865 and of
        the Hargrave family up to 1947. Included are
        materials about the Red River Settlement and
        photographs.

552. DES MEURONS
        List, 1816.
        1 item.   SBHSA (Box 66)

        List of women married to the Des Meurons (Lord
        Selkirk's hired soldiers), giving ages.

553. RED RIVER SETTLEMENT
        Miscellaneous letters and documents, 1823-36.
                                   PAM (MG2 A6)

        Considerable number of references to women in the
        Selkirk settlement in this very long collection.

554. MORRIS, ALEXANDER (1826-89)
        Papers.   PAM (MG12 B1)

        Lieutenant Governor. Correspondence includes
        letters, 1873, from a Mary Carpenter of Bristol,

England, concerning prison contruction and
discipline.

555. RHODES, GERTRUDE A. (1813-94)
Papers. Finding aid.
Originals and microfilm (35
mm)   PAM (MG2 C21 M330-332
                                 and M345)

Prominent Red River Settlement resident.
Correspondence; extracts from church registers;
papers relating to the Hudson's Bay Company;
minutes, accounts and petitions to the Council of
Assiniboia; list of Roman Catholic families in the
Red River Settlement, facts and testimonies in the
Corbitt vs. Dallas trial, 1839; list of marriages,
1864-67; marriage registers, 1813-83.

556. "RIEL FAMILY: HOME AND LIFESTYLE AT ST. VITAL,
1860-1910"

Commissioned study, 1980, Parks Canada Historical
Research Division.
133 pp. Typescript.   PAM (MR 379)

Historical information on the Louis Riel family.
Footnotes; bibliography; maps and diagrams.

557. "THE RIEL AND LAGIMODIERE FAMILIES IN METIS SOCIETY
1840-60"; AND "RIEL HOUSE, ST. VITAL"
Commissioned studies, 1975 and 1977, by Robert
Gosman, Parks Canada Historical Research Division.
2 manuscripts: 139 pp. and 47 pp. Typescripts.
                             PAM (MR 171)

Analysis of Métis society in the Red River
Settlement and the place occupied by the Riel and
Lagimodiere families within it (among "the elite");
a description of the Riel home.

558. ROSS, DONALD (c. 1797-1852)
Papers, 1816-77.
Originals and 3 reels of microfilm (35
mm)   PAM (MG1 D20)

Chief Factor, Hudson's Bay Company, confidential
secretary to Sir George Simpson. Family
correspondence; marriage certificates; letter from
Mary Evans; other materials.

559. "ST. ANDREW'S PARSONAGE, RED RIVER: A STRUCTURAL AND
LAND USE HISTORY"
Commissioned study, 1978 and 1981, by Rodger C.
Guinn, Parks Canada Historical Research Division.
174 pp. Typescript.   PAM (MR 251)

Details of the daily life of William and Anne
Cochran, the Cowleys, and other missionaries.

560. SELKIRK, THOMAS DOUGLAS, FIFTH EARL OF (1771-1820)
Papers, 1803-18.
20 reels Microfilm.   PAM (MG2 A1)

Pioneer settler and founding Governor of the Red
River Settlement. Correspondence; journals and
diaries, 1803-18; Fort William papers, 1816-17;
calendar; index; list of "Free Canadians," wives and
children at Red River, February 1814; names of
settlers at Red River around 1818.

561. SIMPSON, FRANCES R.
Journal, 1830.
1 item.   HBCA (D6/4)

Wife of Governor George Simpson. Daily journal of a
voyage: "From Montreal through the Interior of
Canada, to York Factory on the Shores of Hudson's
Bay," May 2 to June 26, 1830.

562. SUTHERLAND, ALEXANDER
Correspondence, 1815-47.   PAM (MG2 C1-16)

Early Lord Selkirk settler. Correspondence from
Scotland and from Port Talbot, Upper Canada, to A.
Sutherland and his wife, Catherine McPherson, giving
insights into life at the Red River Settlement.

563. TRUTHWAITE, ELIZABETH
Letters, 1843-62.
2 items.   PAM (MG 2C-11)

Letters from Jane Vincent to Elizabeth Truthwaite
from Moose Factory and elsewhere.

564. WEST, JOHN (1778-1845)
Papers, journal.
110 pp., 6 microfilms.   PAM (M67 B1)

References to women (both native and European);
their relationships to traders; education; marriages

of the Des Meurons to women of the newly arrived
Swiss settlers. Journal largely published as The
Substance of a Journal During a Residence at the Red
River Colony, British North America (London: John
West, 1824).

NATIVE LIFE, IMMIGRATION AND ETHNICITY

Native Population

565. BALLANTYNE, MARIE
        Private writings. Restricted.
        In her personal possession, Box 16, 59 Elizabeth
        Road, Thompson, Manitoba, R8N 1X4.

        Articles and essays on native life including
        "Interpretation of Dreams," "Teachings of My
        Elders," and "Finding My Identity,"

566. BRIGDEN, BEATRICE
        Papers.
        Several boxes.   PAM (MG14 C19)

        Among the many other materials in this collection
        are papers relating to the annual Indian and Métis
        Conference, 1954-69, including conference
        proceedings, annual reports, briefs, newsletters and
        correspondence; minutes, reports, and financial
        statements of the Indian and Métis Friendship Centre
        in Winnipeg; intermittent runs of such Indian
        newspapers as the Esterville Free Herald (1967),
        Echo (1962), and Prairie Call (1961-68).

567. FLIN FLON INDIAN AND METIS FRIENDSHIP CENTRE
        (a) Operating files. Restricted.
        Located at 57 Church Street, P.O. Box 188, Flin
        Flon, Manitoba, R8A 1M7. Organized in 1966 as a
        centre for native peoples' activities and as an
        emergency hostel for men and women. Minutes;
        reports; financial records.

        (b) Scattered materials.   FFHS/FFPL
        General history; story of the Métis Friendship
        Centre by Mrs. T. Padgham; articles.

568. FLIN FLON NATIVE OUTREACH PROJECT
Operating files. Restricted.
Located at 57 Church Street, P.O. Box 188, Flin
Flon, Manitoba, R8A 1M7.

Organized in 1979 to encourage native women to
upgrade their education and improve chances for
employment. Minutes; financial records; seminar
reports; client contacts; publications and brochures
from other northern organizations.

569. FLIN FLON NATIVE RELOCATION PROGRAM, LADIES AUXILIARY
Operating files. Restricted.
Located at P.O. Box 267, Flin Flon, Manitoba.

Organized in 1979 to assist native women by teaching
homemaking and child-care skills, giving home
relocation assistance, and helping upgrade their
education. Monthly reports; minutes; financial
statements; client contacts.

570. INDIAN FAMILY CENTRE, INC.
Operating files.
Located at 470 Selkirk Avenue, Winnipeg, Manitoba,
R2W 2M5.

A quasi-religious, socially-oriented organization
designed to meet the spiritual and family needs of
native families.

571. INDIAN HANDICRAFTS OF MANITOBA
Papers, 1959-74. Finding aid.
2'4".   PAM (MG10 C49)

(a) Constitution and by-laws, 1963-68; minutes,
correspondence, financial statements and reports,
1959-72; newsclippings 1959-74; files of Lloyd
Benton, Secretary of the Indian and Métis Committee;
community Welfare Planning Council of Winnipeg,
1961-64.

(b) A.D. Longman collection.
Related materials, 1967-69.   PAM (MG10 C48)

Minutes; correspondence; memos; financial
statements; board meeting minutes; membership data.

572. ISLAND FALLS AND SANDY BAY INDIANS
Tape recordings, 1975. CBC Focus resources.
1 reel (7 1/2").   FFHS/FFPL (Tape)

Oral study and report.

573. JACKHEAD INDIAN RESERVE
        History.   RLDA (DRL-84-26)

        Anglican Women's Auxiliary study of the history of
        women's work.

574. KATERA (KETERI) TEKAWITH MISSION
        Operating files. Restricted.
        Located at 80 Lydia Street, Winnipeg, Manitoba, R3A
        1K8.

        Formerly St. John-Bosco Centre. A ministry of
        social justice for Catholic native people of
        Winnipeg providing liaison with various urban social
        and welfare agencies and providing clothing
        services, community kitchens, and other types of
        support in times of crisis. Minutes and reports;
        financial records; membership lists; project
        descriptions.

575. KINEW HOUSING CORPORATION
        Operating files. Restricted.
        Located at 129-818 Portage Avenue, Winnipeg,
        Manitoba, R3G 0N4.

        Incorporated in 1970 as a non-profit housing service
        for native people in Winnipeg. Minutes; reports;
        lists of homes and addresses; purchases, rentals;
        renovations; financial records.

576. LAHONEN, KATHY
        Diary. Restricted.
        In possession of author, P.O. Box 267, Flin Flon,
        Manitoba.

        Observations by a self-educated native public
        servant on changes among modern native peoples;
        personal reflections.

577. MCALLISTER, MRS. JOHN
        Phonograph, 1950.
        1 record (78 rpm).   PAM (AV C1)

        "Bungi Stories," told by the daughter of Premier
        John Norquay.

578. MANITOBA CONFERENCE BRANCH OF THE WOMEN'S AUXILIARY
        Studies.   UCA-W

Reports and studies of various Indian Study
Committees.

579. METIS LANDS/FAMILIES
        Letters and Public Notices,
        1871-76.   SBHSA (Box 66)

        Letters of and about various Métis families,
        marriages and child-rearing practices. Public
        notices for several Manitoba Roman Catholic parishes
        regarding a grant of 1,400,000 acres of land given
        to children of half-breed heads of families.
        Information provided; name of allotted; number of
        township; description of land; legal sub-division.

580. NATIVE ALCOHOLISM COUNCIL OF MANITOBA
        Operating files. Restricted.
        Located at 203-865 1/2 Main Street, Winnipeg,
        Manitoba, R2W 3N9.

        A counselling service and rehabilitation centre for
        native people with serious alcohol problems.
        Minutes; reports; financial records; lists of staff
        and patients; case histories.

581. NATIVE COMMUNICATIONS, INC.
        Operating files.
        Located at 1 Public Road, Box 5, Thompson, Manitoba.

        Organized to promote the use of native languages
        throughout Manitoba on radio, television, newspaper,
        and other forms of mass media.

582. NATIVE MINISTRY
        Operating files. Restricted.
        Located at 425 Elgin Avenue, Winnipeg, Manitoba, R3A
        1P2.

        A United Church of Canada affiliation comprised
        mainly of women. Board meeting minutes; financial
        records; reports.

583. NATIVE WOMEN'S TRANSITION CENTRE, INC.
        Operating files, 1978-   . Restricted.
        Located at 367 Selkirk Avenue, Winnipeg, Manitoba.

        A home for native women and children requiring or
        seeking change in their present life situations.
        Minutes; reports; financial records.

97

584. NORTHEND COMMUNITY MINISTRY
          Operating files. Restricted.
          Located at 470 Stella Avenue, Winnipeg, Manitoba,
          R2W 2V1.

          An outgrowth of the Old Stella Mission of the United
          Church of Canada, providing emergency assistance,
          clothing depots, programs for children, family
          visiting, and other social action services.
          Minutes; monthly reports; lists of volunteers;
          financial records.

585. THE PAS FRIENDSHIP CENTRE
          Operating files.
          Located at 81 Edwards Avenue, Box 2638, The Pas,
          Manitoba, R9A OH7.

          Organized in 1960 as The Pas Indian and Métis
          Friendship Centre. Offers folk and modern dancing,
          pow wows, teen and senior citizens activities,
          baseball, arts and crafts, cross-cultural awareness.
          Newsletters; minutes; financial records; reports.

Immigration - General

586. GOVERNMENT OF CANADA. IMMIGRATION BRANCH RECORDS
          Departmental files. Finding aid.
                                        PAM (MG4 D1)
          About 650 reels of microfilm, 1865-1908.

          Affiliated with the Department of Agriculture until
          1892, from 1892 to 1917 with the Department of
          Interior, from 1917 to 1936 with the Department of
          Immigration and Colonialization, with Mines and
          Resources until 1949, with Citizenship and
          Immigration from 1944 to 1961, and with the
          Department of Manpower and Immigration from 1966 to
          the present. General Records and passenger ship
          lists.

          (a) Canadian Council Of Immigration Of Women.
          Administrative records, 1922-29.
          Several folders.   PAM (MG4 D1 Vols.
                                        115-116)

          Correspondence and memoranda regarding the Council's
          role and administration; the reception and
          settlement of women immigrants, wages of domestics
          in Ontario, Manitoba and Alberta, problems of
          employing young girls in factories, and several

          98

other immigration-related topics; minutes of various
executive meetings; speech made to the Union Jack
Club of Ottawa by Agnes McPhail; concerns expressed
by various women's organizations regarding national
immigration policies; synopsis of work performed by
the Presbyterian Women's Missionary Society;
reports; proceedings of annual conferences;
activities; and internal memoranda of the Council.

(b) Canadian immigration agents in the United
States.
Correspondence and memoranda. PAM (M64 D1 V. 75)

Gives numbers enroute to western provinces and
includes references to a number of districts in
Manitoba.

(c) Care of immigrants.
Correspondence, 1927-33.   PAM (MG4 D1 V. 140)

Information provided on immigrant trains, complaints
from conductresses about conditions on board
immigrant trains; investigations of domestic
servants leaving trains in northern Ontario;
extracts from train conductress's reports about
immigrant specials.

(d) Customs duties on settlers' effects.
                          PAM (MG4 D1 V. 17)
Correspondence, 1902-07, 1916-25.

Concerning regulations on household furnishings,
canned fruit and clothing.

(e) Deportation cases.
Correspondence and case files, 1893-96.
                          PAM (MG4 D1 Vol. 37)

Specific cases of returning pauper, insane, criminal
and other unacceptable immigrants to their native
countries.

(f) Displaced persons.
Correspondence and policy statements.
                          PAM (MG4 D1 Vol. 31)

Information on the immigration of female domestic
workers into Canada and a 1947 confidential paper
entitled "Entry to Canada of persons now residing in
Germany and Austria."

(g) Distressed Canadians.
Correspondence and memoranda.
                          PAM (MG4 D1 Vol. 52
                          and 53)

Policy and specific cases of repatriation of
Canadians stranded in various countries for a
variety of reasons.

(h) Help for destitute immigrants.
Correspondence and memoranda, 1898-1927.
PAM (MG4 D1 Vol. 133)

Financial assistance and advances to destitute
immigrants and settlers; use of Associated Charities
of Winnipeg to administer relief.

(i) Illness among immigrants.
Correspondence and memoranda. PAM (MG4 D1 Vol. 141)

Appointment of Dr. S.C. Corbett to replace Dr. J.S.
Gray as physician for the Winnipeg immigration hall;
medical treatment and care of immigrants; monthly
visits and cases treated at immigration hall; work
among homeless in the Beausejour district following
prairie fires.

(j) Immigration Act regulations.
Films and correspondence.
PAM (BG4 D1 Vols. 26
and 27)

Copies of the act, amendments and explanatory notes;
regulations concerning criminals, prostitutes, the
insane, paupers, Chinese and other Asiatics;
deportations; medical inspections.

(k) Fumigation.
Correspondence and memoranda, 1893-96.
PAM (MG4 D1 Vol. 20)

Letters and complaints regarding the fumigation of
immigrants' baggage; procedures followed.

(l) Employment bureau, Winnipeg, Manitoba.
Papers, 1893-1915.
PAM (MG4 D1 Vol. 37
and 38)

Correspondence and memoranda regarding the placement
of immigrants in positions as farm labourers in
Carberry and Gladstone, 1904; complaints of
immigrants on treatment received; copies of
advertisements placed by the department in British
newspapers; reports of immigrants wanted for various
positions - Winnipeg Agency, 1897-98; copy of
Manitoba's Labor Bureau Act, 1897; list of places at
which employment agencies have been established,
1893; labour conditions in the West at various
times.

100

(m) Exclusion Order to Prevent Influx of Foreigners.
Correspondence and memoranda, 1919-26.
PAM (M64 D1 vol. 29)

Regulations concerning the prevention of an influx
of foreigners, also skilled and unskilled labour
unless going to farms; widespread opposition
throughout Canada and more particularly in Western
Canada to Doukhobors, Mennonites, Hutterites,
persons guilty of seditious acts or utterances,
Japanese, Chinese, Russian, Germans and Asiatics
generally, Winnipeg General Strike of 1919.

(n) Inspection of immigrants.
Clippings, 1908-09.   PAM (MG4 D1 Vol. 71)

Activities of uniformed American border officials on
Canadian immigrant trains.

(o) Passenger lists.
1892-1902.   PAM (MG4 D1 Vol. 7)

Provides names, age, sex, nationality, latest
residence, destination, occupation and amount of
money in possession of individuals.

(p) Quarantine regulations.
Papers and documents, 1892-1902.
PAM (MG4 D1 Vol. 29)

Correspondence regarding arrangements for quarantine
and vaccination on board ships and immigrant trains
and at quarantine stations; regulations concerning
smallpox, leprosy and typhoid; statements of the
Anti-Vaccination League of Canada (1928 and 1950)
and the Anti-Vaccination and Medical Liberty League
of Canada (1928); explanations of British and U.S.
regulations; handling of displaced persons.

(q) Recruitment.
1905-10,1925.   PAM (MG4 D1 Vol. 38)

"The 1,000 Continental Family Schemes," by the
Employment Bureau, Winnipeg, Manitoba.

(r) Immigration and smallpox.
Correspondence and reports.   PAM (MG4 D1 Vol. 80)

Letters on the outbreak of smallpox on immigrant
trains en route to Winnipeg; "Report of the
Secretary of the Ontario Provincial Board of Health
on the Outbreak of Smallpox"; his visits to Winnipeg
and the state of sewer and water systems in the
city; epidemics and efforts to control them.

(s) Immigrants and illness.

101

Correspondence and other documentation, 1892-1903.
PAM (MG4 D1 Vol. 18)

Correspondence concerning methods adopted for the disposition and treatment of infectious diseases; statistics on patients treated at various times, 1892-93; lists of immigrants accommodated between March and August, 1898.

(t) Naturalization Act.
Correspondence and various documentation, 1896-1916, 1926-28.
PAM (MG4 D1 Vols. 127-128)

Correspondence regarding the naturalization laws and their application to homesteaders, citizenships and aliens of different nationalities; copies of the 1896 and 1913 Naturalization Acts; regulations; difficulties implementing the Act; letters on the issuance of British passports to Italian-born wives of naturalized Italian Canadians; proposed changes in the Act; citizenship status of British women who marry aliens.

(u) Office of Commissioner of Immigration; Winnipeg, Manitoba.
Correspondence, 1909.   PAM (MG4 D1 Vol. 38)

Requests for domestic help and young married couples with small children.

(v) Repatriation of distressed canadians from Brazil
Correspondence and newsclippings,
1891-97.   PAM (MG4 D1 Vol. 33)

Repatriation of Canadians from Brazil; names of returning Canadians; accounts of experiences.

(w) The Western Immigration Association, Winnipeg.
Correspondence and clippings,
1896-98.   PAM (MG4 D1 Vol. 124)

Formation and activities of the Western Immigration Association; alleged ineffectiveness of the organization.

(x) Women's Immigration Branch, Staff.
Correspondence, 1920-22.   PAM (MG4 D1 Vol. 116)

Passage scheme proposed by the governments of Manitoba and Saskatchewan; appointments of train conductresses, ship matrons and women officers.

(y) Women's Protective Immigration Society.

Correspondence and reports,
1892-1914.   PAM (MG4 D1 Vol. 48)

Government grants and bonuses to the Society;
newspaper coverage of the Society's meetings and
functions; reports on conferences of the National
Council of Women of Canada; encouragement of the
immigration of Scandinavian women.

587. CATHOLIC IMMIGRANT SOCIETY
        Correspondence, 1947-49.
        1 folder.   A St-B (Drawer 27)

588. CITIZENSHIP CEREMONIES
        Oral recordings, 1947 CKY.
        Tapes.   PAM (AV A10 Tape
                                        17, tracks 1 and 2)

        Proceedings of citizenship ceremonies in Winnipeg,
        Manitoba, with speeches by Premier S.S. Garson and
        others.

589. IMMIGRANT COUNSELLING SERVICE
        Operating files. Restricted.
        Located at 425 Elgin Avenue, Winnipeg, Manitoba, R3A
        1P2.

        A counselling service and short-term crisis
        intervention centre. Minutes; reports; financial
        statements.

590. INTERNATIONAL CENTRE OF WINNIPEG OF THE CITIZENSHIP
     COUNCIL OF MANITOBA.
        Operating files. Restricted.
        Located at 700 Elgin Avenue, Winnipeg, Manitoba, R3E
        1B2.

        A counselling, language-training and translation
        service. Minutes; reports; financial statements.

591. WINNIPEG CITIZENSHIP DAY
        Film, 1954.
        60' (35mm).   PAM (AV B28)

103

592. CANADA - IMMIGRATION BRANCH RECORDS
General records (1873-1972), passenger ship list
(1865-1905).
PAM (MG4 D1)
About 650 reels of microfilm.

(a) Agent reports.   Reports and correspondence,
1891-1900.   PAM (MG4 D1 Vols. 33,
80 and 135)

E. O'Kelly's inspection trip to Manitoba and his
good impression of the Dauphin, Manitoba, area (Vol.
80); E.J. Wood's correspondence and plan to secure
employment for immigrants to Winnipeg, Manitoba;
posters and leaflets (Vol. 33); A.J. McMillan's
work, 1896-99, in bringing settlers to Manitoba
(Vol. 135).

(b) Annie MacPherson and Pady Homes. Correspondence
and reports, 1890-1912.   PAM (MG4 D1 Vol. 64)

Procedures; lists of children brought to the home;
inspectors' reports; child placements, 1912-25;
published copies of childrens' letters recounting
experiences in Canada; reports of the work by W.J.
Pady; references to the Pady Home (Emerson,
Manitoba); criticism.

(c) Bonus to booking agents (British).
Correspondence and reports,
1914-20.   PAM (MG4 D1 Vol. 60)

Changes in bonus regulations due to supposed surplus
of domestics and farm labourers; demand for female
domestics in principal cities; effects of World War
I; policy on payments of bonus for ex-servicemen.

(d) British Women's Emigration Association.
Correspondence and Reports,
1890-1903.   PAM (MG4 D1 Vol. 45)

Application forms for the "Loan and Employment"
program to enable persons to emigrate and work in
Canada; memoranda of agreement; lists of emigrants
and their destinations; reports from field
inspectors; complaints.

(e) Children's Aid Society (of London, England).
Correspondence; general memo. PAM (MG4 D1 Vols. 65
and 66)

Records of upkeep of the Society's home and
headquarters; correspondence and regulations
outlining the home-inspection process.

(f) Church of England Waifs and Strays Society
Correspondence; references; activities, 1906-08 and
1932-45.
PAM (MG4 D1 Vols.
78-80)

Exchange of letters with the Associated Charities of
Winnipeg; draft copy of employer's agreement;
activities of the Church Army's Receiving Homes.

(g) Criticism. Newsclippings and Criticisms,
1908.   PAM (MG4 D1 Vol. 42)

Primarily British criticism of Canada being touted
as a prime contender for British emigrants.

(h) Dr. Barnardo's Homes, Russell, Manitoba. Files,
1893-1901.   PAM (MG4 D1 Vol. 94)

Correspondence and clippings regarding the Barnardo
Home; jury criticisms of the Home; promotional
literature; lists of individuals brought to court
and of convictions; inspection reports;
testimonials; excerpts from visitors' book; reports
from the Barnardo's Russell, Manitoba, farm (see
also Vol. 133).

(i) East-end Emigration Fund. Correspondence and
reports, 1892-1902.   PAM (MG4 D1 Vol. 80)

Correspondence pertaining to arrival and placement
of immigrants; reports from new immigrants in the
North West Territories and Manitoba.

(j) Emigration from Great Britain. Correspondence
and circulars, 1918-21.   PAM (MG4 D1 Vols. 5
                              and 41)

The domestic labour situation in Canada; efforts to
curtail emigration to only farmers and domestic
helpers; circulars.

(k) English children evacuees. Correspondence and
case files, 1940-46.   PAM (MG5 G4 Boxes
                              32-34 Restricted)

Voluminous approved foster-parent case files;
rejected applications; related correspondence.

(l) Immigration of Children. Inquiries and
Reports.   PAM (MG4 D1 Vols. 67
                              and 129)

Inquiry from Lady Aberdeen concerning policies for
the immigration of juveniles; lists of boys at Dr.
Barnardo's Home; letters from Mr. B. Stewart to the
Pilot Mound Women's Institute (Vol. 129).

(m) Immigration of the deaf and mute.
Correspondence and regulations, 1889-96; 1902-03.
                                    PAM (MG4 D1 Vol. 38)

Jane Groome's efforts to inspire immigration to
Canada; deaf and mute settlers in Manitoba and their
efforts to establish a Home farm for the long winter
seasons; discrimination from other settlers;
donations of land at Wolseley, Saskatchewan.

(n) Immigration literature of the High Commissioner,
London, England. Memoranda, 1893-95.
                                    PAM (MG4 D1 Vol. 83)

Advantages of each province or region of Canada for
settlement; qualifications required of prospective
immigrants.

(o) Liverpool Catholic Children's Protection
Society. Correspondence, lists and complaints.
                                    PAM (MG4 D1 Vol. 65)

A. Brennan of St. Vincent's Receiving Home of
Montreal; Father Berry Homes in Liverpool; lists and
addresses of child immigrants now residing in
Canadian homes; inspection reports; complaints.

(p) Salvation Army. Lists of immigrants and
correspondence, 1895-1937.
                                    PAM (MG4 D1 Vol. 105)

Emigration of domestic female servants;
establishment of hostels in various Canadian cities;
"War Widows' Emigration Scheme," 1916; supervision
of single women and widows immigrating to Canada;
lists and correspondence providing names, family
sizes and destinations.

(q) Scottish crofters and cotters. Files,
1895-1912.   PAM (MG4 D1 Vol. 108)

Reports of Her Majesty's Commissioners appointed to
carry out a scheme of colonization in Canada of
crofters and cotters, which contain information on
the origin of the scheme; individuals as to
location, house, stable, breaking, stock, etc.;
settlements at Killarney, Manitoba, and Saltcoats,
Saskatchewan, 1880-1906; reports of C.N. Speers,
general colonization agent on settlements at
Killarney, Saltcoats, and the Moosomin-Wapella area

of Saskatchewan; names of present settlers at each
place and original settlers at Killarney and
Saltcoats, 1902; reports on twelve representative
settlers, 1908; correspondence between J. Obed Smith
and Lady Cathcart on the origin of the scheme and
the progress of the settlers brought to Canada under
her auspices, 1912.

(r) The Sheltering Homes, Liverpool, England and the
Distributing Home, Knowlton, Quebec. Correspondence
and lists, 1892-1908.   PAM (MG4 D1 Vol. 32)

The placement in Canada as domestic and farm
servants of boys and girls over the age of 18;
correspondence with Louisa Birt of the Distributing
Home, lists of children brought out; requests for
government assistance, Mrs. Birt's scheme to provide
domestic and farm servants to settlers in the
North-West and Manitoba; inspectors' reports.
Several references to Mrs. Birt's schemes for mature
females as domestics in Winnipeg and elsewhere in
western Canada.

(s) Self-Help Emigration Society, London, England.
Self-Help Emigration Society Reports and brochures,
1893-1901.   PAM (MG4 D1 Vol. 72)

"Settlement of Women Workers," Canning Town,
England, 1893; reports on placement and successes
and failures of immigrants; their qualification; the
Society's request for a grant of land in Manitoba
for the establishment of a Home Centre, November
1897 to May 1898.

(t) Southwark Diocesan Education Council and Rescue
Society, Southwark, England. Correspondence lists
and reports, 1895-1908.   PAM (MG4 D1 Vol. 112)

The system used by the Rev. Lord Archibald Douglas,
Southwark Diocesan Education Council, Ottawa, in the
placement of children. Lists of arrivals; visit of
Father St. John and Lord Douglas to Manitoba and the
N.W.T. to secure a site for a receiving home and a
farm in order to create an establishment similar to
the Barnardo Farm at Russell, Manitoba, November
1895; "Across the Sea" Vol. 1, No. 1, July 1896 -
the Society); "Boys and Girls" (Vol. 1, No. 1, July
1896 - the Society); Order-in-Council No. 2478 re
grant of land in TP. 23, Range 17; allegations of
ill-treatment of some children; change of name to
Canadian Catholic Emigration Committee and formation
of a new organization in 1899; copy of letterhead of
the Catholic Emigration Association, which
incorporated all Catholic Emigration Societies in
Great Britain, 1908.

593. IMMIGRATION OF BRITISH CATHOLICS
        One folder, 1925-40.   AWC

594. UNITED SCOTTISH ASSOCIATION
        Papers, 1918-81.
        0.75 ".   PAM (MG10 C72)

        Founded in 1918 to unify the many Scottish societies
        in Winnipeg, Manitoba. Minutes, 1918-79;
        correspondence; financial records, 1920-81.

Immigration - French

595. ASSOCIATION DES INSTITUTEURS DE LANGUE FRANCAISE AU
     MANITOBA ET DE L'OUEST
        1 fd., 1935-48.   A St-B (Drawer #26)

        Correspondence; newsclippings.

596. CENTRE D'ETUDES FRANCO-CANADIENNES DE L'OUEST
        Operating files (French).
        Located at room 1218, 200 ave. de la Cathédrale, St.
        Boniface, Manitoba, R2H 0H7.

        Files on prominent local French-Canadian individuals
        such as Rose-Anna Bérubé, Annette Saint-Pierre and
        Elizabeth Maguet; western French-Canadian folksongs,
        legends and local histories; newspaper clippings
        from and indexes to Western Canadian French language
        newspapers.

597. DANSEURS DE LA RIVIERE ROUGE
        Operating files.
        Located at 340 Provencher Avenue, St. Boniface,
        Manitoba, R2H 0G7.

        A mixed company of French-Canadian folk dancers.
        Correspondence, songs; dance programmes, 1971-72;
        daily routine, newsletters and administration,
        1971-75; Festival du Voyageur minutes,
        correspondence, programmes, advertising, 1971-74;
        CBC Radio Canada, "Programme de la télévision";
        brochures; maps, financial records; "Friends of the
        Dance"; trips to France; dancethon, 1976; annual
        reunions; activities, 1977; list of participants,
        financial report for 1977; performance in Ste.
        Agathe, 1977; membership lists, "des Gais
        Manitobains," provincial appearances of Les

Danseurs, 1977; Folklorama, 1978, "Historique de la
Troupe," membership lists, 1972-75; questionnaires,
1980; songs, music, programmes on CKSB.

598. JEUNESSE CANADIENNE
Correspondence, 1949 (French).
1 folder.   A St-B (Drawer #26)

599. LA LIBERTE
Operating files.
Located at 383 Provencher, St. Boniface, Manitoba,
R2H 0G7.

Children's Aid Society of Eastern Manitoba:
correspondence, October 1970; Manitoba Teacher's
Society: correspondence, 1977-80; Educateurs
Franco-Manitobains: correspondence, 1970; Hôpital
Général de St. Boniface: correspondence: "Les Soeurs
Grises vont-elles se retirer des hôpitaux?",
1976-79; employment records; Centre Cultural St.
Boniface; CCFM: brochures, correspondence, 1970-82;
Cercle Molière: correspondence, information,
1972-82.

600. LA MINERVE
1 folder, 1904-05.   A St-B (BG 7421-7426)

601. PLURI-ELLES
Operating files (French).
Located at 200 ave. de la Cathédrale,
Saint-Boniface, Manitoba, R2H 0H7.

Organized to promote the potential and worth of all
women. Minutes; reports; financial records; names
of resource people; lists of books; films on women
in politics, education, and abused wives; membership
lists; executive minutes and committee lists;
special projects; correspondence.

602. CANADA. IMMIGRATION BRANCH RECORDS
General records, 1873-1972; passenger ship lists,
1865-1908.
                          PAM (MG4 D1)
About 650 reels of microfilm from the Government of
Canada.

(a) French-Canadian repatriation from the United
States. Correspondence, reports, and clippings,
1892-1915.
                          PAM (MG4 D1 Vol. 94)

Activities of the Rev. Father M. Blais in promoting
immigration of French settlers to the Canadian
Northwest; resolutions and recommendations of the
St. Jean Baptiste Society of Manitoba, 1900-01.

(b) French and Belgian immigration. References,
1896.   PAM (MG4 D1 Vol. 106)

French and Belgian immigration to Manitoba and the
North West Territories.

(c) French settlers. Files,
1890-1907.   PAM (MG4 D1 Vol. 106)

Bonuses to settlers taking up land; correspondence
relating to the bonus incentive plans and
regulations governing their payment; list of French
Settlers near Oak Lake, Manitoba; review of the
system.

(d) "Société Générale de Colonization et de
Rapatriement de la Province de Quebec." Files,
1903-05.   PAM (MG4 D1 Vol. 95)

Includes settlement at Bergen, Manitoba, 1905.

Immigration - German

603. CANADA. IMMIGRATION BRANCH RECORDS
     General records, 1873-1972; passenger ship lists,
     1865-1908.
                                         PAM (MG4 D1)
     About 650 reels of microfilm from the Government of
     Canada.

     (a) Carstens, Hugo Correspondence,
     1893-1904.   PAM (MG4 D1 Vol. 34)

     Hugo Carstens' activities in Germany to promote
     immigration to Canada.

     (b) German immigration Correspondence,
     1927-62.   PAM (MG4 D1 Vol. 31)

     Immigration of refugees; the close relative scheme;
     servicemen's wives and fiancées; Polish Army
     veterans; Sudetan Germans, 1948.

604. GERMAN SOCIETY OF WINNIPEG, WOMAN'S SECTION
     Operating files, 1892-   . Restricted.

110

Located at 121 Charles Street, Winnipeg, Manitoba,
R2W 4A6.

A cultural social organization designed to promote
and preserve the German heritage. Minutes; reports;
membership lists; financial records.

Immigration - Jewish

605. B'NAI B'RITH

   (a) Papers, 1925-28.   PAM (MG10 C71)

   Records of the Independent Order of B'nai B'rith,
   Winnipeg Chapter No. 38 of the Order of Aleph Zadik
   Aleph; minute book, 1925-28.

   (b) Operating files. Restricted.
   Located at 2nd. Floor, 319 Graham Street, Winnipeg,
   Manitoba.

   Correspondence; newsclippings; scholarship files;
   financial records; photographs.

606. BROWNSTONE, CANTOR BENJAMIN
   Letter, 1966. Restricted.
   1 item.   PAM (MG10 F3)

   Includes a poem, "Rachel Rejoices in her Children."

607. CHESED SHEL EMES CHAPEL (FUNERAL CHAPEL)
   Death records, 1930-79. Located at 1023 Main Street,
   Winnipeg, Manitoba, R2W 3P9. Restricted.

   In Yiddish until 1947.

608. EZRA CHAPTER - WINNIPEG
   Papers, 1960-75. Restricted.   PAM (M610 F3)

   Minute books; invitations; circular letters.

609. HADASSAH-WIZO COUNCIL OF WINNIPEG
   Papers, 1960-80. Restricted. PAM (MG10 F3)

   Newsletters; invitations; scrapbooks; reports;
   photographs.

610. JEWISH CHILD AND FAMILY SERVICE
          Papers, 1968-78.   PAM (M610 F3)

          Correspondence; reports; paper on Russian
          immigration and budget; minutes; projects; lists;
          constitution; finances, 1976-78; Aging Committee,
          1977-78; paper by Ed. Moscovitch, "Impact of
          Holocaust on Survivors and Their Children";
          historical background; memo on War Orphans report,
          1900-71; correspondence on war orphans, from Thelma
          Tessler, 1947; anniversary dinner; residential
          treatments unit brief; paper by social worker Linda
          Isitts entitled "Settlement of Russian Newcomers,
          1976"; papers on behavioural problems.

611. JEWISH COLONIZATION ASSOCIATION
          Papers, 1920-49.   PAM (MG4 D1 Vol. 82)

          Purpose, function and activities of the Association;
          Russian refugees in Poland; approval of the
          immigration of 100 to 150 boys and girls; their
          placement in Western Canada, 1923; admission of six
          families from Constantinople, 1926; list showing
          locations of recent arrivals, November, 1926; land
          purchases and references to colonies at Narcisse and
          Bender, Manitoba, December 15, 1926; articles from
          various Jewish papers on colonization; historical
          review including statistical data on 16 colonies in
          Manitoba, Saskatchewan and Alberta, November 3,
          1936; dates colonies founded; their progress system
          of land tenure and settlement; rate of interest;
          supervision, 1937; illness of Lyon Cohen, 1937;
          reports of H. Allen of the Land Settlement Branch on
          colonies in 1937; the virtual abandonment of
          colonies in Manitoba at Camper, Moosehorn, Narcisse
          and Lorette and others in Saskatchewan and Alberta;
          achievements of many of the second generation in the
          professions, 1937; statistical data for each colony,
          1937; effects of World War II; efforts of European
          Jews to gain admission to Canada.

612. JEWISH IMMIGRANT AID SOCIETY OF CANADA, AND SETTLEMENT
     OF JEWISH IMMIGRANTS
          Correspondence, 1920-29.   PAM (MG4 D1 Vol. 54)

          Government policy; references to specific cases.

613. JEWISH HISTORICAL SOCIETY OF WESTERN CANADA, INC.
          Historical research files.   JHSA

          Located at 402-365 Hargrave Street, Winnipeg,
          Manitoba, R3B 2K3.

Founded 1968 to document and preserve the Jewish
experience in Western Canada through its archives,
oral history, photographs, and film-making
programmes. Manuscripts; photographs; audio tapes;
motion pictures. Some of its holdings are described
in scattered entries throughout this work.

614. JEWISH OLD FOLKS HOME, WINNIPEG, MANITOBA
Reports, 1920-24; 1945.
2 items.   PAM (MG10 F3)

615. JEWISH ORPHANAGE AND CHILDREN'S AID OF WESTERN CANADA
Papers, 1914-35.   PAM (MG10 F3)

Reports, 1917-35; Certificate of Incorporation of
the Esther Robinson Jewish Orphanage and Children's
Aid Society.

616. JEWISH WOMEN'S MUSICAL CLUB
Papers.
1.5".   PAM (MG10 F3)

Organized 1948 by Mrs. J.J. Lander. Programmes,
1947-62; newsclippings; membership account books;
theatre workshop programmes, 1951-62.

617. MIZRACHI-HAPOEL HAMIZRACH WOMEN'S ORGANIZATION OF
CANADA
Operating files. Restricted.
Contact: Mrs. P.M. Kravetsky, 122 Arrowood Drive S.,
Winnipeg, Manitoba, R2V 2P1.

Organized in 1942 and reorganized 1960 to assist
Israel. Minutes; reports; financial records.

618. NATIONAL COUNCIL OF JEWISH WOMEN OF CANADA
(a) Papers, around 1925-60. Finding
aid.   PAM (MG10 F3)

Organized in 1925 in Winnipeg, Manitoba.
Twenty-five years service report; minutes;
correspondence; reports; clippings; budgets;
policies.

(b) Scattered materials.   PAM (MG10 F3)

Report; correspondence.

113

619. ORGANIZATION FOR REHABILITATION THROUGH TRAINING
        Operating files. Restricted.
        Located at 190 Sherbrooke Street, Winnipeg,
        Manitoba, R3C 2B6.

        Organized in Winnipeg around 1943. Minutes;
        reports; financial records.

620. PIONEER WOMEN'S ORGANIZATION, WINNIPEG CHAPTER
        Operating files.
        Located at 1727 Main Street, Winnipeg, Manitoba, R2V
        1Z4.

        Organized 1925 and closely identified with Labour
        Zionism and the support of Palestine (Israel).
        Membership lists; clippings; photographs of offices;
        correspondence.

621. ROSH PINA SISTERHOOD
        Operating files, 1952. Restricted.
        Located at 123 Matheson Avenue, Winnipeg, Manitoba,
        R2W 0C3.

        Minutes; reports; financial records; activity and
        program notes; membership lists since 1952;
        scrapbook; Bar Mitzvah and wedding arrangements;
        anniversary booklets.

622. SHAAREY ZEDEK LADIES AUXILIARY (SISTERHOOD)
        Operating files, 1890- . Restricted.
        Located at 561 Wellington Crescent, Winnipeg,
        Manitoba, R3M 0A6.

        Synagogue records; High Holiday Ladies' Seats;
        photographs; minutes; reports; financial records;
        activity reports; publications.

623. SHARETH HAPLAITA ORGANIZATION
        Minute books of the ladies auxiliary, 1967-76.
                                    PAM (MG10 F3)

624. SLONIM, ANNE
        Papers.   PAM (MQ0 F3)

        Programmes and scrap book of Jewish Community Choir
        and Jewish Community Orchestra; Programmes of Jewish
        Women's Musical Club Concert and workshop; Peretz
        School programme, invitation; clippings;
        miscellaneous mementos; reports.

114

625. WILDER, H.E.
        Papers.   PAM (MG10 F3)

        Includes documentation on the activities of Mrs.
        H.E. Wilder on behalf of the Jewish Orphanage,
        1928-43.

626. THE WINNIPEG YOUNG HEBREW GIRLS' HELPING SOCIETY
        Programme.
        1 item.   PAM (MG10 F3)

        1916 musical concert for the benefit of Jewish war
        victims.

627. ZIONIST COLLECTION
        Interviews, oral histories, 1961.
        4 reel of microfilm.   PAM (AV A8)

        Rabbi Arthur Chiel interviewing, among others, Mr.
        and Mrs. H. Sokolov.

Immigration - Ukrainian

628. CANADA. IMMIGRATION BRANCH RECORDS
        General records 1873-1972; passenger ship lists
        (1865-1908)
                                         PAM (MG4 D1)
        About 650 reels of microfilm from the Government of
        Canada.

        (a) Emigration from Russia to Western Canada.
        Correspondence and reports,
        1910-25.   PAM (MG4 D1 Vol. 51)

        Promoting emigration from Russia contrary to offical
        Russian policy, 1890s; reports of sailings; lists of
        immigrants; refugees in Rumania, Japan, Turkey and
        elsewhere fleeing post-war Russia, 1918.

        (b) Galacian emigration from Austria.
        Correspondence, lists and descriptions, 1895-1900.
                                         PAM (MG4 D1 vols. 109
                                         and 110)

        References to the desire of Galacians, Poles and
        Ruthenians to settle in Canada; Joseph Oleskow's
        visits to Winnipeg, Morris, Gretna and the Mennonite
        Reserve in Manitoba, 1895; arrival of first group of
        107 persons; lists showing names and ages;

115

description of the Whitemouth area in Manitoba;
investigation by the first arrivals of the
Whitemouth district, 1896; settlements at
Whitemouth, Beausejour, Dominion City, St. Norbert,
Springfield, St. Andrews and Lake Dauphin, 1896;
list of Ruthenian settlers near Dominion City.

629. ST. RAPHAEL'S UKRAINIAN IMMIGRANTS WELFARE ASSOCIATION
OF CANADA
Papers, 1925-38. Finding aid. UCECA

An intermediary between Ukrainian organizations and
the Canadian government in the placement and welfare
of immigrants. Correspondence between the
Association, the Government and applicants from
Ukraine; minutes of the organization; officers'
reports; case files.

630. UKRAINIAN CANADIAN WOMEN'S COUNCIL
Operating files. (Ukrainian).
Located at 456 Main Street, Winnipeg, Manitoba.

Organized about 1940 as a cultural and social
society. Constitution; minute books; reports.

631. UKRAINIAN COOKING
Research paper (unpublished).
Contact Prof. Stella Hryniuk, St. Andrew's College,
University of Manitoba, Winnipeg, Manitoba.

"Ukrainian Home Cookery: There and Here, Then and
Now." Discusses food, cookery, immigration and
settlement experiences, and homes in the Dauphin,
Manitoba, area.

632. UKRAINIAN CULTURAL AND EDUCATIONAL CENTRE
Archives.   UCECA

Founded in 1944 as a repository for Ukrainian
history and culture. Operating files; manuscript
and archival collections of individuals and
institutions of Ukrainian background; art gallery;
museum; library.

633. UKRAINIAN DANCERS
Colour film, silent, 1940s.
1 reel (8 mm; 100').   PAM (M.I.S.)

In traditional dress.

634. UKRAINIAN LADIES SOCIETY OF LESYA UKRAINKA
          Operating files. Restricted (Ukrainian).
          Located at 582 Burrows Avenue, Winnipeg, Manitoba,
          R2W 2A5.

          Formerly organized 1926 as a disseminating agency
          for Ukrainian culture.

635. UKRAINIAN NATIONAL YOUTH FEDERATION
          Papers.   UCECA

          Abundant data on Ukrainian women.

636. UKRAINIAN RED CROSS
          Papers (Ukrainian).   UCECA

          Organized early 1920s to aid war victims in post
          World War I Ukraine. Miscellaneous papers;
          documents; reports.

637. UKRAINIAN REFUGEE CAMPS
          Records, 1946-60.
                                          UCECA

          Records of both cultural and political activities,
          as well as some personal experiences, in the camps.
          The Pictorial Materials section of the archives also
          contains "Ukrainian Refugee Camp Posters." Holdings
          include camp newspapers, periodicals and books.

638. UKRAINIAN WOMEN'S ORGANIZATION - WINNIPEG BRANCH
          Operating files. Restricted.
          Located at 935 Main Street, Winnipeg, Manitoba, R2W
          3P2.

          Current and archival materials.

639. UKRAINIAN WOMEN'S ORGANIZATION - NATIONAL EXECUTIVE
          Papers, 1932-83 (Ukrainian).   UCECA

          Minutes; reports; letters recruiting new members;
          correspondence and printed materials.

640. POLISH CANADIAN WOMEN'S FEDERATION
       Operating files. Restricted.
       Located at 207 Cathedral Avenue, Winnipeg, Manitoba.

       Organized in 1963 as an affiliate of the Canadian
       Polish Congress, Manitoba Division, for cultural and
       charitable purposes. A full complement of
       newsletters from its Toronto headquarters (in
       Polish); minutes; financial records; reports.

641. POLISH COMBATANTS ASSOCIATION
       Operating files, 1930-64. Restricted.
       Located at 1364 Main Street, Winnipeg, Manitoba, R3E
       0Y1.

       Minutes; reports; financial records.

642. POLISH LUTHERAN WOMEN'S GROUP
       Operating files. Restricted.
       Located at Inglis, Manitoba (parish).

       Organized around 1905 as one of the few Polish
       evangelical groups in Canada.

Immigration - Icelandic/Scandinavian

643. CANADA. IMMIGRATION BRANCH RECORDS
       General records, 1873-1972; passenger ship lists,
       1865-1908.
                                     PAM (MG4 D1)
       About 650 reels of microfilm from the Government of
       Canada.

       (a) Baldwinson, B.L., Icelandic agent, Winnipeg,
       Manitoba. Correspondence and memoranda, 1893-1900.

       The arrival of 524 Icelanders on board the ship
       "Lake Huron," 1893; desire of North Dakota
       Icelanders to settle at the Narrows of Lake
       Winnipeg, 1894.   PAM (MG4 D1 Vol. 22)

       (b) Emigration: Scandinavian statistics. Records,
       1893-1903.   PAM (MG4 D1 Vol. 23)

       Statistical data on emigration, especially from
       Sweden but also from Norway and Denmark; emigration

of Swedish conscripts (their origin and
destination); Canadian destinations frequently
provided.

(c) Immigration: Scandinavian and continental
European
testimonials, 1892-1927.   PAM (MG4 D1 Vol. 13)

644. MEDICAL AID IN NEW ICELAND
        History (unpublished).
        7 pp. Typescript.   ERL

        Medical history of Icelanders in the Gimli,
        Manitoba, region including the work of nurses and
        midwives.

645. OTLIN, LOUISE
        Papers, 1885-1909 (Swedish).
        5".   PAM (MG8 B64)

        Correspondence.

646. SISLER, W.
        Papers.   PAM (MG14 C28)

        Material on the early Swedish Colony at Morris Lake,
        Manitoba.

647. VIKING CLUB (CANADIAN SCANDINAVIAN)
        Papers, 1942-71.
        4".   PAM (MG10 C55)

        Founded 1942 to promote closer co-operation between
        Canadians and Scandinavians through social, cultural
        and other activities. Correspondence; minutes;
        bulletins; financial records; dinner programmes.

Immigration - Other

648. CANADA. IMMIGRATION BRANCH RECORDS
        General records, 1873-1972; passenger ship lists,
        1865-1908.
                                      PAM (MG4 D1)
        About 650 reels of microfilm from the Government of
        Canada.

(a) Belgian immigration. Records,
1893-1926.   PAM (MG4 D1 Vol. 94)

Statements, 1901-04, providing names, occupations
and Canadian destinations; "Memorandum re: placing
families of Belgium on farm lands in Canada," 1914;
activities of M.S. Colquhon of Deloraine, Manitoba,
1919.

(b) Dutch immigration. Correspondence and
clippings, 1892-1948.   PAM (MG4 D1 Vols. 38
                                   and 39)

Professor of Dutch immigration; settlement in
Manitoba and throughout western Canada; post World
War I policies and extent of immigration from the
Netherlands; activities, 1928, of the Central
Emigration Foundation; immigration of Dutch farm
labourers, 1920s; placement of Dutch market
gardeners; post World War II developments.

(c) Hungarian immigration. Lists,
1903-04.   PAM (MG4 D1 Vol. 20)

Hungarian arrivals at Winnipeg, Manitoba.

(d) Italian immigration Correspondence, reports and
lists, 1922-73.
                               PAM (MG4 D1 Vol. 130)

Italian immigration statistics; proposed
establishment of Italian agricultural colony in
Canada; visit by Italia Garabaldi to Ottawa and
three prairie provinces, 1923; settlement of Italian
farmers from Piedmont in southern Manitoba; issuance
of British passports to Italian wives of naturalized
Italian immigrants.

649. CANADIAN CZECHOSLOVAK BENEVOLENT ASSOCIATION
     Papers, 1953-71.
     About 2".   PAM (MG10 C65)

     Fiftieth anniversary of founding of the Association,
     1963; reports; programmes; correspondence;
     biographical material, 1953-71.

650. CANADIAN LEBANESE WOMEN'S AUXILIARY
     Operating files. Restricted.
     Located at 834 St. Matthews Avenue, Winnipeg,
     Manitoba.

     Organized in 1960 as a social and charitable
     organization. Minutes; financial records; reports.

651. MENNONITE IMMIGRATION
        Scattered materials, 1874-80. WRL (MG2)

        East Reserve Mennonite immigrants, 1874, with lists
        giving name, age and occupation; West Reserve
        Mennonite immigrants 1875-80, with listings of
        ships, arrival dates and leaders, including name,
        age and occupation of immigrants; clippings on
        various other Mennonites in the Winkler, Manitoba,
        area.

652. CANADA. IMMIGRATION BRANCH RECORDS
        General records, passenger
        lists.   PAM (MG4 D1)

        Mennonite emigration from the United States.
        Correspondence, 1891-1900.   PAM (MG4 D1 Vol. 16)

        Reports on visiting American delegates to Manitoba
        and the Northwest.

WOMEN IN AGRICULTURE

653. BLACK, CHARLOTTE S.
          Papers.
          2".   UMA (A83-1)

          Agriculturalist. Journal of her graduation, 1925,
          from the Manitoba Agricultural College; biographical
          sketch; photographs.

654. CANADIAN COUNCIL OF AGRICULTURE
          Papers, 1910-32.
          Originals (15") and microfilm copy set (2 reels).
          PAM (MG10 E2)

          Women's section minute books, 1919-29; financial
          statements; related materials.

655. 4-H CLUBS
          Resource files.   BCA (MG10 E7)

          Enrollment forms for the Margaret Merrymakers 4-H
          club; materials on the Boissevain and Desford 4-H
          Clubs.

656. MANITOBA FARMERS UNION (NATIONAL FARMERS UNION)
          Papers, 1943-70.
          31'.   PAM (MG10 E19)

          Operating records; minutes; correspondence; reports;
          Farm Women's Week. Files, 1953-69; related
          materials.

657. MANITOBA WOMEN'S CO-OPERATIVE GUILD
          Papers, 1951-71.
          1.5'.   PAM (MG40 G48)

In March 1951, interested women met at the annual
meeting of the Manitoba Co-operative Wholesale
Limited women's conference and, in spite of
controversy, organized a Manitoba Women's
Co-operative Guild. Within a few weeks six groups,
including Flin Flon and Baldur, which had been
formed previously, were active. At the first annual
meeting in 1952, the Provisional Manitoba Council
was appointed, and by 1964 there were sixteen groups
throughout the province.

Education as a means of promoting the co-op movement
and its ideals was central to Guild activities and
therefore relevant films and guest speakers were
often featured at meetings.

The last recorded annual meeting of the provincial
Guild was held at Cypress River 1968. By January
1971, only the Boissevain branch remained active
and, later that year, the Manitoba Women's
Co-operative Guild appears to have been officially
disbanded.

Correspondence, both provincial and national;
minutes of both general and executive committee
meetings; constitutions, by-laws, and resolutions;
mailing and executive lists; project files;
newsletters; correspondence and printed materials
from the Pacific Northwest Cooperator, the
Saskatchewan Co-operative Women's Guild, and other
guilds.

658. MCCARSLAND, ERNIE
        Papers.   BCA (MG14 C81)

        Boys and Girls Swine Club; Calf Club; 4-H Calf Clubs
        of Boissevain, Manitoba.

659. NORRIS, T.C.
        Papers.   PAM (MG13 H1)

        Premier of Manitoba. Papers include materials on
        the Women's Farm Labour Committee and the Women's
        Christian Temperance Union.

660. SIMPSON, WENDY
        Speech.
        1 p. Typescript.   BCA (MG10 E10)

        Concerns the Boissevain, Manitoba 4-H Club.

661. UNITED FARM WOMEN, OAKVILLE
     Papers, 1915-63. Finding aid.
     5".   PAM (MG10 E1-1)

     Minute books, 1915-63; Library Hall Board of Trustee
     minute and account books, 1926-67; other material of
     this Oakville, Manitoba, chapter.

662. UNITED FARM WOMEN OF MANITOBA
     Report, 1931. By Mrs. D.J.
     Clarke.   PAM (MG10 E1)

     "Birth Control and Sterilization."

663. UNITED FARMERS OF MANITOBA INCLUDING UNITED FARM WOMEN
     (UFW) OF MANITOBA AND JUNIOR UNITED FARMERS OF MANITOBA
     Papers, 1903-39.
     9'.   PAM (MG10 E1)

     Administrative and operating files; UFW minute
     books; UFW survey of farm homes, 1922; ledgers; day
     books, 1919-20; membership lists; cash books; other
     materials on the UFW.

664. UNITED GRAIN GROWERS LTD
     Operating files. Restricted.
     Located at corporate headquarters, 433 Main Street
     (Box 6600), Winnipeg, Manitoba, R3C 3A7.

     Corporate records, past and current including the
     following materials on the Women's Section of the
     Canadian Council of Agriculture: cadet training
     question; committee organization; education reports;
     financial statements; first meeting of the
     interprovincial council of women 1919; home
     economics report; immigration reports; international
     council of women; Jr. Work Reports; legislation,
     peace and arbitration reports; marketing reports;
     minutes of annual meetings; National Council of
     Women; public health reports; Social Service and
     Welfare Reports; United Farm Women of Alberta;
     United Farm Women of Manitoba; United Farm Women of
     Ontario; United Farmers of Quebec Women's Section.

WOMEN IN BUSINESS

665. ALPHA-IOTA SORORITY, WINNIPEG, ALUMNAE
     Operating files. Restricted.

     124

Contact: Mrs. Shirley Stewart, 118 Cavell Drive,
Winnipeg, Manitoba, R3J 1P1.

An international honorary business sorority.

666. BOISSEVAIN, MANITOBA, BUSINESSES
Histories.   BCA (MG15 D1)

Histories of Boissevain business, including those
owned and/or operated by women; history, 1981, of
Boissevain; voters lists, 1921,1938.

667. BUSINESS AND PROFESSIONAL WOMEN'S CLUB, WINNIPEG,
MANITOBA
Operating files, 1924-   .
Located at 515-160 Hargrave Street, Winnipeg,
Manitoba, R3C 3H3.

A support group and social activity for women
entering business and professional careers.

668. BUSINESS AND PROFESSIONAL WOMEN'S CLUB,   FLIN FLON,
MANITOBA
Scattered materials.   FFHS/FFPL

Correspondence, 1972; history; conference booklet;
clippings.

669. BUSINESS AND PROFESSIONAL WOMEN'S CLUB, THOMPSON,
MANITOBA
Papers Restricted.
Contact: Margery Ysishen, Thompson, Manitoba.

Organized in 1969 for social and charitable purposes
including working with juvenile offenders and
purchasing hospital equipment.   Minutes;
treasurer's reports.

670. CONSUMERS' ASSOCIATION OF CANADA (MANITOBA)
Papers. Finding aid.
21 boxes.   UMA (MSS 23)

Organized in 1947 to unite consumers to improve
quality of goods and services, to upgrade standards
of living, and to advocate consumer needs and
viewpoints. Executive meetings minutes, 1947-79;
correspondence; membership lists; annual reports;
financial records; reports of special
investigations.

125

671. MANITOBA HOME ECONOMICS ASSOCIATION
        Papers, 1911-81. Finding aid.
        3'.   PAM (MG10 A20)

        Founded 1911 to promote the welfare of the family,
        home and community. Minute books; membership lists
        (1911-); minutes of executive and annual meetings;
        notices of meeting; correspondence; by-laws and
        constitutions; newsclippings.

672. MANITOBA PROVINCIAL ORGANIZATION OF BUSINESS AND
    PROFESSIONAL WOMEN'S CLUBS
        Papers, 1930-78. Finding aid.
        1'.   PAM (MG10 A19)

        Charter member of the Canadian Federation since
        1930. Minutes; papers and proceedings on provincial
        workshops; conferences; organization of new clubs,
        seminars and projects; resolutions.

673. MONARCH LIFE ASSURANCE COMPANY
        Papers, 1904-84.
        30'.   PAM (P201-239)

        The Monarch Life Assurance Company was organized in
        Toronto 1904. In 1906 the head office moved to
        Winnipeg where the company experienced a slow but
        steady growth throughout the 1920s. Though hard hit
        by the Depression, it survived and experienced a
        period of unprecedented and sustained growth
        following World War II. In 1978 all the outstanding
        shares were sold to Can West Capital Corporation.
        In 1983 the North American Life Assurance Company
        purchased these shares from Can West and the two
        companies were amalgamated in 1984.

        Minutes of the Board of Directors, 1904-71, of the
        Executive Committee, 1910-71, and of the Finance
        Committee, 1930-33; financial records including
        general ledgers, 1904-17, record of outstanding
        cheques, 1915-74, and of stop payments; shareholder
        records including share certificates and shareholder
        transactions; printed materials and papers of the
        Heritage Life Assurance Company, 1974-80.

WOMEN AND EDUCATION

674. ALLEN, LILLIAN
        Papers.   UMA (MSS 45)

University of Manitoba professor of home economics;
nature photographer. Diaries of world travels;
correspondence; biographical materials; photographs
(prints and slides).

675. ALPHA OMEGA WOMEN'S ALUMNAE
Operating files, 1958- . Restricted.
Contact: Professor Stella Hryniuk, Saint Andrew's
College, University of Manitoba.

An association of university graduates to promote
and foster Ukrainian culture. Minutes; reports;
financial records; membership lists; projects
supported; booklets.

676. BRANDON UNIVERSITY OFFICE OF THE PRESIDENT
Papers.   BUA

Correspondence concerning women faculty, student
recruitment, developmental education, and furnishing
of women's residence.

677. BRANDON UNIVERSITY. STUDENT ASSOCIATION RECORDS
Papers.   BUA (R79-6)

Student activities in literary, athletic, debating,
publishing and other concerns.

678. THE BRANDON TEACHERS' STRIKE
History, 1971.
200 pp. Typescript.   PAM (MG10 F2 Box K-M)

"The Brandon Teachers' 'Strike.' This Was the
Strike that Was...And Wasn't," by Margaret Mann.
History of this 1921-22 event.

679. BURNSIDE SCHOOL RECORDS
Operating files, 1875-1968.
Contact: c/o Victoria School, 32 Fifth Street, S.E.,
Portage la Prairie, Manitoba, R1N 1J2.

Financial journal, 1875-1946; minutes of school
trustees, 1894-1917; school reunion, 1968.

680. CAMP WHITNEY
Papers, 1935-76.   FFHS/FFPL

Camping facility for Girl Guides, Boy Scouts and
various other groups. Constitution; correspondence;

127

minutes of meetings, 1974-76; regulations; financial
records; plans and projects; camp history;
newsclippings.

681. CARTWRIGHT SCHOOL
Operating files, 1886-1981.
Located at Roblin Municipality building, Cartwright,
Manitoba, and in the office of Cartwright High
School.

Minutes of school board meetings; financial records;
teachers' names and qualifications; miscellaneous
records of schools in East Mountain, 1899-1963, and
in Mylor, 1942-63, Manitoba.

682. CHISHOLM, JEAN ISABEL (1885-1970)
Papers, 1902-10.
7 pp.   PAM (MG8 D27)

Diplomas: teaching certificate; Civil Services
Commission of Canada certificate of proficiency.

683. LE COLLEGE DE ST. BONIFACE
Resource files.
Located at 200, ave. de la Cathédrale, St. Boniface,
Manitoba, R2H 0H7.

Papers, studies and other descriptive materials on
the following: Association canadienne des
éducateurs de langue française; Centre culturel de
Saint-Boniface; Educateurs Franco-Manitobains;
Winnipeg Folk Festival; Festival du Voyageur; Bureau
de l'éducation française; and others. Photographs.

684. DAFOE, ELIZABETH (-1960)
Papers. Largely still in private hands but much of
her professional work documented at the University
of Manitoba.   UMA (UA9)

Director of Libraries at the University of Manitoba,
1937-60.

685. DIBNEY, DORA (c. 1900-67)
Papers.
1 1/2".   PAM (MG14 C17)

Student writer and telephone operator. Papers
relating to the Winnipeg Public Schools Household
and Science Department.

128

686. DAVIS, MATILDA
        Papers, 1837-1937.   PAM (MG2 C24 Box 1
                                     File 2)

        Personal correspondence, 1837-75; invitations and
        notices; Matilda Davis School accounts, 1837-76;
        forty-six general expense notebooks of the school
        covering laundry and ice-house expenses, wheat
        production, milling costs, servants wages and other
        operation expenditures.

687. DUDLEY, MARGARET
        Papers, 1912-71.
        Typescript.   PAM (MG9 A110)

        Professor of botany. Resumé of activities and
        teaching positions at the University of Manitoba,
        Brandon College, and the Correspondence Branch of
        the Manitoba Department of Education; overview of
        her activities in the "Hands Across the Seas"
        movement, 1912-13; accounts of trips to England;
        related materials.

688. EARLY CHILDHOOD EDUCATION COUNCIL
        Operating files.
        Located at Manitoba Teacher's Society, 191 Harcourt
        Street, Winnipeg, Manitoba.

        A non-profit organization dedicated to improving the
        care and education of very young children. Minutes;
        reports; financial records; journals; newsletters.

689. ECOLE NORMALE DE WINNIPEG
        Papers, 1938-43.
        2 folders.   A St-B (Drawer #28)

        Correspondence; photo, 1943.

690. ECOLES DU MANITOBA
        Correspondence, 1907.
        1 folder.   A St-B (Drawer #28)

        Letters to Monseigneur Taché; report of the Sirois
        Commission.

691. FLIN FLON, MANITOBA. EDUCATION
        Scattered materials.   FFHS/FFPL

        History of kindergarten; scholarships, 1946-67;
        minutes of the school board, 1929-71.

        129

692. I.L. PERETZ FOLK SCHOOL
     Files, 1924-69.
     Several boxes.   PAM (MG10 F3)

     Teachers' letters of resignation, 1924-32; teacher
     applications and correspondence, 1924-67; staff
     salaries, 1962-64; Muter Farein notices, 1939-64;
     Muter Farein minutes, 1928-69; Muter Farein Council
     minutes, 1944; book of projects and fees, 1938;
     business calendar, 1934-39; book of events, 1928-39;
     Muter Farein Ladies' Luncheon programs, 1965-67.

693. JOSEPH WOLINSKY COLLEGIATE
     Papers, 1971-74.   PAM (MG10 F3)

     Advisory Board meetings; teachers' files containing
     applications, contracts and salaries.

694. KILLARNEY SCHOOL DIVISION, KILLARNEY, MANITOBA
     Operating files.
     Located in the School Division Office.
     Superintendents' reports; financial records; minutes
     of trustees, 1957-83.

695. MANITOBA ASSOCIATION OF SCHOOL TRUSTEES
     Operating files, 1967.
     Located at 191 Provencher Boulevard, St. Boniface,
     Manitoba, R2N 0G4.

     Minutes; reports; membership forms from all trustees
     (listing name and school district served).

696. MANITOBA EDUCATION
     Scattered files.   PAM (RG19 A1 and F4)

     List of qualified Protestant teachers, 1880-83; list
     of diplomas, 1879-90; court cases involving
     teachers, 1937.

697. MANITOBA EDUCATIONAL ASSOCIATION
     Papers, 1916-70. Finding aid.
     10".   PAM (MG10 B1)

     Founded in 1905. Minutes of the executive, special
     committees and annual meetings; financial records;
     convention speeches; programmes.

698. MANITOBA TEACHERS' SOCIETY
     Operating files. Restricted.

Available at 191 Harcourt, St. James-Assiniboia,
Winnipeg, R3Z 3Z2.

Archives unindexed.

699. MARYMOUND RESIDENTIAL TREATMENT CENTRE
     Operating files. Restricted.
     Located on Scotia Street, Winnipeg, Manitoba.

     Originally established in 1925 as Saint Agnes Priory
     School for wayward girls and older women. Minutes;
     financial records; historical materials.

700. MENNONITE EDUCATION
     2 papers, 1978 and 1979.
     Unpublished.   MHCA (Vertical file)

     "A compilation of Inspectors' Reports from the
     Mennonite School Districts, 1878-1926," by Debra
     Fast; "Manitoba Mennonite Public Schools," by Amanda
     Janzen.

701. MINERVA SCHOOL
     History, 1900-67. Unpublished paper.
                                     ERL

     "Minerva School Reunion." Student lists; names of
     teachers and trustees; photographs; history.

702. MYSTERY LAKE SCHOOL DIVISION
     Operating files, 1956- .
     Located at 408 Thompson Drive N., Thompson,
     Manitoba.

     Student and teacher records; building plans;
     financial records.

703. OAK RIDGE WOMEN'S INSTITUTE
     History, 1928-74.
     Unpublished.   PAM (MG8 A34)

     Compiled by Mrs. S. Rigby. History of school
     district #328; names of teachers.

704. OVERSEAS EDUCATION LEAGUE
     Papers, 1910-64.
     3".   PAM (MG10 B30 and
     B30-1)

Reports; programs; tour and travel itineraries of
the Overseas Education League and the Commonwealth
Youth Movement; memorabilia of a trip to England by
Edith Johnston.

705. PARKHILL-CHEVAL SCHOOL REUNION
        Scattered materials.   SCRLM

        Clippings and reunion pamphlet of Parkhill,
        1879-1965, and Cheval schools, 1901-65; names and
        dates of teachers, students, school trustees and
        inspectors.

706. RAMAH HEBREW SCHOOL (1955-79)
        Papers, 1971-79.   PAM (RG16 B)

        Class and staff lists; lists of board directors;
        photographs.

707. ST. AGNES SCHOOL FOR GIRLS
        Scattered materials.   PAM

        Established in 1925 by the Sisters of the Good
        Shepherd for disturbed and delinquent girls.
        Amalgamated with Marymound in 1969. Self-study
        report; committee reports; minutes miscellany.

708. ST. AUGUSTINE SCHOOL, BRANDON, MANITOBA
        Operating files.
        Located at 322 - 4th St., Brandon, Manitoba, R7A
        3G9.

        Opened by the Catholic School Board in 1906.

709. ST. JOHN'S COLLEGE AUXILIARY (1945-67)
        Papers, 1945-1967.   St. JCA

        Mrs. E.L. Jukes, first president. Correspondence;
        minutes; pamphlets; financial statements;
        presidential reports; constitutions; speeches;
        committee reports; membership lists; addresses;
        donor's lists; fund-raising projects.

710. ST. JOHN'S COLLEGE LADIES' SCHOOL
        (a) Papers, 1877-1930.   RLDA

        Organized 1876 and in 1930 transferred to the
        Corporation of the Archbishop of Rupert's Land.
        Minute books, 1877-1930; course tuitions and

regulations; Ladies' College Endowment fund reports, 1926, 1930; photographs; examinations; early (1880s) press clippings.

(b) Scattered materials.   PAM (MG1 B28;
                                             MG10 B6; MG14 C20)

Register of attendance, conduct and marks, 1881; anonymous description of the school, 1880; H. May Hutchins teaching material.

711. ST. MARY'S ACADEMY
     Operating files and archives.
     Located at 550 Wellington Crescent, Winnipeg,
     Manitoba, R3M 0C1.

     Organized 1869 by the Order of the Grey Nuns but
     assumed by the Sisters of the Holy Name of Jesus and
     Mary in 1874. Chroniques, 1874-1956; tuition
     ledger, 1918; baptism registers, 1880-1951; list of
     gifts and donors, 1924; students' names and
     addresses, 1913-60; St. Mary's sodality records,
     1930-74; guest book, 1945-79; yearbooks, 1932- ;
     photographs. (See also the Françoise-Jeanne
     Papers.)   PAM (MG9 B3).

712. ST. MICHAEL'S ACADEMY
     Operating files. Restricted.
     Located at 10 Victoria Avenue E., Brandon, Manitoba,
     and at the offices of the Four Sisters of Our Lady
     of the Missions, 800 Adele Avenue, Winnipeg,
     Manitoba.

     Organized 1899 by the Four Sisters of Our Lady of
     the Missions.

713. SOUTH EASTERN TEACHERS' ASSOCIATION OF MANITOBA
     Papers, 1913-67.
     15".   PAM (MG10 B2)

     Correspondence; minutes; convention register lists
     and resolutions.

714. SPEECHLY, MARY (1873-1968)
     Selected materials.
     1 folder.   UMA(MSS SC 35)

     Educator. Biographical sketch; tributes, honours
     and awards; speeches; family planning materials;
     correspondence; data on the Women's Institute.

715. STURGEON CREEK SCHOOL DIVISION #30
          School board records, 1908-20. CWA (Area G Row 3
                                          Shelf 74 Item 116B)

716. TRANSCONA SPRINGFIELD SCHOOL DIVISION
          (a) Scattered materials, 1917-82.
                                    TRHM (MG10 B4; BG14
                                    VGP MB10 B4 Box 2;
                                    MG14 B3 file 3-15)

          Minute book, 1917-23; Agreement between School
          Division #39 and Local Teachers Association, 1922;
          newsletters and clippings.

          (b) Board minutes, 1979-82. Located at Transcona
          Public Library

          Minutes of the Transcona-Springfield School Division
          #12.

717. TURTLE MOUNTAIN SCHOOL DIVISION
          Operating files. Restricted.
          Located at Division offices, Killarney, Manitoba.

          Minute books; financial records; inspectors'
          reports; superintendents' reports; school registers;
          teachers' names, qualifications; examination papers.

718. UNIVERSITY OF MANITOBA. ALUMNI ASSOCIATION
          Papers, 1920-77.   UMA (UA19)
          40 boxes.

          Minutes; correspondence; constitutions; fund
          raising; homecomings; scholarships and awards.

719. UNIVERSITY OF MANITOBA. BOARD OF GOVERNORS
          Papers, 1950-83. Unprocessed. UMA (Mfi 6, UASc 29,
                                          UA14)

720. UNIVERSITY OF MANITOBA. FACULTY OF AGRICULTURE
          Women's club.
          Minutes, 1924-64.
          4 volumes.   UMA (UA SC8)

721. UNIVERSITY OF MANITOBA. GENERAL FACULTY COUNCIL
          Papers, 1901-68.   UMA (UA 12)
          4 boxes.

          Correspondence; minutes; reports.

722. UNIVERSITY OF MANITOBA. GLEE CLUB
        Scattered materials.   UMA (UA SC 15)

        Programmes; photographs; newsclippings.

723. UNIVERSITY OF MANITOBA. INFORMATION OFFICE
        Papers, 1969-76.   UMA (UA 16)

        Press releases; clippings.

724. UNIVERSITY OF MANITOBA. OFFICE OF THE PRESIDENT
        Papers, 1913-76.   UMA (UA 20, UA 26)
        126'.

        Covering all aspects of University of Manitoba
        history. Correspondence; reports; minutes of
        committees; reports; briefs; appeals; applications;
        grievances; recommendations; funding; gifts;
        budgets; related materials.

725. UNIVERSITY OF MANITOBA. OFFICE OF THE VICE-PRESIDENT
        Papers, 1934-1976.   UMA (UA 22)
        13'.

        Correspondence; minutes; licenses; applications;
        contracts; policies; reports; plans; regulations;
        financial statements; legal matters; fee structures;
        other administrative concerns.

726. UNIVERSITY OF MANITOBA. REGISTRAR'S OFFICE
        Papers, 1877-1975.   UMA (UA 13)

        Correspondence; records; reports.

727. UNIVERSITY OF MANITOBA. RESIDENCE
        Dietitians' catering records, 1939-62.
        4 volumes.   UMA (UA SC9)

        Records; memoranda; lists; diagrams; brochures.

728. UNIVERSITY OF MANITOBA. SENATE MINUTES
        Minutes of Senate.   UMA (UA 6)
        Minutes of multiple subcommittees of Senate.

        About 60'.

729. UNIVERSITY OF MANITOBA. STUDENT RECORDS
                                     UMA (UA 13)

135

Files of student records. Applications; grades;
reports; graduation.

730. VIRDEN SCHOOL DISTRICT #144, VIRDEN, MANITOBA.
        History, 15 pp.
        Microfilm.   PAM (MG9 A70-2)

        "History of the Virden School District, #144," by
        Ida Clingan.

731. WESTERN MANITOBA TEACHERS' ASSOCIATION
        Papers, 1905-66.
        5".   PAM (MG10 B27)

        Founded in 1883 in Brandon, Manitoba, and ceased in
        1966. Minutes of annual conventions, 1905-66;
        junior high school section minutes, 1928-41;
        convention and registration lists, 1905-41.

732. WINNIPEG WOMEN'S CULTURAL AND EDUCATIONAL CENTRE, INC.
        Operation files.
        Located at 730 Alexander Avenue, Winnipeg, Manitoba,
        R3E 1H9.

        Minutes; financial records; tapes on sexual
        attitudes and sex-role stereotypes.

733. "WOMEN IN THE FACULTY OF SCIENCE - SOME VERY
        PRELIMINARY DATA"
        Unpublished paper, by Professor Charles Bigelow,
        Dean of Science, the University of Manitoba, 1982.
        Available from author.

        Statistical study and overview of women in the
        Faculty of Science at the University of Manitoba.

WOMEN AND HEALTH

734. ARMSTRONG, IDA MANNING (1905-82)
        Papers, 1905-64.
        2'.   PAM (P197-P200)

        Moved from Gladstone, Manitoba, with her family to
        Winnipeg in 1914 when her father was appointed to
        the cabinet of Premier T.C. Norris. She attended
        Kelvin High School and the University of Manitoba,
        obtaining her B.Sc. in 1926. Although she taught

school for some time, her heart was in medicine, and
in 1936 she completed requirements for the M.D.
degree. She spent the next year in England
attending lectures and classes at various hospitals,
which confirmed her interest in women's medicine.
She returned to Winnipeg in 1939, establishing her
own practice chiefly in obstetrics and gynecology.

Correspondence; C.B.C. radio lectures; teaching
certificates; financial records; patient appointment
and treatment files (restricted).

735. BIRTLES, MARY ELLEN
        Papers   BGHA

        First head nurse at Brandon General Hospital, 1892.
        Biographical ramblings; clippings; "Diary of Miss
        Ellen Birtle" (typescript); "Miss Ellen Birtle's
        Recollections" (handwritten); photographs.

736. BLACK, ELINOR, M.D.
        Papers, 1941-71.
        6 folders.   UMA (MSS SC 37)

        Physician. Former head, Department of Obstetrics
        and Gynecology, the University of Manitoba.
        Speeches; journal articles; administrative
        bulletins.

737. BOISSEVAIN, MANITOBA. HOSPITAL LADIES AID
        Papers, 1947-66.   BCA (MG10 B58)

        Financial records.

738. BOISSEVAIN, MANITOBA. HEALTH AND WELFARE
        Miscellaneous collections, 1894-1945.
        90 items.   BCA (MG10 B56)

        Data on local deaths, births and diseases;
        correspondence from area hospitals.

739. BOISSEVAIN, MANITOBA. MEDICAL RECORDS
        Maternity records, 1945-65. Restricted.
        2 notebooks.   BCA (MG10 M60)

740. BOISSEVAIN AND MORTON MEMORIAL HOSPITAL
        Financial statements, 1950-62. BCA (MG10 B66)

741. BRANDON ASSOCIATION OF GRADUATE NURSES
          Papers, 1911-62.   BGHA

          History of the Association; slates of officers, one
          page annual reports, 1911-62.

742. BRANDON ASSOCIATION FOR THE MENTALLY RETARDED
          Operating files. Restricted.
          Available by contacting the Association, Box 774,
          Brandon, Manitoba, R7A 5Z8.

          Minutes; reports; financial statements; published
          materials.

743. BRANDON GENERAL HOSPITAL. CERTIFICATES OF REGISTRATION
          Awards.   BGHA

          Graduations, medals and honours received by various
          members of the Brandon General Hospital School of
          Nursing.

744. BRANDON GENERAL HOSPITAL. MATURE NURSING PROGRAM
          Administrative records; housing; program content
          studies; student records.   BGHA

745. BRANDON GENERAL HOSPITAL. PATIENTS
          Scattered files, 1898-1912.   PAM (MG4 D1 Vol. 43)

          Notices of admission of immigrant patients and
          annual reports.

746. BRANDON GENERAL HOSPITAL. SCHOOL OF NURSING
          Administrative records, guides and programs,
          1965-83.   BGHA

          Student guides and programs for the Nursing Vesper
          Service; administrative records including minute
          books, 1899-1983; lists of graduates, "lady
          superintendents," board chairmen and medical
          personnel.

747. BRANDON GENERAL HOSPITAL. WOMEN'S HOSPITAL AID SOCIETY
          Administrative records,
          1966-80.   BGHA

          Correspondence, 1966-80; membership lists, 1973-80;
          minute book, 1971-80; information on various
          projects sponsored by the Society.

748. BRANDON MENTAL HEALTH CENTRE.   ADMINISTRATION
        Operating records.   BMHCA (SB 28-48;
                                    FC 7-75; SB1 - F2B)

        Financial statements; minutes; operations reports;
        acts and regulations, 1919-80; regulating care of
        the mentally ill; accreditation materials; cemetery
        books, 1925-67; correspondence and lists of patients
        buried; register of patients' valuables, 1909-65;
        correspondence, 1967-77, with the Department of
        Health and Social Development; nursing staff
        records; hospital regulations and manuals;
        entertainment records, 1948-69; ward statistical
        records, 1966-75 showing patient population by sex;
        services to the North; staff salary correspondence,
        1942-67; correspondence on working hours, conditions
        and staff salaries; annual reports, 1891-1944;
        correspondence concerning visitors' books, painting,
        plumbing, the Queen's 1951 visit, etc; newsletters,
        1970-79.

749. BRANDON MENTAL HEALTH CENTRE.   ADMISSIONS
        Tabulations and studies.   BMHCA (SB1 - F13,F14
                                    and F18)

        1975 tabulations of admissions by age, sex and
        diagnosis; statistics on admissions to Manitoba
        Mental Institutions, 1958-64; a study, 1937, by J.
        Wilkes Wright entitled "An Analysis of 560 First
        Admissions to the Brandon Hospital for Mental
        Diseases, with a View to Determining Causative
        Factors in Mental Disorders in Manitoba."

750. BRANDON MENTAL HEALTH CENTRE.   CASE FILES
        Study, 1959. Restricted.
        311 cases.   BMHCA

        "Follow-up study on 311 cases of pre-frontal
        lobotomy" with cases classified as recovered,
        improved, unimproved or deceased (no sex indicated).

751. BRANDON MENTAL HEALTH CENTRE.   HISTORICAL
        Reports and histories.   BMHCA (SB1 -
                                    F1A,3,8-12)

        Research notes on the history of the hospital by Val
        Hippner; various histories on the care of the insane
        in Manitoba; historical reports and correspondence
        on the development of various wards in the hospital;
        history of the Child Guidance Clinic; dietary
        history 1929-47 and 1950-70s; medical staff
        histories, 1891-1945.

752. BRANDON MENTAL HEALTH CENTRE. SCHOOL OF NURSING
        Records, 1923-76.   BMHCA (SB 5-8, SB17)

        Graduation records, 1923-76; staff history prior to
        1950; constitution for student government; uniform
        regulations; course examinations, 1954; procedure
        manuals; class schedules, 1956-75; test results,
        1956-75; laboratory; other education program files.

753. BRANDON MENTAL HEALTH CENTRE. STAFF RECORDS AND
     INTERVIEWS
        Oral histories and
        transcripts.   BMHCA (Tape file)

        Interviews, 1973, with housekeepers Margaret Carter
        and Marjorie Hall, kitchen and laundry staff members
        Kaye and Lexie Denbow, Mr. and Mrs Cliff Sampson,
        and Kate and John Clare; nurses Bill Jones (first
        male attendant), Evelyn McKenzie, Mrs. Frank
        Roberts (began work at the Centre in 1913), and
        Katherine Wilkes Weierman; and therapists Kay
        Dennis, Mrs. Marion Ferguson, and Jessie Rice.

754. CANADIAN ASSOCIATION FOR THE MENTALLY RETARDED (MANITOBA)
        Operating files. Restricted.
        Located at 46-825 Sherbrooke Street, Winnipeg,
        Manitoba, R3A 1M5.

        Twenty-seven Manitoba branches. Minutes; reports;
        financial records; newsletters; extensive
        correspondence; lists of members; project reports
        and analysis; printed resource materials.

755. CANADIAN ASSOCIATION FOR THE MENTALLY RETARDED
     (BOISSEVAIN)
        Papers.
        3 items.   BCA (MG10 B61)

        Chairman's annual report, 1970; 25-year history; a
        minute book, 1957-61.

756. CANADIAN MENTAL HEALTH ASSOCIATION
        Operating files, 1956 present. Restricted.
        Located at 330 Edmonton Street, Winnipeg, Manitoba,
        R3B 2L2.

        Organized in Manitoba in 1956. Minutes; financial
        records; newsletters; submissions; lists of service.

757. CANADIAN NATIONAL INSTITUTE FOR THE BLIND
     Operating files. Restricted.
     Located at 1031 Portage Avenue, Winnipeg, Manitoba,
     R3G 0R9.

     Central Western Division organized in 1919.
     Scrapbook of the Women's Auxiliary of the CNIB
     (since 1920s); newsletters; annual reports; minutes
     and financial reports of the Board; statistical
     analysis of Canada's blind population.

758. CANADIAN PARAPLEGIC ASSOCIATION
     Operating file. Restricted.
     Located at 825 Sherbrooke Street, Winnipeg,
     Manitoba, R3A 1M5.

     Minutes; financial records; reports; lists of
     supporting organizations; correspondence; printed
     materials.

759. CANADIAN RED CROSS SOCIETY (MANITOBA)
     Papers, 1914-74. Finding aid.
     34'.   PAM (MG10 B29)

     Minutes, 1914-66; annual reports, 1914-74;
     correspondence and papers, 1928-70; annual meeting
     files, 1945-68; newspaper cuttings, 1940-69; motion
     picture films, miscellaneous legal and financial
     records, 1919-33; history of the operation of Nurses
     Services Car on the Hudson's Bay Railway; outpost
     hospital records, 1946-61; first aid posts, 1945-68.

760. CANADIAN RED CROSS SOCIETY. DESFORD BRANCH
     Minute book, 1939-65.
     1 item.   BCA (MG10 B55)

761. CANADIAN RED CROSS SOCIETY. KILLARNEY BRANCH
     Records. Available at the residence of Mr. and Mrs.
     V. Britton, Killarney, Manitoba.

     Minute books; reports, 1955-79; minute book of
     Women's Hospital Aid, 1960-65.

762. CANADIAN RED CROSS SOCIETY. MINNEDOSA BRANCH
     Financial records.
     1".   PAM (MG10 B29-1)

     Cash receipt and disbursement journal.

763. CANADIAN RED CROSS SOCIETY. WINNIPEGOSIS BRANCH
          Records, 1918-67.
          1.5".   PAM (MG10 B29-2)

          Minutes, 1918-64; ledgers, 1918-57; war work
          committee reports, 1940-46; miscellaneous reports
          and correspondence, 1945-67.

764. CARTWRIGHT MEDICAL NURSING UNIT
          Financial statements, 1950-63. BCA (MG10 B68)

765. CATHOLIC HOSPITAL ASSOCIATION
          Scattered papers, 1947-49.
          1 folder.   A St-B (Drawer #28)

766. THE CHILDREN'S HOSPITAL OF WINNIPEG
          Papers, 1909-75.
          6'.   PAM (MG10 B33)

          First opened in 1909 through the initiative of Annie
          A. Bond.

          Minutes of the Board of Directors, 1909-72; Finance
          Committee, 1936-68; Building Committee, 1928-53;
          Honorary Attending Staff, 1942-46; annual reports,
          1909-71; cash books, 1911-19; guest registers,
          1932-71; materials and articles on Annie A. Bond;
          newsclippings.

767. THE CHILDREN'S HOSPITAL OF WINNIPEG. ANNIE A. BOND
     GUILD
          Papers, 1928-80.
          5".   PAM (MG10 B35)

          Originally called Junior St. John's Guild. Minutes,
          1928-69; annual reports, 1933-80; constitutions,
          1960; history of the Guild to 1975; quarter-century
          club minutes, 1950; scrapbooks, clippings and
          photographs.

768. THE CHILDREN'S HOSPITAL OF WINNIPEG. NURSES ALUMNAE
     ASSOCIATION
          Papers, 1930-73. Finding aid.
          15".   PAM (MG10 B34)

          Minute books, 1934-66; correspondence, 1953-66;
          reports, 1945-66; photographs.

769. CHOWN, H. BRUCE (1893-   )
        Papers, 1936-   .
        14 boxes.   UMA (MSS 17)

        Correspondence; reports; published articles;
        speeches; lectures; case studies; laboratory records
        concerning his life-long studies of haemolitic
        (blood) diseases of the newborn, especially
        erythroblastosis fetalis and the maternal Rh-factor.

770. CLARKE, HARRIET FOXTON, M.D. (1862-1934)
        Resource material.   UMMFA (Graduate file)

        Physician. First women to graduate (1892) from the
        Manitoba Medical College. Clippings; obituary;
        degrees; correspondence.

771. COALITION OF PROVINCIAL ORGANIZATIONS OF THE
     HANDICAPPED
        Operating files. Restricted.
        Located at 926-294 Portage Avenue, Winnipeg, Manitoba,
        R3C 0B9

        Organized in 1976 and since has become a national
        umbrella organization for self-representation.
        Minutes; financial records; newsletters; addresses of
        affiliated groups; correspondence; newsclippings.

772. COLLEGE OF FAMILY PHYSICIANS OF CANADA (MANITOBA
     CHAPTER)
        Papers, 1954-76.   PAM (MG10 A18)

        Constitutions; correspondence; minutes; reports;
        annual meetings; financial records; papers of the
        Department of Family Practice (Hospitals);
        Department of Family Practice (University of
        Manitoba); Ladies Program, 1976.

773. CONCORDIA GENERAL HOSPITAL
        Operating files. Restricted. (German and English)
        Located at 1095 Concordia Avenue, Winnipeg,
        Manitoba.

        Founded by Mennonite interests in 1927 first as a
        maternity hospital and later (1931) as a public
        general hospital. Minutes; reports; project plans;
        financial records; staff and patient records; 46 pp.
        history, "Concordia Hospital 1928-1978";
        photographs.

143

774. DARRACH, SARAH P. JOHNSTON, M.D. (d. 1974)
        Resource material.   BGHA

        Nurse and supervisor. Biographical data and awards.

775. DEAF ACCESS LINE
        Operating files. Restricted.
        Located at 926-294 Portage Avenue, Winnipeg,
        Manitoba, R3C 0B9.

        Records and materials to assist the deaf to
        information from most public services.

776. DEER LODGE HOSPITAL
        Scattered records.   UMMFA (5.10.2)

        Miscellaneous records.

777. DYNEVOR HOSPITAL
        Papers, 1909-34.   RLDA (DRL-84-162)
        Correspondence, 1940-41.   AWC (Box 3 #6)

        Hospital for Indians at Dynevor, Manitoba.
        Correspondence; register of baptisms and deaths,
        1909-34; synod reports; monthly bulletins.

778. EPILEPTIQUES, MAISON YOUVILLE
        1 folder, 1939-49.   A St-B (Drawer #28)

        Scattered materials.

779. FLIN FLON GENERAL HOSPITAL
        Correspondence, 1972.   FFHS/FFPL

780. HOSPITAL ACCOUNT JOURNALS, WINNIPEG
        Journals, 1932-66.
        Restricted.   CWA (Area D Row 1
                                    Shelf 24-25)

781. INDEPENDENT LIVING RESOURCE CENTRE
        Operating files. Restricted.
        Available at 503-280 Smith Street, Winnipeg,
        Manitoba, R3C 1K2.

        Organized in 1972. Minutes; directors reports;
        financial records; correspondence; government
        services.

782. JACKSON, MARJORIE
        Resource material.   BGHA

        Nurse. Former Director of Nursing at Brandon
        General Hospital. Biographical sketch.

783. KLINIC COMMUNITY HEALTH CENTRE
        Operating files. Restricted.
        Available at 545 Broadway Avenue, Winnipeg,
        Manitoba.
        Processing incomplete.

        Free health clinic specializing in crisis
        intervention and health and drug education.
        Reports; minutes; financial records; patient
        records.

784. MCPHAIL, DON AND ETHEL
        Papers, 1948-76. Restricted. BCA (B57 and P67 E27)

        Physicians. Medical journals; account books; loose
        bills; 1976 photographs of doctors, staff, and the
        Medical Centre at Boissevain, Manitoba.

785. MARTENS, ETHEL G.
        Papers still reside with the creator, except for a
        biography (6 pp.) on deposit at 130 Elliot Street,
        Bird's Hill, Manitoba, R0E 0H0.

        Social worker. Former executive director of the
        Winnipeg Health and Social Services Centre, Inc.

786. MANITOBA ASSOCIATION OF REGISTERED DIETITIANS
        Papers, 1948-80.
        1 1/2".   PAM (MG10 A27)

        Formerly called the Manitoba Branch of the Canadian
        Dietetic Association and the Dietetic Association of
        Manitoba (1956). Minutes, 1948-79; annual reports,
        1972-78; membership list manual, 1949-80;
        newsletter.

787. MANITOBA ASSOCIATION OF REGISTERED NURSES
        Operating file.
        Available at 647 Broadway Avenue, Winnipeg,
        Manitoba.

        Founded in 1905 as the Manitoba Association of
        Graduate Nurses. Minute books, 1913 onward;
        treasurer's cash books; newsletters (Nucleus), an

        145

unpublished, comprehensive history by Beatrice
Fines.

788. MANITOBA DEPARTMENT OF HEALTH AND WELFARE, BOARD OF
HEALTH
Minute books, 1893-1939.
5".   PAM (RG5 A1)

789. MANITOBA DEPARTMENT OF HEALTH AND WELFARE. PSYCHIATRIC
NURSES
Papers. Restricted.   PAM (RG5 F5 and F6)

Minutes of meetings of medical superintendents,
1963-72; reports and papers of examining committee,
1966-80; education advisory committee, 1967-80;
curriculum committee, 1970-80; minutes, 1960-80;
general correspondence, 1972-79.

790. MANITOBA DEPARTMENT OF HEALTH AND WELFARE. PUBLIC
HEALTH NURSING
Papers, 1916-71.
Several boxes.   PAM (RG5 E1)

Annual reports, 1932-69; correspondence, circular
letters, and meeting notices, 1928-71; personnel
lists, 1925-65; tape recordings of conferences;
addresses and lectures; briefs to royal commissions;
Kellogg Foundation and Kellogg Fund Supplies,
1952-64; Sabin Oral Vaccine Program, 1962-64; 50th
Anniversary Celebration file, 1966; nursing manuals
and curricula; Northern Health Services, 1962-65;
Red River flood, 1950; various historical files;
nurses' badges; photographs.

791. MANITOBA LEAGUE OF THE PHYSICALLY HANDICAPPED, INC.
Operating files. Restricted.
Located at 402-280 Smith Street, Winnipeg, Manitoba,
R3C 1K2.

Self-help consumer organization established in 1975
with branches throughout Manitoba. Minutes;
financial records; newsletters; article files.

792. MANITOBA MEDICAL STUDENTS ASSOCIATION, WOMEN'S DIVISION
Miscellaneous materials,
1930-31.   UMMFA (6.2.1)

Includes programmes for graduating classes.

146

793. MANITOBA SCHOOL FOR THE DEAF
        Operating files. Restricted.
        Located at 500 Shaftesbury, Winnipeg, Manitoba, R3P
        0M1.

        Operated by the Manitoba Department of Education.
        Registers; reports; financial records; curricula;
        student and staff lists.

794. MANITOBA SCHOOL FOR RETARDATES
        Operating files. Restricted.
        Available at Third Street N.E., Portage la Prairie,
        Manitoba, Box 1190, R1N 3C6.

        Established in 1890 as "The Home for Incurables" and
        later served as a training centre for psychiatric
        nurses. Now operated by the Manitoba Department of
        Health and Public Welfare. Daily journals, 1956-68;
        graduating exercises; scrapbooks, 1945-   ;
        histories; photographs.

795. MANITOBA SCHOOL FOR RETARDATES, AUXILIARY
        Operating files. Restricted.
        Available at Box 1075, Winnipeg, Manitoba, R3C 2X4.

        A fund-raising public relations support group
        organized in 1966 to assist the Manitoba School for
        Retardates and the mentally handicapped throughout
        the province. Minutes; reports; project
        assessments; lists of volunteers; financial records.

796. MARGARET SCOTT NURSING MISSION (1904-46)
        Papers, 1904-47. Finding aid.
        30".   PAM (MG10 B9)

        Minute books; monthly reports; day book of
        donations; visitors register; correspondence.

797. MENNONITE MEDICINE
        Two unpublished papers, 1981. MHCA (Vertical file)

        "Mennonite Folk Medicine. 'Laughter...the best
        medicine of all!'" by Margaret K. Froese; "201
        Mennonite Home Remedies" by Rick Bergen.

798. MISERICORDIA GENERAL HOSPITAL
        History, 1983.
        Typescript.   HP DEP CW

147

"Misericordia General Hospital, 99 Cornish Avenue,"
by Sheila Grover. History and physical plan of the
hospital.

799. MITCHELL, J.E.
          Papers.   PAM (MG14 C108)

          Includes Lydia E. Pinkham's "Treatise on the Disease
          of Women," 1908.

800. MOUNT CARMEL CLINIC
          Scattered papers and
          references.   PAM (MG2 B10)

          Established in the 1920s as a Jewish-sponsored
          medical and dental facility for newly-arrived Jewish
          immigrants. Minutes of Board meetings;
          correspondence; Baby Week, 1948; Tag Day, 1959;
          account book for the June 1928 emergency campaign.

801. MUNICIPAL HOSPITALS (1912 -)
          (a) Operating files. Restricted.
          Located on Morley Avenue, Winnipeg, Manitoba.

          King George, King Edward and Princess Elizabeth
          Hospitals set aside for the treatment of
          tuberculosis, scarlet fever, typhoid, diptheria and
          other contagious diseases. Annual reports, 1915- ,
          listing patients, diseases and deaths; clipping
          albums, 1911-60; photographs.

          (b) 16-page report, 1983.   HP DEP CW
          "Nurses' Residence, Winnipeg Municipal Hospitals,
          Morely Avenue," by Sheila Grover.

802. NURSING ALUMNI ASSOCIATION
          Papers, 1951-81.
          1 box.   UMA (A85-6)

          Minutes, reports; financial records; history.

803. PORTAGE DISTRICT GENERAL HOSPITAL
          Operating files and archives. Restricted.
          Located at 524 Fifth Ave. S.E., Portage la Prairie,
          Manitoba, R1N 3N8.

          Formally incorporated in 1896; School of Nursing
          established in 1899. Minute book, 1902-14;
          photographs.

804. RENNER, SARAH EFFIE
       Papers, 1931-46.   PAM (MG 114 C113)

       List of births in which she assisted as midwife and
       nurse in the vicinity of Gull Lake, Manitoba; date
       of birth, name of child and parents, and place of
       birth, 1931-45; certificate to practise as a
       licenced practical nurse, 1946.

805. ROSS, CHARLOTTE WHITEHEAD, M.D. (1842-1916)
       Resource file.   UMMFA (12.1)

       Physician. Articles; clippings; 1940 radio talk
       script, by Dr. M. Ellen Douglas, entitled "Dr.
       Charlotte Ross"; biographical sketch (18 pp.) by
       Airdie Bell Cameron; list of awards; obituary. See
       also the Steward McKiechan collection) for an
       article on her work.   PAM (MG14 C88 BOX 22)

806. ST. ANNE HOSPITAL
       1 folder, 1951.   A St-B (Drawer #28)

807. ST. ANTHONY'S HOSPITAL AUXILIARY
       Operating files. Restricted.
       Available at The Pas, Manitoba, R9A 1KA.

       Minutes; financial records; lists of members.

808. ST. BONIFACE HOSPITAL
       Scattered records, 1938-60.
       (a) 4 folders   A St-B (Drawer #28)
       (b) history   SBHSA (Box 40)

       Formerly L'Hôpital Saint-Roch. Salary studies,
       1938-47; history of the St. Boniface Hospital and
       its founding by the Grey Nuns; miscellaneous
       materials.

809. ST. BONIFACE HOSPITAL WOMEN'S AUXILIARY
       Operating files, 1952-   .   Restricted.
       Located at the St. Boniface Hospital, Winnipeg,
       Manitoba.

810. ST. BONIFACE HOSPITAL. HISTORY
       Historical overview, 1983.
       18 pp. Typescript.   HP DEP CW

       "L'Hôpital Saint-Roch, 351 Rue Taché," by Sheila
       Grover.

811. ST. BONIFACE HOSPITAL. REGISTER
          List of patients, 1895-1913. Archives of the Grey
          Nuns, St. Boniface.

          "Régistre des Malades de l'Hôpital Saint-Roch 1895,
          St. Boniface." Patients' ethnic background, age,
          occupation, residence and medical diagnosis.

812. SELKIRK MENTAL HEALTH CENTRE (1886 -   )
          Operating files and library. Restricted.
          Located at Selkirk, Manitoba.

          Administrative records (microfilm) on patients,
          treatments, and personnel; newsletters; several
          unpublished histories; scrapbooks.

813. SELKIRK MENTAL HEALTH CENTRE SCHOOL OF PSYCHIATRIC
     NURSING
          Scattered records.   SMHCL

          Established in 1921. Scrapbook of graduating
          classes; photographs; lists of nurses; programs.

814. SELKIRK HOSPITAL AUXILIARY FOR RECREATION AND EDUCATION
          Papers, 1949-66.
          4".   PAM (MG10 B10)

          A voluntary, non-profit organization formed in 1949
          to assist patients at the Selkirk Mental Hospital.
          Correspondence; newsletters; membership lists;
          reminiscences of founding members; photographs.

815. SHALOM RESIDENCE
          Operating files. Restricted.
          Located at 175 Cathedral Avenue, Winnipeg, Manitoba,
          R2W 0X1.
          Contact: Thelma Brownstone

          A Jewish-sponsored non-profit, non-sectarian home
          for the mentally handicapped.

816. SMALLPOX AT WINNIPEG (1893-99)
          Scattered references.   PAM (MG4 D1 V. 101 F.
                                        14205)

          Correspondence; statistics; financial matters; lists
          of immigrants suffering from the disease; claims.

817. SOCIETY FOR CRIPPLED CHILDREN AND ADULTS OF MANITOBA
        Operating files.   Restricted.
        Located at 825 Sherbrooke Street, Winnipeg, R3A 1M6
        and 340-9th Street, Brandon, Manitoba, R7A 6C2.

        Minutes; reports; financial records; lists of
        participants and volunteers.

818. STEWART, DAVID ALEXANDER, M.D. (1874-1937)
        Papers.   PAM (MG9 A54)

        Physician. Superintendent of the Manitoba
        Sanitorium at Ninette, Manitoba. Data on
        tuberculosis in women; speeches and material by Mrs.
        D.A. Stewart relevant to peace movement of the
        1930s.

819. STEWART, MARGUERITA O.
        Papers, 1945-1955.
        1/2".   PAM (MG14 C41)

        Nurse. Account book, 1945-65; correspondence,
        1945-54, regarding nursing service at Wabowden,
        Manitoba.

820. UNIVERSITY OF MANITOBA MEDICAL COLLEGE
        List of graduates, 1886- , staff appointments, and
        terminations, 1919- .   UMMCA (1.1.1 and
                                        1.3.1)

821. VICTORIA GENERAL HOSPITAL
        Miscellaneous historical
        materials.   UMMFA (5.8.2)

822. VICTORIAN ORDER OF NURSES
        (a) Operating files, 1901- . Restricted.
        Available at 311-167 Lombard Avenue, Winnipeg,
        Manitoba, R3B 0T4.

        Established in Manitoba in 1901. Minute books,
        1901- ; annual meeting reports, 1914-15;
        newsletters; printed reports.

        (b) Additional materials
        1933-37.   PAM (MG10 B12)

823. WEST KILDONAN. PUBLIC HEALTH COMMITTEE
        Minutes, 1921-23. Restricted.
        Finding aid.   CWA (Area B, Row 17,
                                         Shelf 378)

824. WINNIPEG GENERAL HOSPITAL (HEALTH SCIENCES CENTRE)
     (a) Papers, 1871-1973. Finding aid.
     23'. Originals and
     photocopies.   PAM (MG10 B11)

     Established in 1872, it expanded regularly until, in
     1973, the General Hospital amalgamated with the
     Children's Hospital, Manitoba Rehabilitation
     Hospital, D.A. Stewart Respiratory Centre, and the
     Cancer Treatment and Research Foundation to form the
     Health Sciences Centre of Winnipeg. Annual reports,
     1882-1972; minutes of committee board meetings,
     1878-1973; interns' records, 1882-1958;
     correspondence, 1898-1971; miscellaneous files,
     notes, by-laws and agreements, 1878-1958; history of
     the Winnipeg Maternity Hospital and the School of
     Nursing.

     (b) Unpublished history.
     37 pp.   PAM (MG10 F2)

     "A Hundred Years of Health: A Brief History of the
     Winnipeg General Hospital," by Beatrice Fines.

825. "WOMEN IN MEDICINE"
     Resource file.   UMMFA (12.9
                                     Biographical File)

     Correspondence between the University of Manitoba
     Faculty of Medicine and the General Secretary for
     the Overseas Settlement of British Women, 1923; a
     list of medical women on the staff at the Manitoba
     Medical College in 1965, with their qualifications
     and positions held.

WOMEN AND SEXUALITY

826. AIKIN, JAMES MRS.
     Oral interview, 1961.
     Transcript.   PAM (MG10 F2 Box 11
                                     Tape 12)

     In an interview with Lionel Orlikow, she discusses
     birth control in the 1930s and recounts the speeches
     of Dr. H.M. Speechly, Dr. Mary Crawford and others
     to the Labour Women's Group of Winnipeg.

827. COALITION FOR REPRODUCTIVE CHOICE
     Operating files. Restricted.

Contact: Box 51, Station L, Winnipeg, Manitoba, R3H 0Z4.

An organization committed to allowing women the freedom to choose whether or not they will deliver a child (for whatever reason), with abortion as a legal and available alternative.

828. COUNCIL ON HOMOSEXUALITY AND RELIGION
Operating files.
Contact: Box 1912, Winnipeg, Manitoba, R3C 3R2.

829. DIGNITY/DIGNITE
Operating files. Restricted.
Contact: Box 1912, Winnipeg, Manitoba, R3C 3R2.

Reinforces self-acceptance of homosexual men and women and aids them in becoming move active members of the Catholic Church society.

830. GAY COMMUNITY CENTRE
Operating files. Restricted.
Located at 277 Sherbrooke Street, Winnipeg, Manitoba.

A club catering to both male and female homosexuals.

831. GAYS FOR EQUALITY
Operating files. Restricted.
Located at University Centre, University of Manitoba, Winnipeg, R3T 2N2.

An organization designed to meet the needs and supply information on the homosexual community, both male and female.

832. LEAGUE FOR LIFE OF MANITOBA
Operating files.
Located at 579 Des Meurons Avenue, Winnipeg, Manitoba, R2H 2P6.

An anti-abortion association organized in 1970 by Pat Soenen and others committedly opposed to abortion on demand. Minutes; financial records; presidential reports; library of printed materials.

833. LESBIAN MOTHERS' DEFENSE FUND
Operating files.

Located at the Woman's Building, 730 Alexander
Avenue, Winnipeg, R3E 1H9

Organized in 1974 as a support group for mothers in
custody cases.

834. PLANNED PARENTHOOD MANITOBA
Papers, 1966-77. Finding aid.
9 boxes.   PAM (MG10 B28)

Organized initially by Mary Speechly in the 1930s as
the Winnipeg Family Planning Association.
Correspondence; minutes of annual and executive
meetings; financial records; committee papers;
newsletters; campaign records. (See also the Social
Planning Council of Winnipeg Collection.)

835. PLANNED PARENTHOOD MANITOBA RESOURCE CENTRE
Operating files. Restricted.
Located at 1000-259 Portage Avenue, Winnipeg,
Manitoba, R3B 2A9.

Minutes; reports; programmes; printed materials.

836. PREGNANCY COUNSELLING
Operating files. Restricted.
Located at 886 Main Street, Winnipeg, Manitoba, R2W
3P1.

837. PREGNANCY DISTRESS SERVICE
Operating files. Restricted.
Located at 444 Spence Street, Winnipeg, R3B 2R7.

838. PREGNANCY INFORMATION SERVICE INC.
Operating files. Restricted.
Located at 545 Broadway Avenue, Winnipeg, Manitoba,
R3C 0W3.

839. PREGNANCY SERVICE, INC.
Operating files. Restricted.
Located at 304-414 Graham Avenue, Winnipeg,
Manitoba, R3C 0M2.

840. THE WOMEN'S LINE
Operating files.
Located at the Woman's Building, 730 Alexander
Avenue, Winnipeg, R3E 1H9.

Organized in 1974 as a voluntary organization
providing peer counselling and referral for
lesbians. Minutes; reports; financial records;
correspondence.

WOMEN AND LAW, GOVERNMENT AND POLITICS

841. BAYER, MARY ELIZABETH
        Resource files and papers.   LEG LIB (Vertical
                                        file) and PAM
                                        (RG24 Box 65 15-2-3)

        Poet and politician. Deputy Minister for Cultural
        Affairs, 1972. Biographical sketch, vitae,
        scrapbook and centennial speeches.

842. BETTER HOUSING COMMISSION AND COMMITTEE
        Files, 1927-67.   CWA

        Minutes; correspondence; indexes; reports.

843. BRANDON COUNCIL OF WOMEN
        Papers.
        3 boxes plus loose materials. BUA (M80-23)

        A federation of approximately 50 women's groups
        organized in 1952 to sponsor the election of women
        to civic office, to support the Indian-Métis Centre
        and other worthy causes. Proceedings of the
        International and National Councils, 1956-67;
        Provincial Council resolutions and reports, 1964-67;
        Brandon Council and Executive Reports and Minutes,
        1964-67; correspondence; clippings and conference
        kit, 1964-73; scrapbooks; photographs.

844. CANADIAN BAR ASSOCIATION
        Film (b/w silent, mid 1960s).
        1 reel (16 mm)   PAM

        "Garden Party." Visit to Government House by women
        members of the Canadian Bar Association.

845. CO-OPERATIVE COMMONWEALTH FEDERATION (NEW DEMOCRATIC
     PARTY)
        (a) Papers. Finding aid.   PAM (MG14 D8)

(b) Operating records. Located at 656 Broadway
Avenue, R3C 0X3, and 1036 Notre Dame Avenue,
Winnipeg, R3E 0N9.

846. CRERAR, DOROTHY
Recorded address, 1940s.
Disc. 89, (15"). PAM (Tape 3 track 1
and 2)
and PAM (AV A10)

Political talks on the Progressive Conservative and
CCF parties, J.S. Woodworth's pacifism, agriculture,
and the Canadian West. Recorded by CKY.

847. FORT GARRY
Tax rolls and tax sale records, 1908-71.
CWA

848. FORT ROUGE INFORMATION AND RESOURCE CENTRE, INC.
Papers, 1964-77.
6'. PAM (MG10 B26)

Organized in 1966 initially as the Community
Ecumenical Ministry by three local churches to
improve child care and recreational facilities,
youth and information services, and senior citizens'
accommodations. Correspondence; minutes; financial
records; questionnaires; briefs; applications;
mailing lists; newsclippings.

849. GIMLI, MANITOBA
Scattered files. ERL

Voters lists, 1908- ; official photographs of Mayor
Violet Einarson; publications.

850. HALLDORSON, SALOME
Papers, 1936-40.
2". PAM (MG14 B3)

MLA, St. George, 1936-41. Correspondence; speeches;
clippings related to the Social Credit Party.

851. HUMAN RIGHTS COMMISSION
Operating files and case histories. Restricted.
Located at the Dayton Building, 209-323 Portage
Avenue, Winnipeg, Manitoba, R3B 2C1.

Minutes; reports; case histories; data on
legislation and legal precedents.

852. IRVINE, OLIVE
Notes.
1 folder.   UMA (MSS SC 34)

Senator. Obituaries, letter of condolence, and a
map of the Senate Chambers.

853. KONANTZ, MARGARET (1899-1967)
Papers, 1922-67. Finding aid.
11 boxes (about 1700 items).   UMA (MSS 1)

Politician. Diaries, 1944-61; correspondence,
1954-67; notes on trips around the world; reports
and memoranda concerning her work and travels with
UNICEF; newpaper clippings about her and her mother,
Mrs. Edith Rogers; financial records; scrapbooks;
personal certificates and degrees; pamphlets of
nations and places visited; two photographs.

854. L'AMI, CHARLES ERNEST (1896-1982)
Papers and Literary manuscripts, 1930-80. Finding
aid.
36 boxes.   UMA (MSS 25)

Correspondence; unpublished novels; short stories;
plays; poems; articles; CBC radio scripts;
copybooks; research material on the career of this
Winnipeg journalist, broadcaster and fiction writer.
Included also are materials of and about his wife,
Mrs. C.E. L'Ami, also a writer and journalist.

855. LAW SOCIETY OF MANITOBA
Operating files, 1883-1970.
Located on 14th Floor, Lakeview Square, Winnipeg,
Manitoba. (Consult also the Archive of Western
Canadian Legal History at the University of
Manitoba.)

Minute books, 1881-1916; applications for admission
to the bar (post 1930); card index of past and
present lawyers; Law Society scrapbooks, 1883-1970s;
chronological files on Manitoba legal history.

856. LIBERAL PARTY OF MANITOBA
Papers, 1955-80. Finding aid.
71 boxes.   UMA (MSS 18)

157

Correspondence; newsclippings; news releases;
speeches; biographies; minutes; campaign literature;
policy statements; photographs; financial records.

857. MCWILLIAMS, ROLAND FAIRBURN (1874-1957)
      Papers, 1948-63.   PAM (MG12 M2)

      Lieutenant-Governor of Manitoba, 1940-63.
      Collection contains letters from Margaret
      McWilliams, 1917.

858. MANITOBA ASSOCIATION OF WOMEN AND THE LAW
      Operating files.
      Contact: Faculty of Law, University of Manitoba,
      Winnipeg, Manitoba, R3T 2N2.

      Minutes; financial records.

859. NORRIS, TOBIAS CRAWFORD (1861-1936)
      Papers, 1903-47.   PAM (MG13 H1)

      Premier of Manitoba, 1915-22. Correspondence;
      testimonials; reports; studies; material on the
      Civic Charities Bureau; correspondence with the
      National and Local Council of Women about help to
      the blind and mentally handicapped in coping with
      the high cost of living; Salvation Army scheme for
      immigration of British widows; Polish Army in France
      - Ladies Auxiliary notice.

860. PROVINCIAL COUNCIL OF WOMEN AND MANITOBA
      Papers, 1949-80. Finding aid.
      7'.   PAM (MG10 C44)

      Minutes; financial records; reports; research papers
      including "Family Law, 1977-1979." (See also the
      Papers of the National Council of Women.
                                          PAM (MG10 C47)

861. QUEEN VICTORIA PROVINCIAL MEMORIAL COMMITTEE
      Papers, 1901-05
      5".   PAM (MG10 C21)

      Subscription list, 1901; minute book, 1901-04;
      letter books; correspondence, 1901-05.

862. ROBLIN, RODMOND PALEN (1853-1937)
      Papers, 1901-15. Finding aid.
      5".   PAM (MG13 G1)

Premier of Manitoba, 1900-15. Correspondence and papers including 1915 letters from a Mrs. S. Dick concerning the Women's Civic League of Winnipeg, and from a Mrs. R.F. McWilliams regarding the Winnipeg Council of Women.

863. ROGERS, EDITH (1876-1947)
     Papers, 1914-42
     3.5'.   PAM (P183-190)

A Winnipeg social leader and philanthropist. While not in the forefront of the suffrage movement, she was deeply sensitive to the needs of women and children. When asked to run as a Liberal candidate in the election of 1920, she accepted and won, thus becoming the first woman MLA in Manitoba's history. Re-elected in 1922 and 1927, she retired from politics in 1932, having greatly influenced social welfare legislation in the province.

Correspondence relating to political and legislative matters; appeals for social assistance and employment; manuscript and reproduced copies of speeches by Mrs. Rogers and others; reports; estimates, annotated copies of various pieces of legislation; brief and incomplete corresondence files with many of the numerous organizations to which she belonged, including extensive correspondence and receipts for the Save the Children Fund, 1924-26. Incomplete but informative correspondence and case files, 1915-30, for the Soldier's Deserted Wives Fund. This Fund, an arm of the Manitoba Patriotic Fund, was organized at the instigation of Mrs. Rogers. Financial records both personal and relative to the estate of Arthur Rogers; correspondence and congratulatory telegrams on her election, 1920, from such individuals as Margaret King, among many others; newspaper clippings and scrapbooks.

864. STEWART, CRAIG
     Papers, 1968-78. Finding aid.
     45 boxes.   UMA (MSS 31)

Member of Parliament Marquette (Manitoba) constituency. Office files; correspondence from constituents; questionnaires; speeches and writings.

865. WEST KILDONAN CITY HALL
     Records, 1924-77.
     Located at 1760 Main Street, Winnipeg, R2V 1Z7.

159

Account books; by-laws; voter lists; financial
reports; police reports; list of electors.

866. WINNIPEG ASSESSMENT DEPARTMENT
        Assessment rolls.   CWA (Holdings
                                     incomplete)
        For all Winnipeg subdivisions.

867. WINNIPEG CITY COUNCIL

                                  LEG LIB

        Lists of women who served. Jessie Kirk; Margaret
        McWilliams; Hilda Hesson; Maude J. McCreary; Lillian
        Hallonquist; Edith I. Tennont; Inez Trueman; June
        Westbury; Olga Fuga; Florence Pierce; Pearl
        McGonigal; Anne Jorowski; Betty Treton; Evelyn M.
        Reese.

868. WINNIPEG FINANCE DEPARTMENT
        Files. Restricted.   CWA

        Tax sales, 1885-1956; expropriations; home
        assessment records; tax rolls, 1929-66.

869. WINNIPEG MARKET, LICENSE, AND HEALTH COMMITTEE
        Minutes, 1876-1920.   CWA

870. WINNIPEG PARKS AND RECREATION DEPARTMENT
        Papers, 1953-71. Restricted. CWA

        Wage and salary reports; time books; social,
        sporting and recreational activities.

871. "WOMEN IN LOCAL GOVERNMENT"
        A research paper by Caroline Ion.
        115 pp.   IUS/U of W (2H-4)

        A 1974 study on Winnipeg women and their political
        influence.

872. WOMEN IN THE LAW
        Research materials.   AWCLH (A2053)

        267 questionnaires completed by women lawyers and
        other women in the legal profession across Canada
        answering questions on discrimination encountered,
        salary comparisons with male counterparts, type of
        practice, and occupation of spouse. Other

160

miscellaneous files of research conducted by
Professor Cameron Harvey.

873. WOMEN'S MODEL PARLIAMENT, WINNIPEG, MANITOBA
Proceedings, 1972-81.
Typescript.   LEG LIB

3rd, 7th, 10th and 12th sessions.

WOMEN IN NON-TRADITIONAL DISCIPLINES

874. ARTEMIS REPRODUCTIONS
Operating files. Restricted. The Women's Building,
730 Alexander Avenue, Winnipeg, Manitoba, R3E 1H9.

A woman's business enterprise (established in 1979)
in the offset printing business.

875. BELL, DOROTHY
Oral history; photographs.   WCAM (Oral history
collection)

One of Manitoba's first woman pilots.

876. CANADIAN WOMEN'S PRESS CLUB, WINNIPEG BRANCH
Papers, 1906-68.
44".   PAM (MG10 A1)

Founded in 1906 with Catherine Simpson-Hayes as
first president. Minute books (1909-   );
corresondence, clippings; newsletters; scrapbooks;
photographs.

877. EDWARDS, JOAN
Unpublished manuscript. Illustrated.
In possession of the author Box 543, Flin Flon,
Manitoba.

Nurse, artist, author, and trapper. Discusses her
life on the trapline.

878. MEDIA, ARTS, GRAPHICS, IDEAS COMPANY (MAGIC)
Operating files. Restricted. The Women's Building,
730 Alexander Avenue, Winnipeg, Manitoba, R3E 1H9.

161

A women's business enterprise (establised in 1979)
selling a variety of "women-made products."

879. WINNIPEG POLICE ACADEMY
     Located 2799 Roblin Blvd., Winnipeg, R3R 0B8.
     Selected files.

     Mugshots, 1920-   ; recruiting classes, 1945-   ;
     files on officers.

880. WINNIPEG POLICE ASSOCIATION
     Operation files, 1940-79. Restricted.
     Located at 438 1/2 Main Street, Winnipeg, R3B 1B2.

     Police history; women as matrons and later as
     officers; capital punishment files; minutes;
     negotiations; newsletters.

881. "WOMAN PARACHUTIST: SIGNI (STEPHENSON) EATON EARLY
     WINNIPEG AIRSHOW"
     Film documentary, 1928.
     16 mm. (b/w, silent), 3.   WCAM

     Shots of Stephenson field, stunt flying and of Signi
     Stephenson, Winnipeg's first woman parachutist.

882. WOMEN PILOTS: NINETY-NINES INC., INTERNATIONAL
     Operating files. Restricted.
     Contact: Dr. Beth Candlish, 62-1 Snow Street,
     Winnipeg, Manitoba, R3T 2M4.

     An association of women pilots, named after the
     number who met to honour Amelia Erhardt.

883. WOMEN IN TRADES ASSOCIATION
     Operating files, 1979. Restricted. 3-370 Alexander
     Avenue, Winnipeg, Manitoba, R3E 1H9.

     A support system for women in the trades, training
     for the traders, and those seeking employment in the
     trades. Minutes; reports; financial records;
     resource library.

884. ADVENTURE CROSSROADS, INC.
    Operating files. Restricted.
    Located at The Family Centre, 211 Isabel Street,
    Winnipeg, R3A 1R5, Manitoba.

    An inner-city facility sponsored by several
    Mennonite churches to co-ordinate women's interests
    with pre-school child care and family activities.
    Minutes and financial records.

885. BETA SIGMA PHI SORORITY, MANITOBA
    Operating files.
    Located at 2-222 Osborne Street, Winnipeg, Manitoba,
    R3C 1V4.

    Organized in Kansas in 1931 as a social and cultural
    outlet for young women with Manitoba chapters
    established as early as 1938. Each chapter has it
    own files.

886. BETA SIGMA PHI, BOISSEVAIN, MANITOBA.
    Papers, 1966-71.   BCA (MG10 C11)

    Minute books and two cheque books (stubs).

887. BIG SISTERS ASSOCIATION OF GREATER WINNIPEG
    Operating files. Restricted.
    Located at 106-447 Webb Place, Winnipeg, Manitoba,
    R3B 2B2.

    Established in 1926 to assist young, troubled women
    and those looking for employment. Minutes, 1970-
    ; financial records; lists of Big and Little
    Sisters; activity sheets; reports.

888. CANADIAN GIRLS IN TRAINING
    Papers 1918-75.
    2 boxes.   UCA-W

    Sponsored by the United Church of Canada. Minutes
    of Interdenominational Committee, 1918-   ; set of
    the Torch, 1927-69; address lists; constitutions;
    songsheets; 50th and 60th Anniversary files;
    national Camp Committee Minutes, 1966-73; Manitoba
    Camp Council Minutes, 1968-73; photographs and
    slides.

163

889. CANADIAN GIRLS IN TRAINING, FLIN FLON, MANITOBA
        Papers.   FFHS/FFPL

        General information; correspondence, 1972.

890. CANADIAN WESTERN CLUB OF WINNIPEG
        Selected materials, 1937-40.
        93 pp.   PAM (MG10 C13)

891. CANUKEENA CLUB, FLIN FLON, MANITOBA
        Papers.   FFHS/FFPL

        Anthem and holler; history; list of charter members;
        constitution and by-laws, 1967.

892. CHURCHILL LADIES CLUB. CHURCHILL, MANITOBA
        List, 1967.
        0.05".   PAM (MG10 C14)

        Signatures of members, 1967-76.

893. CKY COLLECTION
        Recordings, 1939-48. Finding aid.
        18 tapes.   PAM (AV A10)

        Interviews, speeches, and radio programmes
        documenting certain Manitoba social and cultural
        organizations and events such as the Manitoba School
        Orchestra.

894. FLIN FLON HISTORICAL SOCIETY
        Papers.   FFHS/FFPL

        Letters from Grade 5 students, 1973; correspondence
        of Joyce Henderson, 1972-73, Marge Henry, 1972, and
        of L.B. Merrill and Loretta Yauch, 1972.

895. THE GIMLI READING ASSOCIATION, GIMLI, MANITOBA
        History.
        8 pp. Typescript.   ERL

        Founded in 1911. "'Lestrarfjelagid Gimli' The
        Gimli Reading Association: The Second Icelandic
        Community Library at Gimli," by Anna K. Nordal.

896. GIRL GUIDES OF CANADA. MANITOBA COUNCIL
        (a) Papers, 1922-70.
        3'.   PAM (MG10 C66)

Organized in Manitoba in 1910. Scrapbooks, 1922-62;
history of Guiding; annual reports, 1957-66.

(b) Related materials.
Several items.   PAM (MG10 B20 Box
106)

Correspondence and reports, 1967-68; pilot project;
evaluations; census, questionnaire, and analysis,
1967-68.

897. GIRL GUIDES OF CANADA, BOISSEVAIN, MANITOBA
     Scattered materials.   BCA (MG10 C7)

     Historical sketch, "The Guiding Movement in
     Boissevain 1946-1981" (3 pp.); achievement charts;
     clippings; photographs of Brownies.

898. GIRL GUIDES OF CANADA, FLIN FLON, MANITOBA
     Scattered materials.   FFHS/FFPL

     List of Gold Cord recipients, diary excerpts, 1953,
     of Joyce Douglas; general history.

899. GRISWOLD READING CLUB,   GRISWOLD, MANITOBA
     Papers, 1900-21.
     0.05".   PAM (MG10 C2)

     Minute books, (1910-21); programmes.

900. IMPERIAL ORDER DAUGHTER OF THE EMPIRE (MANITOBA)
     Papers, 1909-82.
     14'.   PAM (MG10 C70)

     Organized in 1909 in Manitoba theoretically to
     render effective assistance to the British Empire
     but in practise to aid educational causes, improve
     libraries and cemeteries, and better health and
     child welfare. Minutes, annual reports and
     scrapbooks of the Provincial, Municipal and Fort
     Garry Chapters; minute books of the Assiniboine,
     General Lipsett, Hudson's Bay, Lake Agassiz, Lord
     Selkirk, Red River and Seven Oaks Chapters; annual
     reports; photographs.

901. JUNIOR LEAGUE OF WINNIPEG
     Operating files.
     Located at 190 Kingsway Avenue, Winnipeg, Manitoba,
     R3M 0H2.

Organized to train women for voluntary participation in community activities. Minutes; financial records; reports.

902. KINETTE CLUB OF THOMPSON, THOMPSON, MANITOBA
Operating files, 1963- . Restricted.
Located with the executive in Thompson, Manitoba.

Originally organized in 1963 as an auxiliary to the Kinsmen and then chartered in 1967 as a service club. Minutes; financial records; reports.

903. MASONIC MEMORIAL TEMPLE
Operating files and archives, 1870- . Restricted.
Located at 420 Corydon Avenue, Winnipeg, Manitoba, R3L 0N8.

Register of members, 1870- ; minutes; photographs; reports; memorial books; visitors' register.

904. MANITOBA CENTENNIAL CORPORATION
Scattered references to women's involvement.   PAM (RG24)

Lectures by Mrs. E.T. Seton and a puppet play by a Mrs. Wylie (Box 48); Steinbach, Manitoba, girls' singing group called Treble Teens (Box 62); women's organizations participating (Box 68 and 69).

905. MANITOBA HORTICULTURAL ASSOCIATION
History, 1948.   PAM (MG10 E22)
Typescript.

"A Half Century and more of Organized Horticulture in Manitoba, 1895-1948"; miscellaneous.

906. MANITOBA WOMEN'S INSTITUTE
(a) Winnipeg, Manitoba. Papers, 1910-80. Finding aid.
23'.   PAM (MG10 C8)

Organized first in Ontario and later in Morris, Manitoba, in 1909 to improve homemaking skills and attitudes among women and to foster educational and cultural development, especially in rural areas. Minutes; correspondence; financial records; annual reports; papers from various districts; file list of district organizations; remembrance books, 1936-63; correspondence, 1963-74, with the Canadian Save-the-Children Fund.

166

(b) Birch River, Manitoba.
Papers, 1934-66.
2.5'.   PAM (P193)

Organized in 1934 as an affiliate of the Manitoba
W.I., with a membership of only nine. Activities
centred around social, educational and community
services and included granting high school
bursaries, hospital and nursing home visitation,
sponsoring rural health clinics, beautifying the
local cemetery, donating funds to the Red Cross and
other charities, and war- relief work.

Minute books and attendance records, 1942-69;
financial records; hospital visiting records,
1952-63; newspaper clippings; record book of the
Manitoba Federation of Women's Institute, 1934-36;
handbooks and other printed programmes.

(c) Fairdale, Manitoba. Papers, 1933-72.
Contact: Jean Froude, Killarney, Manitoba.

Fairdale Sewing circle; correspondence; financial
records; minute books.

(d) Flin Flon, Manitoba. Papers,
1935-43.   FFHS/FFPL

Annual reports; board meeting minutes, 1935-39;
minutes, 1939-45; membership lists, 1938-39;
scrapbooks.

(e) Gimli, Manitoba. Papers, 1917- . Restricted.
Located at offices in Gimli, Manitoba.

Minutes; financial records; presidents' reports.

(f) Hamiota, Manitoba. Papers, 1910-78. Finding
aid.
14".   PAM (MG10 C8-9)

Organized in 1910 as the Household Science
Association; minute books, 1910-78; membership
books, 1941-61; financial records, 1911-16; account
books, 1950-78; annual reports, 1932-78 (incomplete)
and programme cards, 1930-44 (incomplete). The
Atoimah Club records consist of minute books,
1922-38; an account book, 1922-38.

(g) Hullet, Glendenning and Tisdale Branch. Papers,
1929-81.
Located in Killarney, Manitoba.

Minute books, 1929-78; reports; papers, 1929-81.

(h) Mount Vallent, Manitoba. Papers, 1948-83.

167

Contact: local elected executive.

Minute books; treasurer's reports.

(i) Mountain Gap, Manitoba. Plaque and
poem.   PAM (MG10 C7-8)

(j) Myrtle, Manitoba. Papers, 1929-75. Finding
aid.
2.5".   PAM (MG10 C8-10)

Cashbook, 1929-75; minute books, 1946-74.

(k) Norwood, Manitoba Papers, 1923-82.
10".   PAM (MG10 C8-11)

Minute books, 1923-   ; scrapbook; historical
sketch, 1923-65.

(l) Oak Bluff, Manitoba. Papers, 1954-72.
4".   PAM (MG10 C8-3)

Minute books; cash book.

(m) Oak Ridge, Manitoba. Papers, 1928-77.
Contact: Killarney, Manitoba, post office.

Minute books; treasurer's reports; pamphlets;
miscellany.

(n) Pembina-Lakes District. Papers, 1932-76.
circa 4".   PAM (MG10 C8-6)

The district at various times consisted of: Pilot
Mound, Clearwater, Manitou, Belmont, Baldur, La
Riviere, Cartwright, Killarney, Crystal City,
Somerset, Oak Ridge, Northcote, Kaleida, Swan Lake,
Pelican Lake, Treherne, Mount Vallent, Fairdale,
Jacques, Dry River and Glenora. Minutes of
Executive meetings and conventions, 1932-75; minutes
of District Board, 1945-75; account book, 1957-76;
convention, rally and mini-leadership school
registration books, 1936-75; correspondence and
papers, 1957-74.

(o) Pilot Mound District. Papers, 1912-65.
4".   PAM (MG10 C8-6)

Minutes of monthly and annual meetings; minutes of
the executive, 1923-27; correspondence and papers,
1926-65.

(p) Portage District. Papers, 1923-76. Finding
aid.
5".   PAM (MG10 C8-4)

At various times during its existence the following
locals made up the district: Amaranth, Arden,
Arizona, Asprey, Austin, Basswood, Berton,
Clanwilliam, Crocus, Douglas, Durnfries, Eden,
Edrans, Edwin, Flee Island, Gladstone, Helston,
Iroquois, Justice, Katrine, Kelwood, Keyes,
Langruth, Linwood, Livingston, McCreary, McGregor,
Mayfield, Minnedosa, Moore Park, Neepawa, Portage la
Prairie, Sidney, Union. Minutes of District
Conventions, 1923-75; Minutes of District Board,
1925-75; bank book, 1925-36; treasurer's reports,
1934-41; Book of Remembrance, 1948-76; convention
registration book, 1961-75; cheque book, 1963-76;
miscellaneous files.

(q) Roland District Papers, 1941-76.
5".   PAM (MG10 C8-2)

The original local women's institutes forming the
district were Roland, Treherne, Plum Coulee, Carman,
Culross, Morris, Altona, Brunkild, Roseisle, Sanford
and Winkler, and later Gretna, Lowe Farm, Myrtle,
Domain, Fannystelle and Oak Bluff. Minute books,
1941-76; cash books, 1951-76; district register,
1954-76; convention register, 1943-47.

(r) Udall, William V. Papers, 1929-65. Finding
aid.
20".   PAM (MG14 C75)

Correspondence; International Peace Garden.

(s) Winnipeg Interlake Papers, 1932-73
1".   PAM (MG10 C8-8)

Local branches comprising the district are
Beausejour, Chatfield, Dugald, Fisher Branch,
Fisherton, Gimli, Great Falls, Grosse Isle,
Gypsumville, Inwood, Lake Francis, Mount Lildon,
Narcisse, Norwood, Riverton, Rosser, St. Vital,
Teulon, Warren and Winnipeg. Annual, local and
district reports, 1954-73; executive and annual
convention minutes, 1932-69. Deposited by Mrs. C.H.
Turbett, Winnipeg, and Mrs. R. Imlah, Fisher Branch,
Manitoba, 1978.

907. MORDEN-WINKLER DISTRICT GUIDE TO COMMUNITY SERVICES
      Guide, 1977.
      Typescript.   SCRLM

      Lists organizations, churches and service clubs.

908. NINGA CALF CLUB, NINGA, MANITOBA
        Minute books, 1948-65.
        5 volumes.   BCA (MG10 E9)

        Boys' and Girls' Ninga Calf Club.

909. NINGA LADIES COMMUNITY CLUB, NINGA, MANITOBA
        Minute books, 1947-64.
        2 volumes.   BCA (MG10 C4)

        Activities and offices.

910. ORDER OF THE EASTERN STAR, CHIMO CHAPTER, THOMPSON,
     MANITOBA
        Operating files, 1973-   . Restricted.
        Located at Royal Canadian Legion, Thompson,
        Manitoba.

        Minutes; financial records; reports.

911. ORDER OF THE EASTERN STAR, GRAND CHAPTER OF MANITOBA,
     WINNIPEG, MANITOBA
        Operating files. Restricted.
        Located at 52-625 Cathcart Avenue, Charleswood,
        Winnipeg, Manitoba.

        Organized in 1922 by women with families involved in
        the Masonic Lodge. Minutes; financial records;
        reports; records of other Manitoba chapters no
        longer operating.

912. ORDER OF THE EASTERN STAR, KILLARNEY, MANITOBA
        Operating files. Restricted.
        Contact: local executive.

        Minute books, 1947-83; cash books; catering record
        book, 1964; ceremonies notebook; officers, members,
        and visitors' registers, 1953-75; Lodge history.

913. ORDER OF THE ROYAL PURPLE, FLIN FLON, MANITOBA
        Scattered materials.   FFHS/FFPL

        Christmas Cheer Broadcast 1972, 1974; history.

914. ORDER OF THE ROYAL PURPLE, KILLARNEY, MANITOBA
        Papers, 1947-83.
        Located at the Elk's Hall, Killarney, Manitoba.

Women's arm of the Elk's Lodge. Minute books,
1947-83; photographs.

915. PETTAPIECE WOMEN'S COMMUNITY CLUB
     Papers, 1923-71.   UCA-W

     A United Church women's society interested in the
     social work of the church and the welfare of the
     community. Constitution; treasurer's book, 1923-69;
     minutes, 1942-46, 1956-71; membership roll and
     ledger, 1942-64; ledger, 1955-59.

916. PORTAGE AND DISTRICT ARTS COUNCIL
     Operating files. Restricted.
     Located at 160 Saskatchewan Avenue West, Portage la
     Prairie, Manitoba.

     Correspondence and documents, 1940-   .

917. RAY LYNNE HOMEMAKERS
     B3_7 B3_7
     Papers, 1959-70.   BCA (MG10 15)

     Minute books, 1942-76; East Lynne Red Cross minute
     books, 1942-46; cash books, 1959-70; photographs and
     clippings, 1943.

918. REBEKAH ASSEMBLY OF MANITOBA
     Operating files and archives, 1911.
     Located at 293 Kennedy Street, Winnipeg, Manitoba.

     A Sister Lodge of Odd Fellows organized in Manitoba
     1911. Annual journal, 1911-   ; minutes, 1948-   ;
     reports; financial records, 1948-   ; unpublished
     history, 1961 of various Manitoba lodges.

919. REBEKAH LODGE, WA WASTAYO LODGE, THOMPSON, MANITOBA
     Operating files.
     Contact: the executive.

     Organized in 1971 for social and charitable
     activities. Minutes; financial reports;
     correspondence; printed materials.

920. ROSICRUCIAN ORDER, AMORC: CHARLES DANA DEAN CHAPTER,
     WINNIPEG
     Papers, 1926-75. Restricted.
     3".   PAM (MG10 C54)

A non-sectarian fraternal society devoted to the
investigation, study and practical application of
natural and spiritual laws. History of the Chapter;
newsletters; publications; scrapbooks; photographs.

921. SEARCHLIGHT BOOK CLUB
     Papers, 1910-73.
     3'.   PAM (MG10 C51)

     Successively named the Saturday Afternoon Club, the
     Searchlight Art Club, 1912, Searchlight Club, 1930,
     and the Searchlight Book Club, 1970. Minute books
     1910-73; annual reports, 1922-73; papers presented
     by members, 1911-23; constitution, 1943;
     correspondence, 1921-29; newspaper clippings.

922. SOCIAL SCIENCES STUDY CLUB OF WINNIPEG
     Papers, 1913-66.
     5'.   PAM (MG10 C50)

     Organized in 1912 to study and improve local social
     and economic conditions. Minutes of meetings,
     1937-66; programmes, 1913-65; papers read by the
     club, 1916-26,1959-66; short history, 1954;
     newsclippings.

923. "SOUNDINGS"
     Oral history, 1961 (CBC).
     1 reel.   PAM (AV A4)

     Interview with Marjorie Morley, Elizabeth Morton and
     Alberta Letts about regional library development.

924. TOASTMISTRESS CLUBS INTERNATIONAL
     Operating files.
     Located at 871 Kebir Street, Winnipeg, Manitoba, R3T
     1X1.

     Minutes; programmes; lists of offices; printed
     materials.

925. TOASTMISTRESS CLUB, COLLEEN #1747, KILLARNEY, MANITOBA
     Operating files, 1968-78.
     Located at 139 Laurier Avenue, Killarney, Manitoba.

     Financial records, 1968-78; minute books, 1970-78.

926. THOMPSON COMMUNITY CLUB, LADIES DIVISION, THOMPSON,
     MANITOBA
     Minutes, 1959-62   TPL (V1959)

     172

Organized in 1959 for social and fund-raising
activities.

927. THOMPSON LADIES BRIDGE CLUB
        Papers, 1959-   .   TPL (V1959)

        Minutes; correspondence; some Dental Clinic
        correspondence; materials on the founding and
        operation of the Thompson Ladies' Club.

928. THOMPSON MULTICULTURAL CENTRE, THOMPSON, MANITOBA
        Operating files.
        Located at 11 Nelson Road, 2nd Floor, Thompson,
        Manitoba.

        Organized in 1975 to assist in language training,
        employment searches, translation services and other
        needs particularly of local native populations.
        Minutes; financial records; reports.

929. UNITED EMPIRE LOYALIST ASSOCIATION OF CANADA, WINNIPEG
     BRANCH
        Papers, 1880-1976. Finding aid.
        Several boxes.   PAM (MG10 C52)

        Organized in 1901 by descendants of the United
        Empire Loyalists. Archival records; scrapbooks
        maintained by L.A. Bingham.

930. UNIVERSITY WOMEN'S CLUB OF WINNIPEG
        Papers, 1909-78. Finding aid. Restricted.
        13'.   PAM (MG10 C58)

        Established in 1919 to unite all university women,
        to work for the advancement of education, art,
        science, literature and civic reform, and to
        encourage individual development. Minutes of
        meetings, 1909-74; membership lists, 1909-70;
        correspondence, 1914-68; financial records, 1914-73;
        committee papers, 1934-73; scrapbook, 1909-73;
        miscellaneous files, 1909-75; photographs. More
        current materials located at 54 Westgate Street.

931. WEIGHT WATCHERS OF MANITOBA, LTD.
        Operating files. Restricted.
        Located at 202-364 Portage Avenue, Winnipeg,
        Manitoba, R3C 0C5.

        Minutes; reports; records; brochures.

932. WINNIPEG WOMEN'S QUEEN CARNIVAL CAMPAIGN
       Scattered materials, 1941-44. PAM (MG15 B7)

       Cashbook.

933. WOMEN'S CANADIAN CLUB OF WINNIPEG
       (a) Papers, 1907-70. Partially restricted.
       8.5".   PAM (MG10 C11-1 and
                                     C11-2)

       Organized in 1907 "to foster patriotism" through the
       study of Canadian art, literature and history, and
       to work for the "progress of the nation." Minutes,
       1907-64; membership rolls, 1939-70; list of
       officers; financial statements, 1929-64; materials
       on the Winnipeg cenotaph, 1918-23; correspondence,
       1923, pertaining to the publication of the book,
       Women of Red River, by W.J. Healy.

       (b) Scattered materials   PAM (RG19 B1 and MG6
                                    D8)

934. WOMEN'S CHRISTIAN TEMPERANCE UNION
       (a) Papers, 1891-1968. Restricted.
       20".   PAM (MG10 C31)

       Winnipeg chapter organized in 1883 by Mrs. Letitia
       Youmans, later reorganized by Miss Willard, the
       national founder. Annual reports, 1891-1951;
       Provincial executive minute books, 1913-47; cash
       books, 1933-61; Winnipeg district minute books,
       1904-61; local union minute books, 1903-65;
       "Prohibition Watchword," 1923-26; scrapbooks.

       (b) Scattered materials, 1934, 1945-60.
                                    PAM (MG14 C104 File
                                    7)

935. WOMEN'S CHRISTIAN TEMPERANCE UNION, NINGA, MANITOBA
       Minute book, 1934-38.   PAM (MG7 H10 M395)

936. THE WOMEN'S CLUB OF WINNIPEG
       Papers, 1924-71.
       2".   PAM (MG10 C63)

       Organized in 1924 initially as a literary discussion
       group, but in 1932 became affiliated with the
       General Federation of Women's Clubs to better meet
       economic, social and health needs in the community.
       Memorabilia; programmes; newspaper clippings.

937. YOUNG WOMEN'S CHRISTIAN ASSOCIATION
Papers, 1897-1982.   Restricted.
8'. Finding aid.   PAM (MG10 B37)

Minutes of Board of Directors, 1897-1946; minutes of
annual meeting, 1939-69; various committee minutes,
1908-72; annual reports, 1913-82; scrapbooks,
1913-77; photographs.

938. YOUNG WOMEN'S CHRISTIAN ASSOCIATION.   THOMPSON,
MANITOBA
Papers, 1965-85.   Partially restricted.   Finding
aid.
10'.   PAM (P988-1013)

Officially organized in 1969, though various
activities were conducted out of private homes as
early as 1965.   In 1972, the International Nickel
Company of Canada Ltd. donated a building,
furnishings and equipment to the YWCA. Besides
providing counselling and recreational activities,
the "Y" offers residential facilities for women in
transit, women needing emergency medical care or
placement, and for students.

Minutes of the executive, board and various
committees, 1965-85; constitution and by-laws;
correspondence, 1969-82; annual reports; materials
on various projects and programs, 1971-83; papers
relating to the national office of the YWCA;
directories, handbooks, newsletters, and other
printed materials. Desk diaries, 1971-84, and
various staff-related documents which are partially
restricted.

WOMEN AND WAR

939. ADVISORY COMMITTEE ON COORDINATION OF POSTWAR PLANNING
Papers, 1943-46.
8'.   PAM (RG20 B7)

Formed in 1944 to eliminate duplication and conflict
in post-war planning in Manitoba in order to present
a single, well-integrated programme to the federal
government. Topics of greatest concern were
conservation and resettlement, health and education,
town and city planning, industrial reconversion and
employment, agricultural economics, and rural
electrification. Correspondence; minutes;
sub-committee reports.

175

940. CHAPMAN, EDNA, M.
        Papers, 1915-17.
        1".   PAM (MG6 D21)

        Letters from L/Cpl. C.D. Richardson serving in
        England and in France with the 4th University Co.,
        P.P.C.L.I.

941. CANADA. IMMIGRATION BRANCH RECORDS
        (a) Evacuation of British Subjects from Japan and
        Japanese occupied territory.
        Correspondence; cases.   PAM (MG4 D1 Vol.53)

        Case histories of several Manitoba women, including
        Mrs. Verent J. Mills (Alma Eunice May) and her four
        children from Hong Kong; Annie McLachlan, Pipestone,
        Manitoba, from Japan; Dr. Isabelle McTavish
        returning to Newdale, Manitoba, from North China,
        and others.

942. EX-WRENS ASSOCIATION, CHIPPAWA DIVISION
        Operating files. Restricted.
        Located at 51 Smith Street, Winnipeg, Manitoba, R3C
        1J4.

        A naval women veterans' association now meeting
        various social and service need. Minutes; reports;
        clippings.

943. FRANCIS, SARAH MARGARET, PAPERS
        Papers, 1916-19.   PAM (P302-303)

        Correspondence to their "mother" from three "sons"
        with the Canadian Army who served in Canada,
        England, and France during World War I; letters from
        friends, mothers who lost their sons, nephews and
        strangers.

944. JEWISH WOMEN'S WAR EFFORTS COMMITTEE
        Papers, 1943-44.   PAM (MG8 E10)

        Membership lists, 1944; operation of servicemen's
        centre, 1944; minutes and correspondence, 1943-44.

945. LAC DU BONNET, MANITOBA
        Scattered materials.   PAM (MG8 A17)

        "Newsletters to the Lac du Bonnet Boys Overseas," by
        Aileen Small; a series of 22 letters to the men
        recording events at home; booklet, Hello Soldier,
        based on these letters, 1975.

946. MANITOBA WAR INDUSTRIES
Documentary film, 1944.
1 roll (16 mm)   PAM (AV B15)

947. NAVY LEAGUE
Oral history, 1944. CKY.   PAM (AV A10)
1 reel (8").

Interview with Mrs. M.R. Rowands, Secretary, Navy
League of Canada, Manitoba Division, by Wilf
Carpentier, about war, World War I, the Navy League.

948. NURSING SISTERS
Notebook, 1924-46.
Handwritten.   BGHA

Includes minutes and photographs.

949. OSTRY, ETHEL
Journal, 1974.
Typewritten.   UMA (MSS SC44)

Entitled "After the Holocaust: My Work with UNRRA"
and edited by Elizabeth O. Fisher.

950. PATRIOTIC SALVAGE CORPS
Papers, 1941-68.
1'.   PAM (P194-196)

In the summer of 1940 the Central Volunteer Bureau,
a World War II organization, received a call for
glass bottles from a Winnipeg hospital. When the
response to a public appeal proved overwhelming, one
volunteer proposed selling the surplus, and thus the
Patriotic Salvage Corps was born. These Winnipeg
volunteers earned a total of $378,359 during the
five war years.

From 1940-45, volunteers collected, sorted,
telephoned, cleaned, drove the twenty trucks, and
staffed four retail outlets. Monies from these
enterprises were donated to the war effort for such
things as mobile kitchens, prisoners' parcels,
Russian medical relief; a hostel in Halifax for
merchant seamen.

When hostilities ceased the Corps continued
operations, channeling profits to veterans' welfare
and community organizations. In 1967 it ceased
operations and a year later conveyed its assets
unconditionally to the Winnipeg Foundation.

Minute books, 1958-68; general ledger, tax receipts, donations, auditor's reports and other financial records; correspondence; scrapbooks; publications.

951. PERLON, JEANNETTE
Reminiscences (translated from Polish).
PAM (MG10 F3 and MG6 F64)

An account of her experience in the Warsaw, Poland, ghetto, during World War II; the loss of her first child.

952. RADIO PROGRAMS
Recording, 1944. CKY.
2 tape (15"), 2 tracks.   PAM (AV A10)

Prepared for troops overseas, featuring Jessie Owen and Janet Shirley, Murial Leslie, and others.

953. RATION BOOKS
Several volumes, 1943-44.   TRHM (MG4 D3)

For gasoline and other purposes.

954. ROYAL CANADIAN AIR FORCE ASSOCIATION, LADIES' AUXILIARY, FLIN FLON, MANITOBA
Papers.   FFHS/FFPL

Rules and regulations for the Ladies Auxiliary; correspondence; minutes, n.d.; financial records; membership lists.

955. ROYAL CANADIAN LEGION: MANITOBA AND NORTH WESTERN ONTARIO COMMAND
Papers, 1917-75.   PAM (MG10 C67)

Minutes of the Provincial Council, 1961-71; Benefit Fund 1956-71; financial statements, 1948-69; Troop Train Reception Committee (Korean War, 1952); correspondence; photographs and scrapbook of the General Sir John Monash, Prince Edward, East Kildonan, Elmwood, St. James and Transcona Branches; lists of various ladies' auxiliary presidents. (See also PAM MG14 B2 Box 1 for data on the St. Vital Branch.)

956. SILVER CROSS MOTHERS ASSOCIATION
Papers, 1944-67.
2."   PAM (MG10 C9)

Organized in 1942-43 as the mothers of Royal
Canadian Air Force casualties, the club expanded to
include mothers and widows of all servicemen who
lost their lives in the two world wars. Purpose: to
help the children of those who died in war to
receive the education which would have been possible
had their fathers returned. Minutes, 1951-66;
membership lists, 1947-66; financial records,
1944-66; reports, 1959-64; flag; bible;
miscellaneous items.

957. TRANSCONA WAR EFFORTS COMMITTEE
        Scattered materials, 1934-48.   TRHM (MG14 B2 Box 2
                                        file 54-62 and MG16
                                        C10)

        Organized in 1939 as a support group for Transcona
        residents in the armed forces. Correspondence from
        service personnel, 1941-46, which includes some
        women; lists of enlistees from the Transcona area;
        minutes of War Efforts Committee and related
        correspondence, 1940-48; Christmas cards from
        enlistees, 1939-45; cigarette acknowledgement cards,
        1939-45; letters from prisoners of war in Japan
        during World War II.

958. UKRAINIAN WOMEN. "PERSONAL MEMOIRS OF WORLD WAR II"
        Literary entries in a competition.
        80 to 90 papers.   UCECA

        Some relate to women's war-time experiences.

959. VOLUNTARY REGISTRATION OF CANADIAN WOMEN, 1939
        Papers, 1939-   .   PAM (MG10 B16)

        Organized in 1939 (originally called the Greater
        Winnipeg Voluntary Registration Bureau) to
        co-ordinate women's community and war works.
        Correspondence; registration forms; clippings;
        instructions for registrars; membership lists.

960. WAR BRIDES. BRITISH WIVES CLUB OF WINNIPEG
        Operating files.
        Contact: Mrs. K.S. Wilkins, 55 Riverbend Avenue, St.
        Vital, Manitoba, R2M 2N7.

961. "WINKLER WAR SERVICES, 1945"
        History.
        10 pp. Typescript.   WRL

Winkler's contributions to the Victory Loan
Campaigns; the honour roll of those killed in action
with biographical sketches; a list of men and one
woman in active service; the contributions of the
Women's Auxiliary to the Winkler Red Cross; Winkler
Blood Donor's Clinic.

962. WINNIPEG SOLDIERS RELATIVES MEMORIAL ASSOCIATION
Papers, 1920-60.
5". PAM (MG10 C32)

Minute book, 1920-67; correspondence, 1922-59;
commemorative service programme, 1923-67; financial
records, 1924-60; draft of constitution and by-laws,
n.d.

963. WOMEN REGISTRATION
Papers, 1939.
0.25". PAM (MG10 B16)

This organization, also known as the Greater
Winnipeg Voluntary Registration Bureau, was formed
in Winnipeg on October 10, 1939 to coordinate
women's work in the community and in the war effort.

This material includes correspondence, registration
forms, clippings and membership lists.

WELFARE AND SOCIAL SERVICES

Alcohol and Drug Abuse

964. ALCOHOLISM RECOVERY INC.
Operating files. Restricted.
Located at 1 St. Johns Avenue, Winnipeg, Manitoba,
R2W 0W7.

A halfway house for women.

965. ALCOHOLICS ANONYMOUS
Operating files. Restricted.
Located at 567 St. Mary's Road, Winnipeg, Manitoba,
R2M 3L6.

A self-help group for those suffering from
alcoholism.

966. ALCOHOLISM FOUNDATION OF MANITOBA
        Operating files. Restricted.
        Located at 1031 Portage Avenue, Winnipeg, Manitoba,
        R3G 0R8.

        Established in 1956 to assist individuals affected
        by the use of alcohol or other chemicals, to
        distribute information respecting chemical use, and
        to conduct and promote research in the treatment and
        prevention of problems involving chemical use.
        Minutes; financial records; case histories; the
        William Potoroka Memorial Library of printed
        materials on all aspects of chemical use.

967. AL-ANON, THE PAS, MANITOBA
        Operating files, 1956. Restricted.
        Located at 144 Ross Avenue, The Pas, Manitoba, R9A
        1K4.

        Minutes; reports; published materials; oral
        histories with members.

968. AL-ANON, WINNIPEG, MANITOBA
        Operating files. Restricted.
        Located at 811-211 Portage Avenue, Winnipeg,
        Manitoba, R3B 2A2.

        A self-help support group of wives, husbands,
        relatives and friends of alcoholics. Minutes; case
        histories; printed data.

969. ALATEEN
        Operating files. Restricted.
        Located at 811-211 Portage Avenue, Winnipeg,
        Manitoba, R3B 2A2.

        A self-help support group for teenage children,
        relatives and friends of alcoholics.

970. THE ALTRUSA CLUB OF WINNIPEG
        Papers, 1959-84. Inventory.
        40".   PAM (P831-838)

        Organized in 1917 in Tennessee as the first women's
        service club in America, followed in 1959 to serve
        various community needs. In Manitoba, the club has
        supported the Indian and Métis Friendship Centre,

181

established the Family Fund Project, adopted
children, and conducted other support services.

Correspondence, 1961-80; minutes of executive, board
and general meetings, 1959-84; financial records;
project materials; annual and committee reports;
newsletters, yearbooks, and other publications.

971. CHEMICAL DEPENDENCY PROGRAM
Operating and case files. Restricted.
Located at St. Boniface General Hospital, Department
of Psychology, 394 Tache Avenue, Winnipeg, Manitoba,
R2H 2A6.

Established to provide psychiatric supervision and
care for alcoholics, narcotics and persons otherwise
dependent upon prescriptions.

972. CHEMICAL WITHDRAWAL UNIT
Operating and case files. Restricted.
Located at Health Sciences Centre, 75 Emily Street,
Winnipeg, Manitoba, R3E 1Y9.

Medically supervised withdrawal and referral
service.

973. GRACE GENERAL HOSPITAL ALCOHOL PROGRAM
Operating and case files. Restricted.
Located at Grace General Hospital, 300 Booth Drive,
Winnipeg, Manitoba, R3J 3M7.

Assessment and referral; medical detoxication;
counselling.

974. KIA ZAN INC.
Operating files. Restricted.
Located at 60 Balmoral Street, Winnipeg, Manitoba,
R3C 1X4.

A halfway house for young adult men and women
requiring treatment for drug dependency. Minutes;
reports; financial records; lists of programs; staff
members and residents on location.

975. NEW HOPE LODGE (SALVATION ARMY)
Operating files. Restricted.
Located at 205 Arlington Street, Winnipeg, Manitoba,
R3G 1Y6.

A relief home for chronic alcoholics and offering
self-help courses.

Centres for the Aged

976. AGE AND OPPORTUNITY CENTRE, INC.
        Operating files, 1957- .
        Located at 304-323 Portage Avenue, Winnipeg,
        Manitoba, R3B 2C1.

        A social service agency focusing on the retired
        and/or those 60 years of age and over. Operating
        files; minutes; Board of Directors committee books;
        complete reports of activities; a 1976 history of
        the organization; files of executive directors (Rae
        Abernathy, Bernice Tweedie, Evelyn Shapiro, Yhetta
        Gold and Robert Stewart.)

977. BLEAK HOUSE CENTRE
        Operating files, 1978- .
        Located at 1637 Main Street, Winnipeg, Manitoba.

        A drop-in centre for seniors.

978. BOISSEVAIN OLD-TIMERS' ASSOCIATION
        Papers, 1926-41.   BCA (MG10 C5)

        Five minute-books and miscellaneous items.

979. GENERAL CONFERENCE MENNONITE CHURCH. INSTITUTIONS FOR
     THE AGED
        Operating files.
        Located on premises.

        Bethania Home (Winnipeg); Ebenezer Home for the Aged
        (Altona); Bethel Mennonite Care Services Inc.
        (Winnipeg); Salem Home for the Aged (Winkler).

980. MANITOBA SOCIETY OF SENIORS
        Operating files.
        Located at 1102-211 Portage Avenue, Winnipeg,
        Manitoba, R3B 2A2.

        Organized in 1979 by and for senior citizens to
        improve the quality of life for all older people in
        the province. Quarterly newsletters;
        correspondence; minutes; reports; treasurer's
        reports.

183

981. NORTHERN LIGHTS FRIENDSHIP GROUP
          Operating files.
          Located at 226 Mystery Lake Road, Thompson,
          Manitoba, R8N 1S6.

          Organized in 1977 primarily for female senior
          citizens. Minutes; records.

982. "THE SHARON FARM"
          Unpublished paper, by Jack
          Faintuch.   PAM (MG10 F2)

          The history of a Jewish senior citizens' home in
          Winnipeg, Manitoba.

983. "WINNIPEG MEALS ON WHEELS: A PROGRAM EVALUATION AND
     EXAMINATION OF ALTERNATIVE MODELS OF OPERATION"
          Paper by Christine D. McKee. Located at the
          Institute of Urban Studies, University of Winnipeg,
          515 Portage Ave., Winnipeg, Manitoba, R3D 2E9.

          A service provided for the elderly or handicapped by
          volunteers who transport food from the kitchens of
          the Health Sciences Centre to homes.

Child and Home Improvement Associations

984. ALL PEOPLES NORTHEND COMMUNITY MINISTRY, WINNIPEG
          Scattered materials, 1922.   UCA-W

          Kindergarten Club and the Mothers' Club.

985. CAMPBELL, MINNIE JULIA B.
          Papers.   PAM (MG14 C6)

          Includes 1896 notebooks of the Winnipeg School of
          Cookery.

986. CHILDREN'S AID SOCIETY OF DAUPHIN
          Papers, 1914-48. Finding aid.
          Several boxes.   PAM (RG5 G4)

987. CHILDREN'S HOME OF WINNIPEG
          Papers, 1885-1966. Restricted.
          20".   PAM (MG10 B24)

Founded in 1884 by the Women's Christian Union as the first childcare institution in western Canada and in 1950 transformed into a residential treatment centre for emotionally disturbed children. Monthly reports to the Board of Management, 1885-1910; minutes, 1889-1932, 1944-45; by-laws, 1889; visitors books, 1890-1900, 1906; registers of children left with the Home, 1887-1918; registers of children placed in foster homes, 1912-24; inventory of bedding, linen, towels and cutlery (1935-1941); notebooks on buildings and grounds, 1949-60; cash books, 1942-50; scrapbook of newspaper cuttings, 1908-66.

988. PATTERSON, J.C.
     Papers.   PAM (MG12 F1)

     The case of the Children's Aid Society of Winnipeg and Margaret Alice Harrison, 1899-1900.

989. ROBERTSON UNITED CHURCH. KINDERGARTEN
     Papers, 1931-37.   UCA-W

     Minutes and attendance records for both the Kindergarten Club and the Mothers' Club.

990. ST. MATTHEW-MARYLAND CHILD CARE CENTRE
     Operating files, 1972- .
     Located at 641 St. Matthews Avenue, Winnipeg, Manitoba, R3G 0G6.

     Provides care for school-age children before and after school and during holidays.

Crime, Delinquency and Violence

991. COMMITTEE AGAINST VIOLENCE IN THE FAMILY
     Operation files. Restricted.
     Located at 103-61 Tyndall Avenue, Winnipeg, Manitoba, R2X 2T4.

     Minutes; reports; working papers.

992. COMMITTEE AGAINST VIOLENCE TOWARDS WOMEN
     Operation files. Restricted.
     Located at 730 Alexander Avenue, Winnipeg, Manitoba, R3H 1H9.

Minutes; reports; financial reports; correspondence.

993. EMERSON POLICE,   EMERSON, MANITOBA
     Records, 1881-85.   AWCLH (A122)

     List person, charge, plea, verdict and sentence (if
     any).

994. MANITOBA DEPARTMENT OF COMMUNITY SERVICES AND
     CORRECTIONS, CORRECTIONAL CENTRE FOR WOMEN
          Operating files. Restricted.
          Located at 329 Duke Avenue, Portage la Prairie,
          Manitoba, R1N 0S4 and at the Provincial Archives of
          Manitoba.

          Details of women sentenced or remanded by the
          courts.

995. HEADINGLEY CORRECTIONAL INSTITUTE
          (a) Registers, 1874-1968.   PAM (RG5 E1 and H1)

          Prisoner registers and statistics listing sex, place
          and date of birth, colour or race, marital status,
          length of residence in Manitoba, occupation,
          religion, father's full name, occupation and place
          of birth, mother's full maiden name, residence,
          birthplace and occupation.

          (b) Papers, 1874-1978. Restricted for 30 years from
          date of discharge of prisoner. PAM (RG5 H1)

          Prisoner committal ledgers, 1874-1978; punishment
          register, 1930-60; prisoner description register,
          1908-27; prisoner statistics register, 1913-34;
          guard report books, 1892, 1894-95.

996. "THE MANITOBA PENITENTIARY AND ASYLUM 1871-1886"
     Unpublished paper, 1970, by Philip Goldring.
     114 pp. Typescript.   PAM (MR #28)

     The structural features of the penitentiary; staff;
     prisoners; medical and religious services; therapy;
     sexual problems; diagrams; pictures; bibliography.

997. NATIVE CLAN ORGANIZATION
          Operating files, 1971- . Restricted.
          Located at 620-704 Main Street, Winnipeg, Manitoba,
          R3B 1B8 and at P.O. Box 360, The Pas, Manitoba.

A rehabilitation program co-founded by the Indian
and Métis Brotherhood Organization at Stony
Mountain Penitentiary and a Native halfway house.
Minutes; records; reports.

998. OSBORNE HOUSE
Operating files, 1974- . Restricted.
Located at 53 Balmoral Street, Winnipeg, Manitoba,
and at the YWCA.

Organized in 1974 as a crisis shelter for
physically and emotionally abused women and
children; offering a wide range of support and
rehabilitation services. Minutes; financial
records; reports; case files.

999. THE PAS CORRECTIONAL INSTITUTION
Records. Restricted.
Contact: Box 659, The Pas, Manitoba, R9A 1K7.

1000. PROVINCIAL COUNCIL OF WOMEN
Papers.   PAM (MG10 C44)

Includes (box 6) a research paper, "Ad Hoc
Committee on Rape, 1974-76."

1001. RAPE CRISIS CENTRE
Operating files. Restricted.
Located at 545 Broadway Avenue, Winnipeg, Manitoba,
R3C 0W3.

Minutes; financial reports; case histories.

1002. "THE RED-LIGHT DISTRICT IN WINNIPEG: AN ISSUE IN
CIVIC POLITICS, 1903-1920"
Unpublished student essay, 1970, by Joy Cooper.
32 pp.   PAM (MG9 D5)

Political implications of prostitution.

1003. STONY MOUNTAIN PENITENTIARY
Prison registers, 1871-77, and order books,
1874-75.
Located at the prison.

List sex, residence, religion, marital status. See
letter book, 1812-73, of Warden Samuel Bedson in
                              PAM (MG4 D6-1
                              M18-20).

1004. THOMPSON CRISIS CENTRE
         Operating files. Restricted.
         Located at 1-75 Selkirk Avenue, Thompson, Manitoba,
         R8N 0M5.

         Organized in 1977 to assist abused women and
         children. Minutes; reports; financial information;
         brochures; client intake; published reports; film
         and video library on abuse of family members.

1005. WINNIPEG POLICE DEPARTMENT, STATION NO. 5
         Scattered materials. Restricted.
         Located at 219 Provencher Avenue, St. Boniface,
         Manitoba.

         General report book for police activities,
         handwritten, 1882-83; record of doctors' visits to
         jail on Rupert Street, 1921-79; book entitled
         "Prisoners En Route" -- those prisoners passing
         through Winnipeg en route to various detention
         centres in Canada; book of Lodgers in Winnipeg
         police jails ("a hostel type service for the poor")
         giving name, date of stay, home address, age, and
         bag number; night report books; arrest book; jail
         arrest book; robbery report book; occurrence
         reports; letter book; solved and unsolved crimes:
         from the beginning of the century a report of every
         crime in Winnipeg; "subversive files and historic
         data"; "Historic files"; chief constable's annual
         report, 1940-70; press clippings; correspondence;
         police patrol notebooks, 1960; daily journal
         (shifts worked between 1967 and 1974); accident
         reports, 1962-73; lists of people, charges and
         depositions, 1932-78.

Welfare and Social Services

1006. CANADA. IMMIGRATION BRANCH RECORDS
         General records, 1873-1972, and passenger ship
         lists, 1865-1908.
         About 650 reels of microfilm from the Government of
         Canada.

         (a) Canadian Women's Hostel, Winnipeg. Papers,
         1923-36.   PAM (MG4 D1 Vol. 139)

         The work of Margaret Lewis as representative of CWH
         in meeting unaccompanied women and children from
         overseas, 1922-23; correspondence and memoranda on
         course for girls in cooking; grants from Department

to hostels; employment of girls; reports by
Presbyterian WMS immigration workers; activities
and operation of hostel; grants; provision of hot
meals for incoming parties of women immigrants;
resignation of M. Mulheron and appointment of Hope
Atkinson as superintendent, 1926; copy of brochure,
"For newcomers to Canada who are members or
adherents of the Congregational, Methodist or
Presbyterian Churches" (United Church of Canada, 4
pages) financial returns; effect of Depression on
hostel operations; drop in financial assistance
because of the end of passage assistance to
houseworkers; proposed training school for
domestics in Winnipeg; annual reports; leaflet,
"Canadian Women's Hostel, Winnipeg, Manitoba"
(c.1932, 4 pages) discontinuance of Department
grant; opening of training school for houseworkers
at hostel.

(b) Girls' Home of Welcome Winnipeg. Papers,
1897-1920.   PAM (MG4 D1 Vols.
                              118,138, Reel 74)

Organized in 1897 by Rev. Charles W. Gordon, Miss
Fowler and others for the accommodation of single
young girls and older women on their arrival in
Winnipeg; solicitation of funds; opening of Home;
grants made by Department; annual reports; work at
ports with regard to women's immigration by various
denominations and organizations, 1923; Mrs. Helen
Sanford's trip to Great Britain to bring out a
number of girls for domestic service in Canada;
travel arrangements with Canadian Pacific Railway;
list of servant girls and their destinations;
"Emigrant's Application for Ticket" forms, 1908-10;
need for domestic servants in Canada, 1910; making
bonus payments uniform for all organizations
bringing domestic servants to Canada; complaints
from overseas booking agents against Mrs. Sanford;
curtailment of domestic servants to Canada with the
outbreak of war; elimination of commissions and
bonuses, 1914; postwar regulations on the
immigration of women to Canada; advancement of
fares through the Employment Service of Canada.

1007. BROADWAY HOME
        Operating files. Restricted.
        Located at 155 Spence Street, Winnipeg, Manitoba,
        R3C 1Y2, and in departmental files.

        Operated by the Community Services and Corrections
        Department, Government of Manitoba, to accommodate
        female clients of the Vocational Rehabilitation
        Program.

        189

1008. CANADA DEPARTMENT OF EMPLOYMENT AND IMMIGRATION.
WOMEN'S EMPLOYMENT COUNSELLING CENTRE
Operating files. Restricted.
Located at 324 Kennedy Street, Winnipeg, Manitoba.

Designed to help women assess their capabilities,
explore occupation, education and training
opportunities, and to prepare for the job search.
Copies of minutes; reports; financial records.

1009. COMMERCIAL GIRLS' CLUB
Papers, 1931-77.
2.5".   PAM (MG10 B21)

Minutes; list of members; presidents' reports of
the Social Welfare Committee; copies of The
Commercial Girls' Commentator for July and
September, 1940; an historical sketch of the Club
by Mrs. E. Wolmersley, Winnipeg, 1978.

1010. "EBEN-EZER GIRLS' HOME, WINNIPEG, 1926-1959"
Unpublished paper, 1977. Compiled by Eric Rempel.
                          CMBC
Typescript.

A short history of this home for immigrant and
rural Mennonite girls working in Winnipeg and
efforts to prevent assimilation.

1011. EMPLOYMENT OF WOMEN IN MANITOBA
Unpublished report, 1939, by A. Oddson for the
Economic Survey Board.
Typescript, 8 sections.   LEG LIB

1012. HARGRAVE HOUSE
Operating files. Restricted.
Located at 62 Hargrave Street, Winnipeg, Manitoba,
R3C 1N1, and with the YWCA.

A residence for single women from 18 to 28 years of
age.

1013. MANITOBA ASSOCIATION OF SOCIAL WORKERS
Papers, 1943-84. Finding aid.
4'.   PAM (MG10 A33)

Begun as the Manitoba Branch of the Canadian
Association of Social Workers in 1930, the
objectives of the Association include the
improvement of salaries, general working conditions

190

and employment standards, and to improve social
conditions in the community. Minutes, 1947-79;
account ledgers, 1943-76; constitution and by-laws,
1967-79; reports, 1961-72; newsletters, 1967-84;
program file, 1978-79; correspondence; briefs.

1014. MANITOBA. DEPARTMENT OF COMMUNITY SERVICES EMPLOYMENT
SERVICES PROGRAM
Operating Files. Restricted.
Located at 206-460 Portage Avenue, Winnipeg,
Manitoba.

Originally designed for treaty Indians on reserves
but currently also involved with women in urban
areas, and mother's allowance. The services are
very comprehensive and include problem solving and
relaxation techniques, nutrition, and a follow-up
program women who have entered the work force.
Minutes; case records; policy papers on premises.

1015. MANITOBA. DEPARTMENT OF LABOUR
(a) Papers.   PAM (RG14 A1)

Voluminous government papers including
correspondence, statistical studies and letters of
application, 1940-41, collected by the Women's
Division of the Department as well as
correspondence, 1931-46, and reports from the
Employment Service of Canada.

(b) New careers program.
Operating files.
Located at Provincial Building, 59 Elizabeth Road,
Thompson, Manitoba, R8N 1X4.

Minutes kept on location; financial records sent to
the Department of Labour.

(c) Union membership in Manitoba.
Files. Restricted.
Located at Research and Planning Branch, 409-401
York Avenue, Winnipeg, Manitoba, R3C 0V8.

(d) Women's Bureau.
Operating files.
Located at 241 Vaughan Street, and at PAM
("Government Documents").

A multi-faceted counselling and resumé service for
women, offering a wide range of services including
employment assistance, skill, ability evaluation,
referrals, speaker's bureau, displays, print and
audio-visual services, and other forms of
assistance.

1016. MARY-MARTHA HOME AND TABEA VEREIN
        Papers, 1916-37 (mostly in German).
                                MBA (BC 271)

        Winnipeg centre for rural and immigrant Mennonite
        women and girls working in the city, under the
        supervision of Anna Thiessen. Minutes, 1916-37;
        photographs; scrapbook; handwritten early history;
        Reports on the Home found in M.B. Conference
        Reports until 1959.

1017. ST. JOHN'S COLLEGE LADIES' SCHOOL
        Minute book, 1877.   RLDA

        Salaries of staff.

1018. SNYDER, HARRIET E. (1855-73)
        Account book.   PAM (MG16 A12)

1019. TAYLOR, SAMUEL
        Journal, 1849-73.   PAM (MG2 C13)

        Discusses women employed by the Hudson's Bay
        Company of Moose Factory to make coverings, bags
        and shoes.

1020. UNIVERSITY OF WINNIPEG, COUNSELLING SERVICES: WOMEN'S
      SEARCH
        Operating files.
        Located at 515 Portage Avenue, Winnipeg, Manitoba,
        R3B 2E9.

        Designed for women who wish to explore new goals in
        career or academic areas. Minutes; reports;
        discussion summaries.

1021. WOMEN'S EMPLOYMENT COUNSELLING SERVICE
        Operating files. Restricted.
        Located at 503-352 Donald Street, Winnipeg,
        Manitoba, R3B 2H8.

        A counselling service designed to help women
        without work or on low incomes, those entering
        non-traditional jobs or re-entering the work force,
        and women in need of other employment assistance.
        Minutes; reports; clients' records; financial
        materials.

Social Services -
Welfare Association and Relief Agencies

1022. ASILE RITCHOT
Operating files, 1903-   . Restricted.
Located at 3514 Pembina Highway, St. Norbert,
Manitoba, R3V 1A1.

Founded in 1903 as an orphanage for babies of unwed
mothers and operated by the Sisters of Mercy (Les
Soeurs de la Misèricorde).

1023. BRACKEN, JOHN.
Office correspondence, 1924-39. Finding aid.
Several boxes.   PAM (MG13 I2)

Premier of Manitoba, 1924-39, and later federal
leader of the Progressive Conservative Party.

Box 7: "Unemployment" file contains 1924-25
"Report of Emergency Unemployment Relief
Committee:, which was established by City Council
in 1924 to relieve the Social Welfare Commission of
destitute cases due to unemployment; 15 pages of
statistics primarily on men but some information on
the numbers of wives and children involved, and
percentage of working wives.

Box 16: "Health and Public Welfare - Dr. E.H.
Montgomery"; compilation of welfare institutions in
Manitoba and their maintenance costs for 1927;
statistics on dependent relief, i.e. wives and
child welfare, milk depot; numbers of mothers and
children maintained under Children's Aid Act.

Box 21: "Public Welfare - Hon. Dr. E.W.
Montgomery"; "Third Annual Report of the Child
Welfare Division of the Department of Public
Welfare, 1926-1927"; statement on policies for
children who are neglected, dependent, bereaved or
adopted, or whose parents are unmarried;
statistical tables include numbers of children
under care, religion and age of mother, father's
occupation, amount of money mother is expected to
earn for varying family sizes, municipalities in
which families reside.

Box 22: "Seasonal Unemployment in Canada: A
Report, 1928"; "Women and the Employment Service,"
an historical sketch with a few statistics.

Box 36: "Health and Public Welfare - Deputy
Minister": 1928-29 Annual Report of the Department

of Health and Public Welfare, 207 pages; 15-page
section on Child Welfare Division citing statistics
on numbers of children, mothers' religion and
nationality.

Box 51: Scattered information and statistics on
numbers of unemployed single women on or off relief
in Winnipeg and District.

Box 81: "Unemployment - Comparative Statements";
"Report of Operations and Costs Year Ending
December 31, 1933 - City of Winnipeg, Unemployment
Relief Committee" (25 pages).

Box 98: "Unemployment Relief": 2-page summery of
costs, enrolment, wages, revenue and disbursements
of Winnipeg School for Household Assistants, 19
March to 31 August 1936.

Box 115: "Unemployment Relief - Miscellaneous
Cases": personal letters to Premier asking for
relief, many by women.

Box 120: Health and Public Welfare Department:
"Summary, Annual Report : Department (of) Health
and Public Welfare, 1938"; Assistance - Unorganized
Territory" which details cases; headings include
"Widows" and "Unmarried Mothers" and break-downs by
nationality.

Box 124: "Unemployment Relief": copy of the
Dominion-Provincial Material Aid and Civic
Improvements Agreement Appendix "B", 1939; policies
and definitions of "unemployable," "partially
employable" and "employable" persons and outlines
how women fit into the first category.
"Unemployment Relief - Youth training": Statistics,
reports, correspondence, newspaper clippings on
youth training for 1938-39; report of
"Dominion-Provincial Youth Training Programme"
includes male/female breakdowns.

1024. CANADIAN COUNCIL ON CHILD AND FAMILY WELFARE
        Correspondence, 1933.   PAM (RG5 G4)

1025. CANADIAN WELFARE COUNCIL
        Annual reports, 1920-71.   LEG LIB

        Includes a report on the Public Welfare Department,
        City of Winnipeg, 1955.

1026. CHILD WELFARE BOARD
Minutes and agendae,
1924-1958.   PAM (RG5 G4 boxes
                                1-7)

1027. CHILDREN'S AID SOCIETY, CITY OF WINNIPEG
Payable records, 1953-79.
Restricted.   CWA

1028. CHRISTIAN WOMEN'S UNION OF WINNIPEG
Papers and reports,
1895-1956.   LEG LIB (Rbc Hv-700)
                                and PAM (MG10 B13)
                                1903 20 pp.

Annual reports, 1885, 1889-1906, 1946-47;
president's, addresses; reports of religious
instruction; secretaries reports; related data.

1029. CHURCH HOME FOR GIRLS/MCMILLAN HOUSE
Papers and reports.   RLDA (See also MG10
                                B20)

Organized in 1925 by the Presbyterian and Methodist
Churches to assist unmarried mothers; renamed
McMillan House in 1972. Reports; questionnaires;
statements of policy; constitution; budgets; 1975
programmes and services; reports on referal
statistics; staffing and problems; minutes of
annual meetings, 1976; list of board of directors,
1975-76; related materials.

1030. CITY OF WINNIPEG. UNEMPLOYMENT RELIEF COMMITTEE
Papers, 1926-77.   CWA

Minutes, 1926-77; Committee's correspondence,
reports, financial statements; registration of the
numbers of married and single men, and single and
married women who are unemployed and seeking aid;
in 1931 a "Women's Department" is added
(reorganized in 1940 as the Public Welfare
Committee); correspondence, 1932, from the
Department of Public Works suggests placing single
women on relief into domestic service, similar to
the plan in which single men are placed on farms; a
petition from Working Women's League "asking for
consideration of cash allowances to unemployed
persons"; correspondence from the Council of Women
of Winnipeg in regard to the organizing of women on
relief into a "co-operative group for the purposes
of mending, sewing, etc"; policies on various

phases of relief; over-age children in receipt of
Mother's Allowance; Extension of Parent's
Maintenance Act; training single women for
housework.

1031. CITY OF WINNIPEG. CIVIC CHARITIES
        Scattered materials, 1927-70. CWA

        Minutes; correspondence; requests for endorsement
        of charities, 1955-74; Civic Charities Endorsement
        Bureau.

1032. CITY OF WINNIPEG. CITY COUNCIL COMMUNICATIONS
        Petitions.   CWA

        Several hundred petitions from city residents
        petitioning City Council for redress,
        consideration, alterations and other action to
        improve their property, lifestyle, and standard of
        living.

1033. FAMILY SERVICES OF WINNIPEG
        Operating files. Restricted.
        Located at 4th Floor, 287 Broadway Street,
        Winnipeg, Manitoba, R3C 0R9.

        Funded by the United Way to assist families to cope
        with the problems and stresses of modern family
        life. Minutes; annual reports.

1034. GERMSCHEID, DARLENE (1938-)
        Papers, 1957-82. Finding aid.
        52".   PAM (Unprocessed)

        Native of Neepawa, Manitoba. Active in the
        Mother's Allowance Group, the Neighborhood Services
        Centre, Winnipeg Community Communications, the
        Social Planning Council of Winnipeg, the Manitoba
        Institute of Registered Social Workers, the YWCA,
        the National Council of Welfare, the Community
        Educator Project, the Manitoba Rent Stabilization
        Board, and the Manitoba Human Rights Commission.
        Correspondence; minutes; financial records;
        speeches; printed matter.

1035. HELPING HAND, INC.
        Operating files, 1973- .
        Located at 160 Saskatchewan Avenue West, Portage la
        Prairie, Manitoba R1N 0M1.

196

Meal delivery organization for senior citizens.
Correspondence.

1036. "HIGHLIGHTS IN WINNIPEG'S WELFARE SERVICES, 1844-1949"
      Listings.
      10 pp.   LEG LIB

      Dates of establishment and general work of various
      relief and welfare services in Winnipeg; specific
      groups and organizations.

1037. LANGUAGE BANK OF WINNIPEG
      Operating files. Restricted.
      Located at 700 Elgin Avenue, Winnipeg, R3E 1B2.

      Volunteer interpreters to assist victims of rape,
      legal problems, accidents, family crisis and
      arrests. Sponsored by the Altrusa Club of Winnipeg
      and the International Centre.

1038. MANITOBA. CHILD WELFARE DIVISION
      Papers, 1912-78. Finding aid. Restricted.
      18.5'.   PAM (RG5 G4)

      Agendas, 1924-72; Mothers' Allowance Commission
      papers, 1916-74; Military Dependents' Allowance
      case files, 1940-46; English Children's Evacuees
      papers; Children's Aid Society of Dauphin papers,
      1914-48; Children's Aid Society of St. Adelaid
      papers, 1912-42.

1039. MANITOBA. HEALTH AND WELFARE: WELFARE SUPERVISION
      BOARD
      Papers, 1908-72. Finding aid.
      8'. 19 boxes.   PAM (RG5 G2)

      Materials concerning the Welfare Supervision Board
      and a large number of health and welfare-related
      institutions, societies, and agencies throughout
      the province concerning a multiplicity of
      health-related topics. The description below,
      while not inclusive of all concerns, provides a
      fairly exhaustive listing - alphabetically arranged
      - of the resource materials available in this
      extensive, multi-faceted collection.

      Box 1: Asile Ritchot; Brandon General Hospital;
      Brandon Hospital for the Insane, 1921; Birtle
      Hospital, 1921-22; Canadian Council on Child and
      Family Welfare, 1933; Canadian National Institute
      for the Blind, 1925-46.

197

Box 2: Canadian Red Cross Society, 1916-42; Canadian Women's Hostels, 1929-35; Carman General Hospital, 1921; Charitable Institutions, 1911-37; Child Welfare, 1917-42.

Box 3: Children's Aid Society of St. Adelard, 1905-33, Brandon, 1929-37, Dauphin, 1920-33, Winnipeg, 1930-41, Children's Bureau of Winnipeg.

Box 4: Children's Home of Winnipeg, 1921; Children's Khaki Club, Winnipeg, 1918, Civic Charities Bureau, 1917-18; Community Welfare Council of Ontario, 1930; Custodial Care of Girls, 1928-30; Dauphin Gaol, 1922; Delinquent Girls, Winnipeg, 1925-27; Deloraine Hospital, 1921; Desertion, 1920-31; Detention Home, 1920-23; East Kildonan Home.

Box 5: Ethelbert Hospital, 1921; Grace Hospital, 1919-45; Greater Winnipeg Welfare Association, 1931-34; health education and insurance, 1929-31; Home of the Good Shepherd, West Kildonan, 1919-37; hospitals and nursing 1913-33.

Box 6: Indigent Persons, 1930; Infant and Social Health Service, Toronto, Ontario, 1936-41; Inter-Children's Aid Societies Conference, 1929-43; Jewish Children's Home, 1943-70; Jewish Orphanage and Children's Aid Society, 1918-33; Kindergarten Settlement Association of Winnipeg, 1918-20.

Box 7: Libraries; Maison St. Joseph, Otterburne, 1918-38; Manitoba Home for Girls West Kildonan, 1930-33; Margaret Scott Nursing Mission, 1917-32.

Box 8: Marriage, 1928-31; Middlechurch Old Folks' Home, 1911-33; Military Dependents' Allowance Commission, casefiles, 1940-46; Misericordia General Hospital, 1921; Mothers' Allowance, 1917-32; Mount Carmel Clinic, 1932; Municipal Hospitals, Winnipeg, 1908-21; National Council of Mental Hygiene.

Box 9: National Conference of Social Work; National Probation Association, 1928-33; Neepawa General Hospital, 1921; Old Age Pensions, 1911-30.

Box 10: Old age pensions; Old Folks' Home, 1921-37; the poor, 1918; Portage la Prairie General Hospital, 1921; Provincial Gaol, 1922-23; Russell Sage Foundation.

Box 11: St. Agnes Priory School, 1929-38; St. Benedict's Orphanage, Arborg, 1917-29; St. Boniface Hospital, 1921; St. Boniface Orphanage, 1918-39;

St. Boniface Orphanage and Old Folks' Home,
1930-33; St. Joseph's Orphanage, 1917-33.

Box 12: Salvation Army Home, Brandon, 1922-36;
Selkirk General Hospital, 1921; Selkirk Hospital
for the Insane, 1921; Shoal Lake Cottage Hospital,
1920-22; Social Service Council of Canada, 1926-34;
Social Welfare Commission, Winnipeg, 1930-33;
Social Work - conferences and councils, 1926-35;
Souris Municipal Hospital, 1920-21; sterilization,
1927-32; Survey Magazine.

Box 13: Tribune Empty Stocking Fund; tuberculosis
- Canadian Tuberculosis Association, 1930-31;
tuberculosis - Manitoba Sanitorium, Ninette, 1929;
United Farm Women of Manitoba, 1927; venereal
disease, 1930; Victorian Order of Nurses, 1915-46,
Virden Hospital 1921; Winnipeg Community Chest and
Foundation, 1928-44; Winnipeg General Hospital,
1917-21; Winnipeg Health League, 1929-39; YMCA,
Winnipeg.

Boxes 14-16: Correspondence and papers, 1919-29.

Box 17: Accounts, grants, expenditures, 1927-45.

Box 18: Reports, surveys, 1929-45.

Box 19: Minutes, 1942-46; agenda, 1927-33; annual
reports, 1922-45; summaries of board meetings,
1925-43.

1040. MANITOBA. INDUSTRIAL WELFARE AND WOMEN
         Scattered materials,
         1884-1925.   PAM (RG3 C1-3)

      Manitoba Department of Attorney-General files.

1041. MANITOBA. PUBLIC WORKS DEPARTMENT
         Files relating to the provincial welfare system,
         1900-1954.
                                 PAM (RG18 A4)

      Correspondence concerning welfare recipients;
      "unemployment relief" files and attendant studies,
      reports and resolutions; report of the Personal
      Service League, 1933; statistical studies; food
      scheduling; resolution of the Conference of Workers
      Unity League; application for relief (Relief
      Assistance Case Files) which list assistance sought
      and granted, family size, nationality and
      occupation; numerous special requests; deputy
      minister correspondence and case
      files   PAM (RG18 B2-3).

1042. MARRIED WOMEN ALONE
       Papers, 1970- .
       Located at the YWCA, Winnipeg.

       Discussion and social activities.

1043. MIDDLECHURCH HOME OF WINNIPEG
       Papers, 1883-1980. Finding aid.
       20".   PAM (MG10 B32)

       Organized in 1883 to provide a temporary home for
       female immigrants and servants and to care for the
       aged. Annual reports, 1885-1980; monthly
       operations reports, 1908-18; visitors report books,
       1899-1925; record of admissions, 1943-77;
       newsletter, 1955-63; committee papers.

1044. THE PROVINCIAL COUNCIL OF WOMEN OF MANITOBA
       Papers, 1949-80.
       7'.   PAM (MG10 C44)

       Minutes; correspondence; reports; financial
       statements; briefs; notice of meetings;
       resolutions; cash book; constitutions; scrapbooks.

1045. SOCIAL SERVICES ADVISORY COMMITTEE
       Operating files. Restricted.
       Located 202-323 Portage Avenue, Winnipeg, R3B 2C1.

       Established in 1959 to appeal decisions made by the
       director of Social Services concerning pensions,
       resident care, municipal assistance, and in other
       ways act as an intermediary between citizens and
       various government bureaucracies.
       Minutes; case histories; annual reports;
       statistics.

1046. THE SOCIAL PLANNING COUNCIL OF WINNIPEG
       Papers, 1893-1977. Restricted. Finding aid.
       127'.   PAM (MG10 B20)

       The Central Council of Social Agencies was formed
       in Winnipeg in 1919. It consisted of thirty-eight
       affiliated agencies whose aims were to develop a
       better co-operation among existing agencies, to
       further new activities, to provide for united
       action in the administrative or legislative fields,
       and to carry out a systematic programme for social
       development.

The Central Volunteer Bureau was formed in 1939 and
united with the Council of Social Agencies in 1945,
but retained the status of a separate division
within the Agency. The Welfare Council of Greater
Winnipeg came into being in 1951, combining the
aforementioned agencies. In 1961 the Welfare
Council became known as the Community Welfare
Planning Council of Greater Winnipeg. In 1973 the
name was changed to the Social Planning Council of
Winnipeg.

Since the collection is so vast and connects into
almost every welfare relief agency in the province,
a more detailed listing is given below arranged in
alphabetical order. Much of their described
materials was generated as part of the agency's
normal work in dialogue with the Social Planning
Council.

Alcoholism Foundation of Manitoba - reports,
    projects, and clippings.
Age and Opportunity Centre, Inc. - reports and
    memos.
Bethany Home, Salvation Army - questionnaires and
    statistics, 1957-74.
Central Volunteer Bureau - correspondence; reports;
    minutes, 1939-71.
Child Care and Family Division - correspondence;
    reports; studies of child labour; minutes,
    1941-72.
Children's Bureau of Winnipeg - statistical
    studies, 1941-42.
Children's Aid Societies of Manitoba -
    correspondence; minutes, 1943-1952.
Children's Aid Society of Winnipeg - reports,
    1942-43.
Day Care for Children - lunch and after-four
    programme-minutes, 1970.
Day Nursery Centre - statistics and reports,
    1965-72.
Day Nursery Centre, Inc. - statistics on income of
    female workers.
Day Nursery Committee of the Council of Social
    Agencies - minutes, 1943.
Delinquency Study Committee - minutes, 1949.
Department of Health and Public Welfare - annual
    report, 1940.
Elizabeth Fry Society of Manitoba, Inc. -
    newsletter, report, 1969.
Family Bureau of Winnipeg - report.
Family and Child Care Division - minutes, 1943-44.
Family Day Care Project - reports, 1965-77.
Family Division - minutes, 1942-43.
Girls' Hostel - minutes, 1944.

Girls of Indian Descent Committee - minutes, 1953-74.
Health Division - minutes, 1943.
Home Welfare Association - annual reports, 1941-44.
Home Welfare Council - minutes, 1941-42.
Homemakers Services - description of services, 1966.
Homemakers Training Program - minutes, 1970.
Income Maintenance Schemes - reports; statistics, 1972.
Indian and Métis Conference - minutes, 1954.
Juvenile and Adult Offenders Committee - minutes, 1955-76.
Kindergarten Settlement Association of Winnipeg - reports; minutes; brochures, 1915-76.
Knox Day Nursery - report, 1970.
Lindenview Home (Salvation Army) - studies and reports.
Manitoba Camping Association - minutes.
Manitoba Home for Girls - audit; questionnaire.
Marriage Guidance Committee - correspondence.
Marymound Residential Treatment Centre for Adolescent Girls - reports; brochures; correspondence, 1967-78; questionnaire.
New Canadians Committee - minutes, 1948-49.
Overseas Children's Care Committee - minutes, 1941-42.
Patriotic Salvage Corps, Winnipeg - references, 1940.
Pregnancy Counselling Service - clippings; reports, 1974; working papers; statistics.
Psychotic Women - minutes, 1948-49.
Protestant Girls' Needs Committee - minutes, 1949.
Reports of the Social Planning Council - annual reports and surveys.
River House (operated by Alcoholism Foundation of Manitoba).
Roslyn House Association - annual reports; correspondence.
Single Women's Committee - minutes, 1942.
Sisters of Service Girls' Residential Club - annual reports; correspondence; brochures.
Unmarried Mothers in the Forces (World War II) - minutes, 1942.
Unmarried Mothers of Manitoba - Annual Council and Agency reports, 1936-43.
Unmarried Mothers - Special Committee - minutes, 1941.
Unmarried Parent Services of Children's Aid Society of Winnipeg.
Victorian Order of Nurses - reports; correspondence.
Villa Rosa (formerly Rosalie Hall) - correspondence; by-laws; questionnaires.
Volunteers in Hospitals - minutes, 1941.

Welfare Council of Greater Winnipeg –
correspondence and papers on unmarried mothers.

1047. PAUL, A.
      Papers.   TRHM (MG4 B1)

      Includes minutes, 1931-32, and financial records of
      the Transcona Social Welfare Committee.

1048. TRANSCONA. SOCIAL SERVICES WEEKLY STATISTICAL REPORTS
      1974. Restricted.   TRHM (MG15 B20.4)

      Employable persons on assistance; unemployables.

1049. VILLA ROSA
      Operating files, 1898-1982. Restricted.
      Located at 784 Wolseley Avenue, Winnipeg, Manitoba,
      R3G 1C6.

      Organized in 1898 under the direction of the
      Sisters of Misericordia (Soeurs de la Misèricorde)
      to provide residential care for the unwed pregnant
      woman of any religion or nationality. Registers of
      mothers and children, 1898-1944; admissions,
      1960-74; clinic books, 1927-75; index of patients,
      1928-65; re-admissions, 1953-72; financial records,
      1898-1972; St. Norbert Infant Home, 1921-46;
      Misericordia Hospital patient records, 1952-77;
      correspondence and financial records, 1959-63;
      regulations for baptism of illegitimate babies;
      Home of the Good Shepherd, 1951; Jewish Child
      Services; correspondence on adoption, 1958-70;
      monthly reports; daily events, 1955-70.

1050. WINNIPEG. UNEMPLOYMENT RELIEF COMMITTEE
      Papers, 1926-30.   CWA (Book 1A)

      Reports; minutes; financial statements, 1926-29,
      which include discussion on single women and aid
      (individual cases and recipients).

1051. WEST KILDONAN. RELIEF COMMITTEE
      Minutes, 1921-23, 1933-42. Restricted.
      Finding aid.   CWA

1052. WIDOW'S CONSULTATION CENTRE
      Operating files, 1974- . Restricted.
      Located at the YWCA, 447 Webb Place, Winnipeg,
      Manitoba, R3B 2P2.

      203

Established in 1974 to assist widows in coping with
emotional and practical problems. Minutes; case
files.

1053. WINNIPEG COUNCIL OF SELF-HELP, INC.
        Papers, 1970-78. Inventory.
        3.0'.   PAM (P839-845)

        Originally organized in 1970 to represent various
        related groups interested in improving conditions
        of life for people living in poverty but
        reorganized in 1973 to allow for individual as well
        as group membership. The Council published a
        newsletter, Orbit, provided referral and grievance
        services, and in other ways promoted the concerns
        of the poor to the general community.

        Minutes, 1971-76, of council and board meetings;
        address lists; objectives and history, 1970-71;
        policies and procedures, 1970-76; reports, receipts
        and taxation forms, 1971-77; files pertaining to
        related and participating associations such as
        Mothers Allowance Groups and Mothers Action
        Committee; issues of the quarterly newsletter,
        Orbit from 1973 to 1976, related materials.

1054. WINNIPEG PUBLIC WELFARE COMMITTEE
        Papers, 1905-71. Finding aid.
        Several shelves.   CWA

        Organized in 1940 out of the former Unemployment
        Relief Committee and chaired by Margaret
        McWilliams. Minutes, 1940- ; reports, 1940-
        citing number of family cases, single women,
        mothers' allowance, and homeless women; Health
        Committee communications; correspondence.

1055. WOMEN'S RESOURCE CENTRE
        Operating files. Restricted.
        Located at the YWCA, 447 Webb Place, Winnipeg,
        Manitoba, R3B 2P1.

        Steering agency to guide women in emergencies to
        most appropriate relief agencies.

1056. YWCA, THOMPSON, MANITOBA
        Operating files, 1969- .
        Located at 39 Nickel Road, Thompson, Manitoba, R8N
        0Y5.

Organized in 1969 and opened its 105-bed hostel in 1972. Reports; minutes; financial records; "The Diary" - a register of daily events since 1972; briefs presented to various commissions; housing for native people.

WOMEN AND RELIGION

The Anglican Church

1057. ANGLICAN CHURCH.   ANGLICAN DIOCESE OF BRANDON
      (1924 TO PRESENT)
            Diocesan. Parish records. Uncatalogued.
            Restricted.
            Located at the Synod Office, 341-12th Street,
            Brandon, Manitoba, R7A 4P8.   DBA

            The first proposals for the information of the
            diocese of Brandon were discussed by the Rupert's
            Land Synod in 1911 and boundaries were set to
            include that part of Manitoba "west of the line
            between ranges nine and ten west of the principal
            meridian, and west of Lakes Manitoba and
            Winnipegosis." However, the World War I
            intervened, and it was not until 1924 that
            Archbishop Matheson opened the first Synod of the
            Diocese of Brandon, which in turn elected the
            Venerable W.W.H. Thomas as its Bishop.

            A year later, the Brandon Diocesan Woman's
            Auxiliarly was organized, with the Rupert's Land WA
            dividing the surplus balance of funds as well as
            the Missionary Library with the new Auxiliary.
            Early years were characterized by a special
            emphasis on Indian missions and welcoming new
            settlers, a work in which St. Faith's Mission and
            its Bishop's Messengers were very active. The
            Mothers' Union began locally in Russell (about
            1925) and was organized as a Diocesan Council in
            1929.

            (a) Parish records of individual churches;
            Approximately 12 parishes,
            1898-1972.   DBA

      206

St. Matthew, Brandon, 1907; St. George, Elton,
Manitoba, 1945; Anglican Women's Auxiliary, Cyprus
River, Manitoba, 1952; St. George, Birtle,
Manitoba, 1964; St. Agnes, Carberry; Manitoba; and
St. James, Flin Flon.
Also three typescript histories: "Remember When:
History and Memories, 1890-1980" (Holy Trinity,
Killarney, Manitoba); "An Historical Record of the
Diamond Jubilee of St. Thomas Church, Rapid City,
Manitoba, October 6, 1940" (St. Thomas, City,
Manitoba); and one of the Neepawa District.
Also several unidentified account and minute books,
1911-47 of the Women's Auxiliary throughout the
Brandon Diocese.

(b) St. Faith's Mission, Swan Lake, Manitoba.
Papers, 1931-72.   DBA

Financial statements, 1963-74; Guild letters,
1930-49; Montreal branch minute books, 1947-75,
1966; newsletters, 1956-79, 1971) Ottawa branch
(disbanded 1972) minute books, reports and
financial statements, executive reports,
miscellaneous correspondence, 1945-79; photograph
album from St. Luke's Mission and Griswold Sioux
Indian Reserve; photograph (mounted) of Marguerita
Fowler; photographs of the various stations served
by the Messengers, most undated; reports from
Cormorant, Herb Lake and Wabowden, 1931-43 and from
the Sioux Indian Reserve at Griswold, 1943-46.

(c) Papers relating to diocesan women and women's
auxiliaries Several items,
1908-72.   DBA

A history ("The Open Door"), 1885-1967; reports;
memorial rolls; minute books; newsletters; reports
to Synod, 1965-76; cash books, 1935-38, 1958-69;
synoptic skills, 1944-72; audited financial
statements, 1938-73; executive committee minute
book, 1927-34; ledger sheets, 1935-78; booklet on
the Scattered Members' Branch, 1959; printed works;
auxiliary reports and bulletins.

(d) Female priest files.   DBA

Among the substantial number of biographical files
on priests located at the Synod office are the
following materials on women priests: the Reverend
Allayson Barnet-Cowan (The Pas) the Reverend Kay
Hill (Cormorant), the Reverend Marjorie Kennon
(Carberry); Cannon May Stockford (Brandon); the
Reverend Thelma Tanner.

207

1058. ANGLICAN CHURCH.   ANGLICAN DIOCESE OF BRANDON.
ANGLICAN CHURCH AT THE PAS, MANITOBA

DBA

Bishop's Messengers of St. Faith's, minute book,
1961-79; letters of appreciation from many parts of
Canada, written by persons who experienced in some
way the work of the Messengers; newsletters,
1930-76; guild letters, 1949-78; photograph
collection of Bishop's Messengers work from all the
various stations, 1928-79; "A proposal for
evaluating experimental activity in connection with
the observance of the Rule of Life"; reports; St.
Faith's Chapel, Vestry Book, 1937-78 giving date,
day of Christian year, hour, service, officiant,
number in congretion, number of communicants; St.
Faith's Guest Book, 1955-79; and an article, "Women
in the Clergy," by Janice Tyrwhitt describing the
work of Reverend Kathleen Hill.

1059. ANGLICAN CHURCH.   ANGLICAN DIOCESE OF KEEWATIN (1899
TO PRESENT)

DKA

(a) Diocesan and parish records.   Uncatalogued.

Geographically the largest of the three Anglican
dioceses in Manitoba, the population of the Diocese
of Keewatin, almost evenly divided between native
and white, is by far the smallest, the most
scattered and the most inaccessible.   T.C.B. Boon
termed it the "Diocese of the Pre-Cambrian Shield,"
for it includes an area from just west of Lake
Superior to just east of Lake Winnipeg and north to
the boundaries of Hudson Bay and the North West
Territories.   Although constitutionally founded in
1899, because of financial difficulties the Diocese
became a reality only in 1902 with the election of
the Venerable Joseph Lofthouse as Bishop.   While
Kenora, Ontario, was chosen as the administrative
centre, the following points of the Diocese are
located in Manitoba: Churchill, Norway House,
Gillam , Ilford, Split Lake, York Landing,
Thompson, Pikwitonei, Thicket Portage, Hole River,
Manigatogan, Whitemouth, Lac du Bonnet, Little
Black, Pine Falls, Piney and Shamattawa.

As everywhere else, the women of the Diocese had
been gathered together under various names, but the
first parochial branch of the Women's Auxiliary was
organized at Fort Frances, Ontario, in 1903, two

years before the Keewatin Diocesan Board of the WA appeared in Kenora. Local branches could affiliate in that first year for ten cents, one cent of which went to the General Board. The first Indian women to affiliate (in 1913) were those of Split Lake, where missionaries had translated the Members' Prayer into Cree.

(b) Parish records from within the Diocese.
Several items, 1850-1965.   DKA

St. Paul's Mission, Churchill, record book, 1860-1934, of Indian names, new Christian names, and baptisms; parish register, 1850-34. Fort Alexander (Lansdowne), parish record, 1904-36, listing sermon topics, texts, attendance, offering, officiating clergymen, confessions (especially of native women); St. Mark's Church (Jack River, Manitoba) mission journal at Norway House, 1926-45, kept by W.H.J. Walter describing day-to-day accounts of life among the Indians; parish record of services, remarks, confirmations, offerings and funerals, and lists of families; inventory, 1910-32 of church goods and property. Norway House – Parish register, 1902-37; baptisms, confirmations, marriages, burials and a brief handwritten parish history, 1900-on. Thicket Portage register of births, 1869-1965; marriages, 1906-76; family allowances. York Factory parish registers, 1864-1952; marriages with many names in syllabics; York Factory baptisms, marriages and deaths, 1903-30.

(c) Papers relating to Diocesan women and women's auxiliaries (WA)
Several items, 1893-1974.   DKA

WA Diocesan annual reports, 1924-26, 1947-73; annual reports from branch auxiliaries, 1952-72; minutes of the Board of Management of the WA of the Keewatin Diocese, 1955-70; reports to the Synod of the Diocese, 1907-73 financial records to the Synod of the Diocese, 1907-73; financial records and cash books, 1952-74; minute books of the WA, 1924-74; handbooks; brief histories; leaders' guides; correspondence from branch auxiliaries and missionary wives; executive meeting reports and financial statements; photographs and slides, 1954-; questionnaires on meetings, attendance and fund-raising projects; reports of various annual meetings; related material.

1060. ANGLICAN CHURCH.   ANGLICAN DIOCESE OF RUPERT'S LAND
      (RLDA) (1820 to Present)
            (a) Diocesan records and holdings.   Uncatalogued.
      Located at Anglican Centre, 935 Nesbit Bay,
      Winnipeg, Manitoba.

                              RLDA

      Although this western Canadian Anglican Diocese was
      formed in 1849 with David Anderson as Bishop,
      girls' and women's activities were fostered soon
      after the arrival of the Rev. John West in 1820.
      At first under the tutelage of Mrs. George
      Harbidge, a schoolmistress, then under successive
      missionaries' wives, and finally in each parish as
      it was organized, women's groups, if they had any
      name at all, were known as sewing classes, ladies'
      aid societies, mothers' meetings, guilds, or by
      various other designations.   In 1885, however, the
      Women's Auxiliary came into being in Ottawa, and in
      1887 an auxiliary was formed in Winnipeg for the
      Diocese of Rupert's Land, with Mrs. John Grisdale
      as president.

      The work of the infant organization initially was
      "to supply every parish in the Diocese with church
      furnishing," as well as to repack bales of clothing
      sent form eastern Canada for distribution among
      various Indian missions.   The organization quickly
      expanded its horizons to include a multitude of
      charitable works as diverse as the Dorcas
      Department, which looked after material needs, took
      responsibility for the management of Dynevor
      Hospital, and established a library.

      In 1896 senior parochial branches were established
      in Winnipeg and, with several rural organizations
      already in existance, the Auxiliary expanded
      rapidly until virtually every rural parish was
      organized and most urban churches boasted two
      active branches - a senior and a junior auxiliary,
      the latter usually meeting in the evening.   Other
      groups fostered by the WA were Little Helpers,
      Girls' Auxiliary, Junior Girls, and the Church
      Boy's League.

      When the Woman's Auxiliary was founded in 1885 it
      was the only avenue of Christian service open to
      women of that day.   From 1885 onward there has been
      a gradual development of opportunity for women in
      the church, culminating at the end of 1973 with the
      integration of programs and finances of Anglican
      Church Women with those of the Diocese.

      In 1966 the Constitution of the Synod of Rupert's
      Land was amended to allow women to be members of

      210

Synod, vestries, etc. In 1967 the formation of
Anglican Church Women united a number of parish and
diocesan women's groups into one structure. Now
included were parish guilds, the Mother's Union,
prayer groups and the structured Woman's Auxiliary.
This action opened the way for a resolution passed
at the 1969 Diocesan Synod which endorsed the
policy of the eventual total integration of the
finances, personnel and program of Anglican Church
Women into the mainstream of the life of the
Diocese.

(b) Records of individual churches.
44 Churches, 1820-1971.   RLDA

Parish records from the following Winnipeg
churches:
Christ Church Anglican, 1884-1972; Emmanual Church,
1917-33; Grace Church, 1965-75; St. Alban Anglican,
1910-70; St. Andre Anglican, 1908-44; St. Ann
Anglican, 1913-74; St. Barnabas Anglican, 1925-71;
St. Brysostom Anglican, 1912-69; St. Cuthbert
Anglican, 1903-73; St. David Anglican Church,
1921-71; St. George Anglican Church, 1884-76; St
George (Transcona), 1912-67; St. James Anglican
Church, 1906-76; St. John's the Baptist Anglican
Church, 1934-73; St. Jude Anglican Church 1906-75;
St. Luke Anglican Church, 1910-77; St. Margaret
Anglican Church, 1908-77; St. Mark Anglican Church,
1915-66; St. Martin-in-the-Fields, 1907-72; St.
Mary Anglican Church, 1922-79; St. Mary Magdalene
Anglican Church, 1926-77; St. Patrick Anglican
Church, 1912-77; St. Paul Anglican Church,
1850-1960; St. Peter Anglican Church, 1893-1932;
St. Philip Anglican Church, 1900-77; St. Saviour
Anglican Church, 1914-77; St. Stephen Anglican
Church, 1929-77; St. Thomas Anglican Church,
1907-70; St. Timothy Anglican Church, 1928-73.

Parish records from the following non-Winnipeg
churches:
All Saints, Dominion City, 1914-79; All Saints,
Drinview, 1940-77; All Saints, Gunnville, 1939-73;
All Saints, St. Peter, St. Matthew, Hodgson-Peguis
Area, 1946-78, 1953-63, 1944-69; All Saints,
Morris, 1884-1920; All Saints, Scotch Bay, 1938-74;
All Saints, Whytewold, 1905-42; Christ Church,
Selkirk, 1905-77; Christ Church, Stony Mountain,
1881-1929; Church of the Ascension, Stonewall,
1889-1964; Gordon Anglican Mission later St. James
Church, Jackhead Indian Reserve, 1893-37; St.
Helen's Church, Fairford Reserve; Gypsumville,
1938-79; Hodgson-Peguis Anglican Church of St.
Philip, 1912-48; Holy Trinity, Headingley,
1857-1945; Lansdowne Anglican Parish, Lansdowne,

1864-93; Oak Point Anglican Parish, Oak Point,
1906-79; Queen's Valley, Queen's Valley, 1911-13.

(c) Papers relating to diocesan women and women's
auxiliaries. Several items. RLDA

Annual reports; minutes of annual meetings of the
WA, 1914-77; WA monthly bulletins, 1915-76; WA
scrapbooks of clippings and other data, 1886-1973;
women and ministry reports, 1971-79; WA histories
of forty-five difficult churches and areas within
the Diocese; presidents' addresses; synod journals
(particularly those discussion about ordination of
women to the priesthood); diocesan histories;
correspondence; Keewatin handicrafts sale, 1978;
printed materials (including "Bulletins of the
Council for Social Service for the Church of
England in Canada").

(d) Miscellaneous materials. RLDA

Minutes of the Selkirk Deanery WA, 1913-37;
material of the Yellow Knife Conference of Indian,
Eskimo and non-native women, 1974; synod reports,
1909-10); Synod journals providing much on marriage
and divorce.

1061. ANGLICAN CHURCH. ALL SAINTS ANGLICAN CHURCH
      Operating files and church records, 1860-1983.
      Located at 175 Colony Street, Winnipeg, Manitoba,
      R3C 1W2.

      Register of services, 1884-1966; parish records
      1884- ; register of marriage banns, 1860, 1927-71;
      WA Book of Remembrance, 1927-74; WA minutes,
      1923-60; WA cash book and attendance, 1957-73; WA
      Reports, 1956-62; Diocese of Rupert's Land WA
      annual reports, 1884-1949; Women's Guild Record
      (scrapbook), 1884-1949; records of women's work,
      1883-1947; Women's Guild: attendance, 1939-78;
      minutes and correspondence, 1932-77; History of All
      Saints Mothers' Union, 1951; Chancel Guild: minute
      book, 1909-29; cash books, 1908-28, 1931-49;
      reports and correspondence, 1926-43; St. Cecelia's
      Guild (in charge of music), correspondence,
      1930-78; Sunday School records; Brownie cash book
      and attendance, 1961-73; correspondence; membership
      roll and attendance at Annual Meetings, 1915-83;
      short histories; photographs.

1062. PEGUIS ANGLICAN CHURCHES
      Histories.   RLDA

St. Peter's; All Saints; St. Matthew's.

1063. ST. ALBAN'S ANGLICAN CHURCH
        Selected materials.   BCA (MG7 B2)

        WA minute book; minute book and cash book;
        correspondence.

1064. ST. JOHN'S CATHEDRAL PARISH
        Parish records, 1906-1965. Restricted.
        Located at 135 Anderson Avenue, Winnipeg, Manitoba.

        Minutes of Ladies Auxiliary, 1906-36; Ladies Aid
        correspondence and annual reports, 1932-43; minutes
        of WA with lists of members and records and
        expenditures, 1937-49; Altar Guild minutes,
        1925-40; Annual Meeting, Ladies Auxiliary, 1949;
        Ladies Aid minutes, 1944-75; Evening Branch,
        1945-66; "The History of St. John's Cathedral
        Women's Auxiliary," compiled by L.A.P. Smith, n.d.;
        letter to Mrs. Doope concerning church affairs,
        1926; photographs.

1065. ST. MARY'S LA PRAIRIE ANGLICAN CHURCH
        Selected materials, 1908-72.
        Located at 2nd Street S.W., Portage la Prairie,
        Manitoba.

        St. Mary's Altar Guild daily journal and ledger,
        1945-75; minutes, 1968-72; cash books and honour
        roll, 1948-75; St. Mary's Ladies Aid, 1908-71; WA,
        1935-54; Evening Branch, (1954-75); photographs;
        "An Oldtimer's Recollection of the Red River
        Colony."

1066. ST. PHILIP'S ANGLICAN CHURCH, SCANTERBURY
        History.   RLDA (Drawer 1)

        History of women's work in the church.

The Greek Orthodox Church

1067. GREEK ORTHODOX CHURCH. RUSSIAN GREEK ORTHODOX HOLY
        TRINITY CATHEDRAL
            Operating files. Church Records.

213

Located at 643 Manitoba Avenue, Winnipeg, Manitoba,
R2W 2H1.

Within this cathedral congregation several women's
groups are active and control their own archival
materials, some of which are housed in the
cathedral; however most are in the hands of
individual groups. Contact may be made through the
cathedral office.

1068. GREEK ORTHODOX CHURCH. ST. DEMETRIOS GREEK ORTHODOX
CHURCH LADIES PHILOPTOCHUS SOCIETY
          Operating files.
          Contact: 2255 Grant Avenue, Winnipeg, Manitoba.

1069. GREEK ORTHODOX CHURCH. UKRAINIAN GREEK ORTHODOX HOLY
TRINITY CHURCH
          Operating files and church records (mostly in
          Ukrainian).
          Located at 1175 Main Street, Winnipeg, Manitoba,
          R2W 3S4.

          This central cathedral of the Ukrainian Greek
          Orthodox faith in Winnipeg also houses a museum
          containing Ukrainian folk art and crafts brought
          from the Ukraine by early pioneers. Included is
          the traditional dress of various regions. The
          cathedral congregation includes several active
          women's groups who control their own archival
          materials, some of which are stored in the
          cathedral museum, some in the consistory at 9 St.
          John's Street, and some in the possession of the
          elected representatives.

1070. GREEK ORTHODOX CHURCH. UKRAINIAN WOMEN'S ASSOCIATION
          Operating files.
          Contact: Ukrainian Greek Orthodox Church
          Consistory, 9 St. John's ave. R2W 1G8, Winnipeg,
          Manitoba; also the Holy Trinity Cathedral Museum,
          1175 Main Street, Winnipeg, R2W 3S4.

1071. ROMANIAN ORTHODOX CHURCH. GENERAL. ST. GEORGE'S
ROMANIAN ORTHODOX PARISH.
          Church records, 1962-79.
          Located at 123 Harvard Avenue, Transcona, Manitoba,
          R2C 0L9.

          Yearbooks; ladies auxiliary record books and
          minutes of meetings; baptisms; marriages; funerals;
          video and audio cassettes of church functions.

214

1072. LUTHERAN CHURCH.   BRAETHRA LUTHERAN CHURCH,   RIVERTON,
      MANITOBA
            Selected materials.   PAM (MG7 E2)

            Ladies Aid Report, 1961.

1073. LUTHERAN CHURCH.   LUTHERAN COUNCIL IN CANADA
            Operating files.
            Located 500-365 Hargrave Street, Winnipeg,
            Manitoba, R3B 2K3.

            A joint agency for the three major Lutheran bodies
            in Canada. Correspondence and reports of K.
            Petersons, Lutheran Church port worker in Montreal,
            1949-79; "women - organizations and ordination";
            microfilms of materials on Lutheran Church women,
            divorce, family, and International Women's Year,
            1975.

1074. LUTHERAN CHURCH.   LUTHERAN WOMEN'S LEAGUE.
            Papers.   UMA (Icelandic
                                           Library)

            Reports, 1925-77; executive reports of the Sunrise
            Lutheran Camp, 1947-76; general reports, 1955-66.

1075. LUTHERAN CHURCH.   PEACE LUTHERAN CHURCH, MOOSEHORN,
      MANITOBA
            Selected materials.   PAM (MG7 E1)

            Secretaries book of ladies' group, meeting notes,
            1949-78 (German); constitution of ladies' group and
            meeting notes, 1924-48 (German); Women's Mission
            Society, secretaries reports, 1950-76 (English);
            ladies' group, 1957-70 (English).

The Mennonite Church

Mennonites first entered Canada in 1786 as "late loyalists"
from the United States, settling in various parts of southern
Ontario. In 1874 1,533 immigrants, mostly of Dutch extraction
but domiciled in Russia, arrived in Manitoba, settling in an
area around Steinbach (the East Reserve) but expanding to the
West Reserve, centred in the Gretna-Winkler-Altona area as
early as 1875. The present Mennonite population of Manitoba
is estimated at between 60,000 and 65,000, Winipeg having the
world's largest concentration approximately 25,000.

The Mennonites are a homogeneous religious group only in a
broad sense and, like the Lutherans, are organized into
numerous conferences, differing one from another largely in
matters of practice rather than in basic doctrine. In
Manitoba the two main groups, both with their Canadian
archives located in Winnipeg, are the Conference of Mennonites
in Canada (General Conference), and the Mennonite Brethren.

The Gretna First Mennonite Ladies Aid (General Conference),
believed to be the first formally organized women's group, was
organized about 1895 or 1896, while the women of the Mennonite
Brethren in Winkler followed suit soon after. The General
Conference women, after undergoing numerous name changes, are
presently known as the Manitoba Mennonite Women in Mission,
while the Mennonite Brethren women remain the Manitoba
Mennonite Brethren Women's Conference.

In addition to these two conferences, women of other Mennonite
groups in Manitoba are known by a great variety of names, and
generally keep their archival materials with an elected
executive committee. Contacts with these groups may be made
through the pastor of any given congregation.

1076. MENNONITE CHURCH CULTURE. BERGTHALER MENNONITE CHURCH
      OF MANITOBA
            Church records.   MHCA (Vols. 718-726)

            Church registers of family, birth, baptisms and
            deaths, 1890-1953.

1077. MENNONITE CHURCH CULTURE. BERGTHALER MENNONITE CHURCH
      OF MANITOBA
            Unpublished papers.   MHCA (Vertical file)

            This file includes several unpublished papers on
            the history of the Manitoba Bergthaler Church,
            including "The Women's Right to Vote in the Morden
            Bergthaler Church," 1981, by Paul Peters.

1078. MENNONITE CHURCH CULTURE. CONFERENCE OF MENNONITES IN
      CANADA
            Various Church Records (in German or English).
            Being microfilmed.   MHCA

            Church membership, baptisms, marriages, deaths and
            activity records of the following Mennonite
            churches including date of first record:

            Altona Bergthaler, 1951; Altona Mennonite, 1971;
            Arnaud, 1890; Bergthal (South Russia) and
            Chortitzer (Manitoba), 1836; Bethel Mennonite,
            1937; Blumenort Mennonite, 1834; Carman Mennonite,

1968; Charleswood Mennonite, 1963; Elim
Mennonite,(Grunthal), 1885; First Mennonite,
(Winnipeg), 1924; Fort Garry Mennonite Fellowship,
1967; Glenlea Mennonite, 1932; Grace Mennonite
(Steinbach), 1961; Graysville, 1927; Homewood,
1939; Home Street (formerly Winnipeg Bergthaler),
1957; Morden Bergthaler, 1932; Northdale
(Winnipeg), 1974; North Kildonan, 1889; Sargent
Avenue (Winnipeg), 1949; Schoenfelder (Pigeon Lake)
(1927); Springfield Heights (Winnipeg) (1964);
Springstein, 1929; Steinbach, 1943; Trinity
Mennonite Fellowship (Mather) (1977); Whitewater,
1927;

1079. MENNONITE CHURCH CULTURE. MANITOBA WOMEN IN MISSION
(Name changed in 1975 from Manitoba Women's Missionary
Association.)
Papers, 1967-   .   MHCA (Vols. 670-773;
1402-1403)

Correspondence; annual questionnaires on
membership, finances and projects of each group;
constitutions; presidential reports; financial
materials; program outlines; minutes of executive
meetings; booklets relevant to women's groups.

1080. MENNONITE CHURCH CULTURE. MISSIONS - NAHVEREIN (SEWING
CIRCLE)
1 box.   MHCA (XX11 F5 Vol.
2271)

Copies of Unser Missionsblatt, a four-page
newsletter published monthly in Altona, Manitoba,
by the Missions-Nahverein of the Conference of
Mennonites in Canada; in German, Gothic type.

1081. MENNONITE CHURCH CULTURE. WOMEN IN CHURCH VOCATIONS
Selected materials, 1955-79. MHCA (XX11 F4)

Handbook; minutes of executive and committee
meetings; reports.

1082. MENNONITE CHURCH CULTURE. EVANGELICAL MENNONITE BRETHREN
Listings, n.d.   MVMA

List of church members.

1083. MENNONITE CHURCH CULTURE. EVANGELICAL MENNONITE CHURCH
Selected materials.   MHCA (XX 45)

Memoirs, 1942-75, of Heinrich and Helena Reimer;
oral history of Helen H. Rempel of Rosenort,
Manitoba; correspondence and information on the
Peter and Margareta Kroeker family of Rosenort and
Morris, Manitoba; autobiography of Katherine H.
Regehr; handwritten booklet by Suzanne Hamm on the
Russian Steppes.

1084. MENNONITE CHURCH CULTURE. EVANGELICAL MENNONITE
MISSION CONFERENCE COLLECTION
    Papers.   MHCA (Microfilm
                                      220-222)

Church registers; regulations; an index; a full run
of Der Leitstern, 1944-77, its monthly publication.

1085. MENNONITE CHURCH CULTURE. GNADENTHAL VILLAGE RECORDS
    Family register, 1884- .   MHCA (Microfilm 188)

Village family registers with household
inventories.

1086. MENNONITE CHURCH CULTURE. MENNONITE BRETHREN CHURCHES
IN MANITOBA
    Various church records.
    Several files.   MBA (BC 500)

Each church has a "Ladies Fellowship: or a "Women's
Missionary Society," and while many records remain
with the executive of an elected committee, the
following (some in German, some in English) are on
microfilm at this location: minutes; lists of
members; lists of officers; financial records;
annual reports for the churches listed: Alexander,
Fort Garry, Niverville, Arnaud, Horndean, North
Kildonan, Boissevain, Justice, Portage Avenue
(Winnnipeg), Brandon, Kronsgart, Rivereast
(Winnipeg), Brooklands, Killarney, Salem
(Winnipeg), Carmen, Manitou, Steinbach, Domain,
Marquette, Winkler, Elm Creek, Morden, Winnipeg
Central, Elmwood, Newton, Westview (Portage la
Prairie).

1087. MENNONITE CHURCH CULTURE. MENNONITE BRETHREN
COLLEGIATE INSTITUTE COMMITTEE: WOMEN'S AUXILIARY
    Papers.   MBA (BC 243)

Minutes; reports.

1088. MENNONITE CHURCH CULTURE. MENNONITE BRETHREN
        Journals.   MBA

        Mennonite Brethren Herald, 1962-85 Mennonite
        Observer, 1955-71 Mennonitische Rundschau,
        1880-1924 (U.S.), 1924 to present (Canadian).

1089. MENNONITE CHURCH CULTURE. MENNONITE BRETHREN, MANITOBA
        WOMEN'S CONFERENCE
        Papers, 1954-77.   MBA (BC 370)

        Correspondence; membership lists; projects for
        mission work, 1954-77; executive meeting minutes,
        1967-77; presidents' reports; constitution.

1090. MENNONITE CHURCH CULTURE. MENNONITE COLLEGIATE
        INSTITUTE, GRETNA, MANITOBA
        Operating files.
        Located in Gretna, Manitoba.

        The oldest Mennonite high school in Manitoba.
        Student records; year books; school concert
        programmes; music; miscellaneous papers.

1091. MENNONITE CHURCH CULTURE. MENNONITE FAMILIES
        Unpublished paper, 1977, by Norman Klippenstein.
        Typescript.   MHCA (Vertical file)

        "Mennonite Family Studies: An Annotated
        Bibliography."

1092. MENNONITE CHURCH CULTURE. MENNONITE FUNERALS
        Unpublished Paper, 1979, by Charlotte Rempel.
        Typescript.   MHCA (Vertical file)

        "The Changing View of Mennonite Funerals."

1093. MENNONITE CHURCH CULTURE. MENNONITE GENEALOGY, INC.
        Operating files and research library.
        Located at Autumn House, 790 Wellington Avenue,
        Winnipeg, Manitoba, R3C 2H6.

        Research library specializing in Prussian-Russian
        Mennonite family records, with help available for
        those interested in tracing their own family
        history.

1094. MENNONITE CHURCH CULTURE. MENNONITE HOMES
        Unpublished paper, 1951, by Dorothy M. Schmidt
        Typescript.   MHCA (Vertical file)

        219

"The Mennonite Home."

1095. MENNONITE CHURCH CULTURE. MENNONITE HOME LIFE
        Oral history (English).
        45'.   MVMA (E391)

        Interview with Helen Rempel, Altona, by LaVerna
        Klippenstein.

1096. MENNONITE CHURCH CULTURE. MENNONITE WOMEN
        Selected Information. Unindexed.
        In original or in microfilm
        format.   MHCA (Vertical file)

        Material by or about:
        Baerg, Anna; Bergen, Esther C.; Dyck, Anna Reimer;
        Friesen, Wanda Regier; Hamm, Susanna; Heese, Lena;
        Hooge, Kathe; Kirkpatrick, Debbie; Krahn, Elizabeth
        Wiens; Loewen, Mary J. Petkau, Irene Friesen;
        Pries, Jacob and Agathe; Rempel, Olga; Thiessen,
        Helene; Warkentin, Mary; Wiebe, Justina Teichroeb;
        Teichroeb, Peter.

1097. MENNONITE CHURCH CULTURE. MENNONITE DEACONESSES
        Unpublished paper, 1980, by Joan Driedger.
        Typescript.   MHCA (Vertical file)

        "Mennonite Women in Service: the History of the
        Deaconess Movement."

1098. MENNONITE CHURCH CULTURE. MENNONITES IN MANITOBA
        Unpublished papers/essays.
        39 items.   MHCA (Vertical file)

        Histories of Mennonite communities.

1099. MENNONITE CHURCH CULTURE. MENNONITES FROM MANITOBA IN
        BOLIVIA, MEXICO, PARAGUAY AND URUGUAY
        File.   WRL (MG2)

        Clippings and printed material on conservative
        Manitoba Mennonites emigrating for religious
        reasons. Many of these came from the Winkler area.

1100. MENNONITE CHURCH CULTURE. REINLAENDER MENNONITE CHURCH
        REGISTER("Old Colony Mennonite Church")
        Church records, 1875-1922.
        Microfilm.   MHCA (Microfilm 91)

Names, births, baptisms, marriage and death dates
of Mennonite families of Southern Manitoba from
1875-1922; alphabetical index of all those included
in the register; women's maiden names given.

1101. MENNONITE CHURCH CULTURE. SERVANTHOOD
       Translation of diary, 1895.
       15 pp.   MHCA (Vertical file)

       "The Servanthood Position of Mennonite Women," a
       translation of a diary of Catherine (Friesen)
       Schultz. Translation by Laverna Klippenstein.

1102. MENNONITE CHURCH CULTURE. SOMMERFELD VILLAGE, MANITOBA
       Selected materials, 1860-   . MHCA (Microfilm 91,
                                         microfiche 4)

       Village record ledger; family book; "Papers of
       Altester David Stoesz of the Chortitzer Mennonite
       Church, East Reserve, Manitoba; and the
       Waisenverordnug of the Sommerfelder Mennonite
       Church, Manitoba."

1103. MENNONITE CHURCH CULTURE. SOMMERFELD MENNONITE CHURCH
       Papers, 1893-1929.   MHCA (Microfilm 351)

       Registers and papers 1929, including materials from
       Mexico.

1104. MENNONITE CHURCH CULTURE. THIESSEN, ANNA
       Papers. Unpublished paper
       (German).   MBA

       "Die Entstehunh und Entwikelung der Mennoniten
       Bruder Gemeinde in Winnipeg, 1907-1966."

1105. MENNONITE CHURCH CULTURE. UNRAU, GERTRUDE
       Autobiographical notes.   MHCA (XXV B Vol.
                                         1073)

       Long-time missionary under the Mennonite Pioneer
       Mission.

1106. MENNONITE CHURCH CULTURE. WEST RESERVE ("OLD COLONY
       MENNONITE CHURCH" OR "REINLAENDER MENNONITE CHURCH")
       Church registers (1880-).   MHCA (Vols 1107 and
                                         2267)

221

1107. MENNONITE CHURCH CULTURE. WINKLER, MANITOBA
      Clipping files, scrapbooks.   WRL

          Return to Winkler of South American Mennonites;
          "Mennonite Settlement: West Reserve; with
          references to women's dress, house plans, roof
          thatching, brick heaters, etc.

1108. MENNONITE CHURCH CULTURE. "WINKLER CHURCHES AND
      RELIGIOUS FIGURES"
          Selected materials.   WRL (MG1)

          Clippings; yearbooks; directories; other data on
          the Bergthaler Mennonites, Evangelical Mennonite
          Brethren, Evangelical Mennonite Mission, Reinlander
          Mennonite, Old Colony Mennonite, Winkler Mennonite
          Brethren, and Trinity Evangelical Lutheran
          Churches.

1109. MENNONITE CHURCH CULTURE. WOMEN IN CHURCH
          Unpublished paper, 1959, by Helen Letkeman.
          Typescript.   MHCA (Vertical file)

          "Women in Church Work"

1110. MENNONITE CHURCH CULTURE. WOMEN'S LIBERATION
          Unpublished paper, 1978, by Adelia Neufeld.
          Typescript.   MHCA (Vertical file)

          "Women's Liberation in the Mennonite Church: A
          Survey." A bibliography of Mennonite periodicals
          from 1968-77 and their published articles relating
          to women.

The Roman Catholic Church

With the arrival of Fathers Joseph Norbert Provencher and
Sevère-Nicholas Dumoulin at Red River in 1818, the Roman
Catholic Church became the oldest Christian denomination
permanently and officially to locate in Manitoba. In 1844
Pope Gregory XVI created a vicariate apostolic of Hudson Bay
and James Bay, and in 1847 Pius IX founded the Diocese of the
Northwest, appointing Provencher its Ordinary. Provencher,
feeling that "Bishop of the Northwest signifies nothing,"
successfully petitioned for a change of name to
Saint-Boniface. In 1871 the Diocese was made into an
Archdiocese, while the Archdiocese of Winnipeg, in turn, was
erected upon the division of St. Boniface after the death of
Archbishop Langevin in 1915.

Officially Catholic women's work in Red River had its
beginnings when Angelique Nolin inaugurated girls' education
at St. Boniface in 1829, and shortly thereafter extended the
work to include St. François-Xavier. Her curriculum stressed
French, English, and domestic sciences, described as "weaving
and other domestic arts." Madame Mulaire's school in Ste.
Agathe was another early educational endeavour specifically
geared to women and girls.

However, the most concentrated efforts by or for women in
Catholic areas have traditionally been carried on by women in
various religious orders. Although there has been a marked
decline in recent years, evidence of their energetic activity
is still available in the Canadian Catholic Church Directory,
1983, which lists the Archdiocese of St. Boniface as having
585 nuns (compared to 213 priests, deacons and brothers), and
the Archdiocese of Winnipeg with 355 (compared to 160 men).

In addition the Catholic Women's League is active in most
English-speaking parishes, and La Ligue des Femmes
Catholiques, les Dames de Sainte-Anne, and other groups, in
French-speaking areas. Both French and English speaking
organizations are concerned also with children's work, such as
the Children of Mary (Enfants de Marie). Their archival
materials, however, are not at present generally deposited in
a central location, but remain in the possession either of the
parish of of an elected executive. This can be determined
upon inquiry in any local parish office, although the
Inventaire Sommaire des Archives Paroissiales, located with
the Head, Moving Images and Sound Section, PAM, is very useful
for French-speaking parishes.

The selective lists of descriptives which follow have been
arbitrarily divided into three subclassifications:
"Archdiocesan and Diocesan"; "Religious Orders"; and "General"
which incorporates all data not easily included in the other
groupings.

A.   Roman Catholic Church.   Archdiocesan Records

1111. ROMAN CATHOLIC CHURCH.   ARCHDIOCESAN AND DIOCESAN
      RECORDS, ARCHDIOCESE OF ST. BONIFACE
            (a) Administrative records (French).
            Unless otherwise noted, available at the
            Archdiocese of St. Boniface Archives, 115 rue de la
            Cathédrale, St. Boniface,
            Manitoba.   A St-B

            Mission correspondence; priests' correspondence;
            reports of spiritual growth and activity throughout
            the diocese.

      223

(b) Parish registers and ordinance records
(primarily in French).
Unless otherwise noted, available at the
Archdiocese of the St. Boniface Archives, 151 rue
de la Cathédrale, St. Boniface, Manitoba, R2H
0H6.   A St-B

Listing of earliest known vital statistics in early
Manitoba and Northwest Territories, 1818-70, giving
baptisms, marriages, deaths and populations SBHSA,
Box 40); prenuptual and marriage records including
correspondence, authorizations, consent forms, and
marriage registers, 1901-75; baptism registers,
1833-1927; confirmation registers for St. Boniface,
1881-1957; selected parish records; statistical
study of the Diocese, 1937.

(c) Statistical, resource and miscellaneous
historical materials. Unless otherwise noted,
available at the Archdiocese of St. Boniface
Archives, 115 rue de la Cathédrale, St. Boniface,
Manitoba.

                     A St-B

Reports and correspondence from the various
parishes; statistics, 1944-72, on baptisms,
confirmation, marriages and deaths; statistical
studies on essential aspects of most parishes in
the Archdiocese; photographs, 1935; several folders
of general church business, 1891-1958; temperance
activities.

1112. ROMAN CATHOLIC CHURCH. ARCHDIOCESAN AND DIOCESAN
RECORDS, ARCHDIOCESE OF WINNIPEG

        (a) Administrative records, 1916-76 Unless
        otherwise noted, available at the Archdiocese of
        Winnipeg Chancery Archives, 50 Stafford Street,
        Winnipeg, Manitoba, R3M 2V7. AWC

        Pastoral and circular letters by Reverend A.A.
        Sennott, 1916-29; parish annual reports, 1970-76;
        marriage applications, 1977-79.

        (b) Statistical, resource and miscellaneous
        historical materials, 1895-1977. Unless otherwise
        noted, available at the Archdiocese of Winnipeg
        Chancery Archives, 50 Stafford Street, Winnipeg,
        Manitoba, R3M 2V7.

        Correspondence; "Save the Children" Diocesan
        Bazaar, 1921; reports and statistics on various
        parishes, 1915-24; annual report of St. Edward's
        parish, 1916-17; reports, Archbishop circulars,

224

sisters' reports, and questionnaires of various religious vocational schools, 1934-36; data on several estate investments, 1938-78; foreign missions folder, 1931-38; correspondence regarding various Indian missions and the Oblate Fathers; correspondence regarding marriages in various parishes, 1895-1965; photographs; printed sources including anniversary booklets, the <u>North-West Review</u>, 1855-1948, <u>The Manitoba Ensign</u>, 1953-76, and other imprints.

(c) Parish registers and ordinance records. Unless otherwise noted, available at the Archdiocese of Winnipeg Chancery Archives, 50 Stafford Street, Winnipeg, Manitoba, R3M 2V7.

Parish registers of St. Laurent Missions, 1864-83, St. Adelard, St. Cecilia of Inwood, Manitoba, St. John Vianniy of Teulon, Christ the King of Stonewall, Manitoba, and the Immaculate Conception, 1891-1915; marriage records, including descriptions and revalidations, 1916-82; dispensations for mixed religion marriages, 1950-72; mixed religion and consanguinity marriage files, 1930-46.

B. Roman Catholic Church.   Records of Religious Orders

1113. ROMAN CATHOLIC CHURCH.   RELIGIOUS ORDERS
       Confessions, ordinary and extraordinary for
       religious communities, 1920-36.
       1 folder.   AWC

1114. ROMAN CATHOLIC CHURCH.   RELIGIOUS ORDERS.
       CONGREGATION DE LA STE-VIERGE
       3 folders, 1949-71 (French).   A St-B (Drawer #26)

1115. ROMAN CATHOLIC CHURCH.   RELIGIOUS ORDERS.
       CONGREGATION DE NOTRE DAME DE CHARITE DU BON
       PASTEUR
       1 folder, 1906-1911 (French). A St-B
                                     (L26155-26165)

1116. ROMAN CATHOLIC CHURCH.   RELIGIOUS ORDERS.
       CONGREGATION DES ENFANTS DE MARIE
       1 folder, 1949-1951 (French). A St-B (Folder #27)

1117. ROMAN CATHOLIC CHURCH. RELIGIOUS ORDERS. FIDELES
COMPAGNES DE JESUS
Selected materials
3 folders, 1901.   A St-B
(L27262-27352)

1118. ROMAN CATHOLIC CHURCH. RELIGIOUS ORDERS. FILLES DE LA
CROIX
(a) Operating files.
Located at 66 Moore Street, Winnipeg, Manitoba, R2M
2C4.

Founded in 1805 in France, the Order came to
Manitoba in 1904, having temporarily the care of
the Archbishop's Palace and the sacristy of the St.
Boniface cathedral as their responsibility. Later
they taught schools in St. Adolphe, St. Malo, Fort
Alexander and Sandy Bay, among other places.

(b) Unpublished articles and newsclippings. SBHS
(Box 59) (c) Various historical files.
13 folders, 1905-1914.   A St-B (L27353-27585
and L29087-29145)

1119. ROMAN CATHOLIC CHURCH. RELIGIOUS ORDERS. FILLES DE
JESUS CONGREGATION
Selected materials.
1 folder, 1902-03.   A St-B
(L26136-26154)

1120. ROMAN CATHOLIC CHURCH. RELIGIOUS ORDERS.
FRANCISCAINES MISSIONNAIRES DE MARIE
Operating and archival files.
Located at 311 boul. Provencher, St. Boniface,
Manitoba, R2H 0G8.

Founded in 1877 in India, this Order sent their
first sisters to Manitoba in 1897 to teach at St.
Laurent and to engage in charitable work. They
were especially active among the Ruthenians of
Winnipeg.

1121. ROMAN CATHOLIC CHURCH. RELIGIOUS ORDERS. GREY NUNS
(SOEURS GRISES DE MONTREAL)
(a) Operating files and archival records.
Located at Provincial House, 151 rue Despins, St.
Boniface, Manitoba, R2M 0L7. GNPHA

The Order was founded 1738 in Montreal by the widow
Marguerite d'Youville with the object of providing

a refuge for the aged and infirm, for education and
for care of the sick. At the time of the founding,
Madame d'Youville's uncle La Verendrye erected Fort
Rouge at the forks of the Red and Assiniboine
rivers, and it was to this new settlement that four
nuns came in 1844 at the invitation of Bishop
Provencher.

Letters; diaries; yearly <u>Annual</u> biographical
materials on all sisters who ever served the Order
in Manitoba; photographs; scrapbooks; reports;
artifacts; relics; operating files of the Order's
various institutions including the following:
St. Boniface General Hospital; the General Hospital
(Ste. Rose, Manitoba); Tache Nursing Centre; St.
Boniface Home; St. Amant Centre; The Valade Vitae
Service; Sara Riel Inc.; Youville Foundation Inc.;
Centre Laurent.

(b) Selected biographical   SBHSA (Box
                                 6,19,26,73)

Letters and typewritten historical sketches on
Sister Marguerite (the first Grey Nun novice in the
West), Sister Mary Curran, Sister Marie-Josephine
Nebraska, Sister Mary Murphy, and Sister Valade,
the first superior of the Grey Nuns at Red River.

(c) Sisters of Charity
Papers, 1741-1941. Finding aid.
Microfilm 5 reels.   PAM (MG7 D2)

Letters; notes; journals. (See also AWC for
original files.)

(d) Selected materials (Soeurs Grises)
5 folders, 1843-1905   A St-B

Correspondence, 1843-78; constitutions; land
records; records from Lorette, Manitoba, and St.
Vital, Manitoba.

1122. ROMAN CATHOLIC CHURCH.   OBLATE MISSIONARIES OF MARY
      IMMACULATE
           (a) Operating files.
           Located at 601 rue Aulneau, St. Boniface, Manitoba,
           R2H 2V5.

           Founded in 1904 in St. Boniface by Bishop Langevin.
           Films; assorted footage.

(b) Selected materials,
1925-37.   AWC

Correspondence; newsclippings.

1123. ROMAN CATHOLIC CHURCH. RELIGIOUS ORDERS. OBLATE
SISTERS OF THE SACRED HEART AND MARY IMMACULATE
    (a) Correspondence, 1917-72.
    7 folders.   AWC

    Correspondence with Mother House, 1927-71; St.
    Charles Convent, 1917-36; Dunrea, 1925-79;
    Camperville, 1936-64; Cayer, 1953-77; Duck Bay,
    1953; Pelican Rapids, 1957-72.

    (b) Selected materials.
    11 folders, 1902-49.   A St-B (Drawer 28
                                   and 28745-28899
    School records of Ecole Notre-Dame; photographs;
    reports.

1124. ROMAN CATHOLIC CHURCH. RELIGIOUS ORDERS. PETITE
MISSIONAIRE D'OTTERBURNE
    Selected materials, 1924-38.
    1 folder.   A St-B (Drawer #25)

1125. ROMAN CATHOLIC CHURCH. RELIGIOUS ORDERS. PETIT
MISSIONAIRE ST. JOSEPH
    Selected materials, 1959.
    1 folder   A St-B (Drawer #25)

1126. ROMAN CATHOLIC CHURCH. RELIGIOUS ORDERS. RELIGIEUSE
NOTRE-DAME DES MISSIONS
    Papers, 1901-15.
    13 folders.   A St-B (L28522-28744)

1127. ROMAN CATHOLIC CHURCH. RELIGIOUS ORDERS. RELIGIOUS OF
THE SACRED HEART
    Selected materials, 1924-74.
    1 folder.   AWC

    Correspondence; clippings; confidential report.

1128. ROMAN CATHOLIC CHURCH. RELIGIOUS ORDERS. SISTERS
ADORERS OF THE PRECIOUS BLOOD
    Selected materials, 1929-72.
    Restricted.   AWC

Index; Monastery of the Precious Blood, 1929-70;
Precious Blood Men's Auxiliary, 1930-72.

1129. ROMAN CATHOLIC CHURCH. RELIGIOUS ORDERS. SISTERS
FRANCISCAN OF MARY-MISSIONARIES
(a) Selected materials,
1896-1940.   AWC

Index; correspondence from Maison Notre Dame de la
Miséricorde, St. Laurent, 1896-1940; Camperville,
correspondence, 1911-21.

(b) Other materials.
1 folder, 1912-14.   A St-B (L26166-26186)

1130. ROMAN CATHOLIC CHURCH. RELIGIOUS ORDERS. SISTERS OF
CHARITY (SISTERS OF OUR LADY OF CHARITY OF THE GOOD
SHEPHERD)
Operating files.
Located at St. Joseph's Convent, 491 College
Avenue, Winnipeg, Manitoba, R2W 1M7.

Founded 1651 by Blessed John Eudes, the Order was
given new impetus in 1835. Both contemplative and
active, its work is "one of reformation and
protection, effected by means of thorough religious
and moral training." St. Agnes Priory School,
opened in 1925 as an orphanage, remains as one of
its primary concerns, although both its name and
emphasis have changed.

1131. ROMAN CATHOLIC CHURCH. RELIGIOUS ORDERS. SISTERS OF
CHARITY HALIFAX
Correspondence, 1929-72.
2 folders.   AWC

Microfilm material by Swan River Hospital, 1931;
correspondence between Msgr. Sinnott and Mother
House, 1929-72.

1132. ROMAN CATHOLIC CHURCH. RELIGIOUS ORDERS. SISTERS OF
CHARITY OF THE IMMACULATE CONCEPTION
Correspondence, 1919-35.   AWC

1133. ROMAN CATHOLIC CHURCH. RELIGIOUS ORDERS. SISTERS OF
MISERICORDE
(a) Selected materials, 1915-76.
4 folders.   AWC

229

Founded 1848 at Montreal and invited to Manitoba by
Bishop Langevin in 1847 for hospital work. Their
first home of 1898 eventually expanded into the
present Misericordia Hospital. Index; Misericordia
Hospital financial statements; correspondence.

(b) Other materials
8 folders.   A St-B
                                   (L26262-26412)

1134. ROMAN CATHOLIC CHURCH. RELIGIOUS ORDERS. SISTERS OF
    OUR LADY OF CHARITY OF THE GOOD SHEPHERD
         Papers, 1911-72.   AWC

    Monastery of the Good Shepherd, 1916-72;
    correspondence with Mother House, 1925-40;
    correspondence and documents from St. Boniface,
    1911-14.

1135. ROMAN CATHOLIC CHURCH. RELIGIOUS ORDERS. SISTERS OF
    OUR LADY OF THE MISSIONS
         (a) Operating files. Restricted.
    Located at St. Edwards Convent, 800 Adele Avenue,
    Winnipeg, Manitoba, R3E 0K6.

    Founded in Lyon, France, in 1861, especially for
    educational work in foreign missions, the Sisters
    first arrived in Manitoba in 1898 and 1899 to teach
    at Grande Clairière where they combined the active
    life with the contemplative in semi-cloister. At
    present they have four schools and convents in the
    province, with the Provincial Superior resident at
    St. Edward's Convent.

    Attestations; biographical files on each of the
    Sisters of the Order giving birth dates and places,
    parents, confirmation, date of entrance to the
    Order, education, and related background
    information data; blueprints of many houses; "Book
    of First Vows" containing the vows made by
    individuals entering the Order; "Book of Perpetual
    Vows" (containing final vows and dates); "Book of
    Renovation of Vows"; chapter minutes, 1913-78;
    constitutions; financial records, 1902-   ;
    Biography of the Boundaries, 1902-75; historical
    and miscellaneous papers from various Houses;
    history of the vicars and provincials, 1902-80;
    minutes of meetings, 1902 to present; minutes of
    the, province and of local houses, 1899-   ;
    canonical visitations, 1920-   ; noviate journals
    (handwritten day-to-day records of convent life,
    1919-70s; "Registre des Postulantes"; oral

histories with older sisters; personnel lists;
programmes and printed materials; scrapbooks,
clippings; files and photographs; typed case
history of exorcism by Gabrielle Chaput; liturgy
and prayers.

(b) Selected materials.
Unpublished paper.   SBHSA (Box 73)

"The Sisters of Our Lady of the Missions," by
Antoine Lussier. Background data on the Ste.
Rose-du-Lac, Brandon, St. Eustache, Letellier,
Elie, St. Joseph and Winnipeg convents.

(c) Correspondence and dispensations from vows.
10 folders.   AWC

Correspondence from St. Michael's Academy of
Brandon, 1917-78, Ste. Rose du Lac Convent,
1919-71; St. Edward's Convent of Winnipeg, 1920-79,
Portage la Prairie Convent, 1920-34, Grande
Clairière, 1921-36, St. Eustache Convent, 1922-79;
and Elie Convent, 1937-66.

1136. ROMAN CATHOLIC CHURCH. RELIGIOUS ORDERS. SISTERS OF
PROVIDENCE OF KINGSTON
    Selected materials.
    1 folder.   AWC

Correspondence of Archbishop Sinnott with Mother
Superior: invitation to establish in Winnipeg,
1922-75; revision of Constitution; correspondence
with first postulant; request to take Brandon
hospital and refusal of Sisters, 1934; transfer of
St. Joseph's Orphanage to Sisters, 1937.

1137. ROMAN CATHOLIC CHURCH. RELIGIOUS ORDERS. SISTERS OF
SERVICE
    (a) Operating files. Restricted.
    Located at The Convent, Camp Morton, Manitoba, R0C
    0N0.

Founded in 1922 in Toronto primarily to serve
immigrants, the Order also was concerned with the
protection of single girls away from home. In
Manitoba they were also in charge of several
schools in the Camp Morton area.

(b) Selected materials.
3 folders.   AWC

CWL Hostel financial statement, correspondence;
Mother House correspondence, 1922-38; Camp Morton
Convent, letters marked confidential, 1925-39.

1138. ROMAN CATHOLIC CHURCH. RELIGIOUS ORDERS. SISTERS OF
ST. BENEDICT
Operating files. Uncatalogued. Restricted.
Located at St. Benedict's Priory, 225 Masters
Avenue, Winnipeg, Manitoba, R3C 4A3, and at 13
Coral Crescent, St. Boniface, Manitoba, R2J 1V6.

The Benedictine Sisters arrived in Winnipeg from
Duluth, Minnesota, in 1903, especially to teach
children of Polish immigrants. When the Mother
House wished to withdraw them in 1912, Bishop
Langevin instituted an indigenous Benedictine
Community which these Sisters joined, and in which
they continued to serve in education, nursing, and
the care of orphans.

1139. ROMAN CATHOLIC CHURCH. RELIGIOUS ORDERS. SISTERS OF
ST. JOSEPH OF ST. HYACINTHE
(a) Selected materials, 1918-36.
2 folders.   AWC

Correspondence; Indian Boarding School at Sandy
Bay.

(b) Other materials, 1901-15.
8 folders.   A St-B (L26583-26751)

(c) Historical notes and
pamphlets.   SBHSA (Box 73)

1140. ROMAN CATHOLIC CHURCH. RELIGIOUS ORDERS. SISTERS OF
ST. JOSEPH D'OTTERBURNE
Selected materials, 1954-79. A St-B (Drawer #25)

1141. ROMAN CATHOLIC CHURCH. RELIGIOUS ORDERS. SISTERS OF
ST. JOSEPH OF TORONTO
Selected materials, 1922-73.
5 folders.   AWC

Correspondence; reports concerning St. Joseph's
Hospital, Salter and Pritchard Street, Winnipeg,
1922-73; St. Mary's Convent, Sifton, 1929-34.

1142. ROMAN CATHOLIC CHURCH. RELIGIOUS ORDERS. SISTERS OF
THE GOOD SHEPHERD (SISTERS OF OUR LADY OF CHARITY OF THE
GOOD SHEPHERD OR GOOD SHEPHERD SISTERS)
Operating files, 1911-   .
Located at 442 Scotia Street, Winnipeg, Manitoba,
R2V 1X4.

Founded in France in 1641 by St. John Eudes, the
Order has branches throughout the world whose
present apostolates are treatment centres for
emotionally disturbed girls, probation work,
special education, counselling, child care and
social work. The Sisters came to Manitoba in 1911
at the request of Judge Daly, founder of the
Juvenile Court, to establish St. Agnes Priory and
Marymound Schools.

Because the Congregation embraces two societies,
the contemplation and the apostolic, the Tourrière
Sisters attended to public duties such as shopping
and funerals, until about 1940; the lay sisters,
who did not recite Divine Office, worked in the
kitchen and did the housekeeping while the Lady
Helpers of the Good Shepherd, first mentioned in
1912, were secular women who helped with public
duties forbidden to the cloistered nuns and with
financial support. The Canadian Mother House is at
3650 Wells Street, Windsor, Ontario, N9C 1T9.

Annual reports and minutes from 1911 to present;
Book of Vows, Renewal of Vows; Scrapbook; "Archives
of the Convent"; photographs; historical sketches
of new beginning; documents; clippings files;
convent annuals, 1911 to present (a record of daily
life in the convent); printed brochures,
information literature.

1143. ROMAN CATHOLIC CHURCH. RELIGIOUS ORDERS. SISTERS OF
THE IMMACULATE CONCEPTION (RUTHENIAN)
Correspondence, 1921.
1 folder.   AWC

1144. ROMAN CATHOLIC CHURCH. RELIGIOUS ORDERS. SISTERS OF
THE PRECIOUS BLOOD
Operating files. Restricted.
Located at 3507 Vialoux Drive, Winnipeg, Manitoba,
R3R 0A5.

An English-speaking branch of the Adoratrices du
Precieux-Sang.

1145. ROMAN CATHOLIC CHURCH. RELIGIOUS ORDERS. SISTERS OF
THE CROSS OF ST. ANDREW
Correspondence, 1922-33.   AWC

233

1146. ROMAN CATHOLIC CHURCH. RELIGIOUS ORDERS. SISTERS OF
THE HOLY NAME OF JESUS AND MARY
Selected materials.
6 folders, 1912-77.   AWC

Canonical visitations; correspondence; list of
obediences; final profession ceremony, final
profession vows; clippings. (Personal papers of
Sister Geraldine MacNamara, founder of Rossbrook
House, in possession of the Order.)

1147. ROMAN CATHOLIC CHURCH. RELIGIOUS ORDERS. SISTERS OF
THE ORDER OF ST. BENEDICT
Selected materials, 1916-71.
1 folder.   AWC

General correspondence; investments.

1148. ROMAN CATHOLIC CHURCH. RELIGIOUS ORDERS. SISTERS OF
THE PRECIOUS BLOOD CORPORATION OF WINNIPEG
Promises of payment, 1941-47. AWC

1149. ROMAN CATHOLIC CHURCH. RELIGIOUS ORDERS. SOEURS
CARMELITES
Selected materials, 1908-15. A St-B
                             (L26210-26239)

1150. SOEURS DE DULUTH
Scattered materials.   AWC

Brochures; correspondence.

1151. ROMAN CATHOLIC CHURCH. RELIGIOUS ORDERS. SOEURS
DOMINICAINES DE L'ENFANT-JESUS
Selected materials, 1910-15.
3 folders.   A St-B
                             (L27638-27675)

1152. ROMAN CATHOLIC CHURCH. RELIGIOUS ORDERS. SOEURS
FILLES DE MARIE DE LA PRESENCE DE BROONS
Selected materials.
2 folders; 1902-03.   A St-B
                             (L27586-27637)

1153. ROMAN CATHOLIC CHURCH. RELIGIOUS ORDERS.
MISSIONAIRES DE MARIE
Selected materials.
2 folders, 1901-13.   A St-B
                             (L26539-26582)

1154. ROMAN CATHOLIC CHURCH. RELIGIOUS ORDERS. SOEURS DE
LA CHARITE DE LA PROVENCE
Selected materials.
4 folders, 1905-12.   A St-B
(L26457-26500)

1155. ROMAN CATHOLIC CHURCH. RELIGIOUS ORDERS. SOEURS DE
LA CONGREGATION
10 pamphlets of their centenary, (1877-1977).
A St-B

1156. ROMAN CATHOLIC CHURCH. RELIGIOUS ORDERS. SOEURS DE
NOTRE DAME DE LA CROIX MURINAIS
3 folders, 1905-11.   A St-B
(L26413-26456)

1157. ROMAN CATHOLIC CHURCH. RELIGIOUS ORDERS. SOEURS DE
LA PRESENTATION DE LA BONNE VIERGE-MARIE
Selected materials.
1 folder; 1906-14.   A St-B
(L26515-26538)

1158. ROMAN CATHOLIC CHURCH. RELIGIOUS ORDERS. SOEURS DE
LA SAINTE-FAMILLE
Selected materials.
2 folders, 1911-12.   A St-B
(L26240-26261)

1159. ROMAN CATHOLIC CHURCH. RELIGIOUS ORDERS. SOEURS DES
SAINTS NOMS JESUS ET MARIE
(a) Operating files. Restricted.
Located at 321 ave. de la Cathédrale, St. Boniface,
Manitoba, R2H 0J3.

The order of the Soeurs des Saints Noms de Jésus et
de Marie (Sisters of the Holy Names) was founded
1843, and came to Manitoba in 1874. The archives
contains material relating to the order and its
work in Canada, the U.S.A., Lesotho, Brazil, Peru
and Haiti. Most of the collection relates to
Manitoba and, especially, to the administration of
schools and convents. Cash-books; correspondence;
tape recordings; photographs; the book of entrants
dating from 1844; nomination books (1895 to the
school inspectors' reports, 1911-16; and lists of
pupils, by school, dating from 1883.

(b) Selected materials.   A St-B
9 folders, 1901-74.   (L28363-28521535
and L59513-79)

235

Reports; centennial celebration materials,
histories.

(c) Other materials.
Partial box.   SBHSA (Box 73)

Newsclippings; speeches and addresses; histories;
data on St. Joseph Collegiate Institute; St.
Mary's Academy, St. Mary's College, St. Joseph's
Collegiate, Holy Cross School, Immaculate
Conception School and St. Mary's School.

1160. ROMAN CATHOLIC CHURCH. RELIGIOUS ORDERS. SOEURS DU
      SAUVEUR
            Selected materials.
            30 folders, 1902- .

            Rules and regulations;
            services.   A St-B(L26752-27261)

1161. ROMAN CATHOLIC CHURCH. RELIGIOUS ORDERS. URSULINE
      SISTERS (SOEURS URSULINES)
            (a) Operating files.
            Located at Our Lady of Victory Convent, 227 Arnold
            Avenue, Winnipeg, Manitoba, R3L 0W4.

            In 1912 four Ursulines from different convents but
            all of German origin came to Manitoba to take
            charge of St. Joseph's parish school. The Order
            has remained active in education.

            (b) Correspondence, 1919-38.
            2 folders.   AWC

            (c) Selected materials.
            1 folder, 1901-14.   A St-B
                                      (L28900-28915)
                                      and SBHS (Box 23)

1162. ROMAN CATHOLIC CHURCH. RELIGIOUS ORDERS. URSULINE
      SISTERS OF TILDONK
            (a) Operating files.
            Contact: Provincial Superior, 44 River Road,
            Winnipeg, Manitoba, R2M 3Z2.

            Founded in Belgium in 1831, the Urselines arrived
            in Bruxelles, Manitoba, in 1914 to establish a
            school and later a convent in St. Alphonse.

      236

(b) Constitution.   A St-B

C. Roman Catholic Church. General Records

(Most records in this "General" category are specific
churches, church-related or church-sponsored auxiliaries and
associations, and of particular individual.)

1163. ROMAN CATHOLIC CHURCH. GENERAL. ASSOCIATION
      CATHOLIQUE DES HOPITAUX CANADIENS
            Selected materials, 1938-71.
            1 folder.   A St-B (Drawer 24)

1164. ROMAN CATHOLIC CHURCH. GENERAL. BELCOURT, GEORGES
      ANTOINE
            Correspondence.
            9".   SBHSA (Boxes 1 and 2)

            A 1858 letter referring to Soeur Saint
            François-Xavier and Les Soeurs de la Propagation de
            la Foi; correspondence concerning the Grey Nuns;
            letter about Mary Fairclough, 1969; information on
            the Sisters of the Propogation of the Faith.

1165. ROMAN CATHOLIC CHURCH. GENERAL. BLESSED SACRAMENT
      ROMAN CATHOLIC CHURCH
            Operating files.
            Located at 710 Roanoke Street, Transcona, Winnipeg,
            Manitoba.

            Baptismal, first communion, confirmation, marriage
            and funeral records, 1960-   ; Blessed Sacrament
            School records, 1958-78; "Search for Christian
            Maturity," Catholic Youth Education Organization
            correspondence and financial records, 1976-   .

1166. ROMAN CATHOLIC CHURCH. GENERAL. CARIGNAN,
      FRANCOISE-JEANNE
            Selected materials.   PAM (MG9 B3)

            Materials on the La Congrégation des Soeurs des
            Saint-Noms des Jésus et de Marie.

1167. ROMAN CATHOLIC CHURCH. GENERAL. CATHOLIC DAUGHTERS OF
      AMERICA
            Scattered material, 1926-77. AWC

237

1168. ROMAN CATHOLIC CHURCH.   GENERAL.   CATHOLIC IMMIGRATION
AID OF WESTERN CANADA
     1 folder, 1951-74.   AWC

1169. ROMAN CATHOLIC CHURCH.   GENERAL.   CATHOLIC WOMEN'S
LEAGUE OF CANADA LTD.
     (a) Operating files, 1920-   .
     Located at 3081 Ness Avenue, Saint
     James-Assiniboia, Winnipeg, Manitoba, R2Y 2G3.

     The League had its beginnings in 1920 as an
     organization to unite Canadian Catholic women on
     the national, provincial, diocesan and parish
     levels. Its aims were to support "a constructive
     programme of spirituality, press activity,
     legislative study and vigilance" by promoting
     education, study and discussion groups,
     scholarships, sponsoring child and social welfare,
     and many other activities. The League came to
     Manitoba shortly after its inception.

     (b) Selected materials, 1943-71 (French).
     1 folder.   A St-B (Drawer 26)

     Correspondence; constitution.

     (c) Other materials, 1917-76.
     1 folder.   AWC

1170. ROMAN CATHOLIC CHURCH.   GENERAL.   CONVERSIONS AU
CATHOLICISME
     Listings.   A St-B

     Formule d'abjuration, 1952.

1171. ROMAN CATHOLIC CHURCH.   GENERAL.   DAMES DE HOLY CROSS
STE-ANNE
     Questionnaire, 1950.
     1 folder.   A St-B (Drawer 26)

1172. ROMAN CATHOLIC CHURCH.   GENERAL.   DAMES DE STE-ANNE:
LA BROQUERIE PAROISSE
     Selected materials, 1936-77. A St-B (Drawer 26)

     Members, 1936-77; financial records, 1937-67;
     historical brochure, 1936-77.

1173. ROMAN CATHOLIC CHURCH.   GENERAL.   DAMES DE STE-ANNE
(PAROISSIALE)
     Operating files (French).

Contact: Mme Alma Perreault, Ste-Anne, Manitoba,
R0A 7R0.

Minutes of the Congregation des Dames de Ste-Anne,
Manitoba, 1969, 1960-78; account books, 1965-73;
1968-78; Members of the Ligue des Femmes
Catholiques, 1976-79; principal activities,
1969-78; reports; minutes of reunions.

1174. ROMAN CATHOLIC CHURCH.   GENERAL.   ENFANTS DE MARIE
Selected materials, 1957.   A St-B (Drawer 26)
1 folder.

Parish history; brochures; manuals.

1175. ROMAN CATHOLIC CHURCH.   GENERAL.   GUIDES CATHOLIQUES
DU CANADA
(a) Operating files (French).
Located at 466 1/2 rue Aulneau, St. Boniface,
Manitoba, R2H 2V2.

Membership lists from approximately 25 parishes and
churches throughout Manitoba; pledges; membership
requirements; papers from local chapters and
churches; applications and nominations; printed
Guide materials; constitutions; administration
records, 1973-80; financial records;
correspondence; working papers.

(b) Selected materials, 1953 (French).
1 folder.   A St-B (Drawer 26)

Correspondence; brochures; clippings.

1176. ROMAN CATHOLIC CHURCH.   GENERAL.   HOLY CROSS ROMAN
CATHOLIC CHURCH
Operating files.   Restricted.
Located at 252 Dubuc Street, St. Boniface,
Manitoba.

Church registers, 1921-   ; 50th Anniversary
Booklet, 1972; Parish Diary, 1942-49; (became
scrapbook, 1949-77); Holy Cross Parishioner (weekly
bulletin), 1946-72; Catholic Women's League
minutes, 1950-72; Sodality of the Children of Mary
minutes, 1948-49; Catholic Women's League scrapbook
of clippings, 1946-71; 1958-73; records,
photographs, school board minutes of Holy Cross
Parochial School; Parish registers of St. John
Fisher Roman Catholic Chaplaincy, 1956-76.

1177. ROMAN CATHOLIC CHURCH. GENERAL. IMMACULATE
CONCEPTION ROMAN CATHOLIC CHURCH
Operating files. Restricted.
Located 181 Austin Street North, Winnipeg,
Manitoba, R2W 3M7.

Built in 1883, the church was destroyed by fire in
1978. Many documents were lost, but plans for the
new building include specific space for a church
archives. Immaculate Conception School was served
by the Sisters of the Holy Names of Jesus and Mary
until its closing. Its records are located at 231,
ave. de la Cathédrale, St. Boniface, R2H 3C6.
Since 1978 the church has become the parish of the
Portuguese community in Winnipeg, with present
archival material still on the premises. Contact
parish office for details of women's activities.

1178. ROMAN CATHOLIC CHURCH. GENERAL. LA BROQUERIE PARISH
Operating files, (French).   Restricted
Located at La Broquerie, Manitoba, R0A 0W0.

Parish bulletins, 1964-77; Registers to baptisms,
marriages and deaths, 1884-1983; Grey Nuns,
1884-1912; register of families, 1883-1959.

1179. ROMAN CATHOLIC CHURCH. GENERAL. POLISH NATIONAL
CATHOLIC CHURCH OF ST. MARY
Church records (in Polish until 1940).
Available at 361 Burrows Avenue, Winnipeg, R2W 1Z9.

Baptisms; marriages; funerals; files of the Maria
Kopnopnicka Association.

1180. ROMAN CATHOLIC CHURCH. GENERAL. PRENOVAULT, SOEUR.
Video. Colour.
1 item.   CBWFT CSB

1181. ROMAN CATHOLIC CHURCH. GENERAL. PROVENCHER,
JOSEPH-NORBERT (MSGR)
Correspondence, 1851-73.
Several items. Typewritten. SBHSA (Box 22)

Package of letters with frequent mentions of the
Grey Nuns at the Red River Settlement; historical
newsclippings on the 1844 coming of the Grey Nuns.

1182. ROMAN CATHOLIC CHURCH. GENERAL. ST. FRANCIS DE SALES
CATHOLIC CHURCH OF THE DEAF
Operating files.

Located at 329-285 Pembina Highway, Winnipeg,
Manitoba, R3L 2E1.

1183. ROMAN CATHOLIC CHURCH, GENERAL. STE-ANNE PARISH
Operating files, 1898-1967 (French).
Located at Ste. Anne, Manitoba, R0A 1R0.

Membership lists; minutes; history; women's
auxiliaries.

1184. ROMAN CATHOLIC CHURCH, GENERAL. ST. CHARLES ROMAN
CATHOLIC CHURCH
Census book, 1904-12.
Located at 310 St. Charles Street, Winnipeg,
Manitoba, R3K 1V2.

Annual censuses.

1185. ROMAN CATHOLIC CHURCH. GENERAL. ST. EDWARD'S ROMAN
CATHOLIC CHURCH RECTORY
Operating files, 1908-77.
Located at 818 Arlington Street, Winnipeg, R3E 2E2.

Catholic Women's League minutes and correspondence,
1964-77; baptism and marriage records from 1908;
first communion and confirmation from 1914;
photographs; records of St. Edward's School. The
church has a large Filipino congregation.

1186. ROMAN CATHOLIC CHURCH. GENERAL. ST. MARY'S ROMAN
CATHOLIC CATHEDRAL
Church, registers, 1876.
353 St. Mary Ave., Winnipeg.

Registers of baptisms, first communions,
confirmations, marriages and funerals.

1187. ROMAN CATHOLIC CHURCH. GENERAL. SOCIETE ST-ADELARD
Selected materials.
0.3".   SBHSA (Box 73)

Founded in 1905 by Archbishop Langevin, its goals
were to: (1) administer dependents, allowances for
wives and children of men in service; (2) care for
children neglected by carelessness or misfortune of
parents; (3) find support for, assume guardianship
or set up adoption for illegitimate children; (4)
supervise overseas children during the war.
Correspondence; mission statements; reports.

1188. ROMAN CATHOLIC CHURCH. GENERAL. WESTERN CATHOLIC
CONFERENCE
Report, 1976.
1 item.   SBHSA (Box 75)

"Report of the Western Regional Committee on Women
in the Catholic Church," a study on attitudes of
Catholic Women on family life, decision-making,
education, and the ministry.

The Ukrainian Catholic Church

1189. UKRAINIAN CATHOLIC CHURCH. BLESSED VIRGIN MARY
UKRAINIAN CATHOLIC PARISH
Operating files. Church records, 1925-
(Ukrainian).
Located at 969 Boyd Avenue, Winnipeg, Manitoba, R2X
0Z9.

Minutes; reports; financial records; membership
lists of both the church and the Women's League.

1190. UKRAINIAN CATHOLIC CHURCH. ST. IVANS UKRAINIAN
ORTHODOX CATHEDRAL: LADIES SOCIETY OF OLGA
KOBYLANSKY
Operating files. Restricted.
Located at 939 Main Street, Winnipeg, Manitoba, R2W
3P2.

Historical files.

1191. UKRAINIAN CATHOLIC CHURCH. SISTERS SERVANTS OF MARY
IMMACULATE
Operating files.
Located at 131 Aberdeen and 600 Cathedral Avenue,
Winnipeg, Manitoba, R2W 0Y5.

A Ukrainian order devoted to instructing children,
the care of the sick, and other charitable duties,
these sisters came to Winnipeg from the western
Ukraine in 1905. They are presently attached to
the archdiocese of Winnipeg, and are in charge of
the Immaculate Heart of Mary School in Winnipeg, as
well as the Holy Family Nursing Home. Although
some records are kept locally, most documents of
historical value are sent to the Mother House in
Toronto.

242

1192. UKRAINIAN CATHOLIC CHURCH. UKRAINIAN CATHOLIC WOMEN'S
      LEAGUE
        Operating files for the regional and provincial
        levels.
        Located at 418 Aberdeen Street, Winnipeg, Manitoba,
        R2W 1V7.

        The League was organized formally in 1944 although
        individual parish women's groups existed long
        before this time. On the parish level each
        organization maintains its own records, to be found
        in the possession of the elected executive.

The United Church of Canada

(The United Church of Canada, Manitoba and Northwest Ontario
Conference)

The union of the Congregational, Methodist, and most
Presbyterian churches in Canada in 1925 resulted in the
formation of the United Church of Canada, all the founding
denominations in Manitoba having their own women's
organizations already in place.

The Women's Foreign Missionary Society (WFMS) of the
Presbyterian Church in Canada was organized in Winnipeg in
1884. The Portage la Prairie Presbyterian women banded
together as the Women's Indian Missionary society, and joined
the new group in 1886. From this time on, expansion
throughout the province proceeded with some rapidity both in
rural and urban areas. The Woman's Home Missionary society
(WHMS), also Presbyterian, came to Manitoba in 1903, forming a
presbyterial in Winnipeg by 1908. Only in the Dauphin
presbyterial (1913) were all auxiliaries member jointly of the
WFMS and the WHMS, but when the two societies amalgamated
nationally in 1914, the provincial councils quickly followed
suit to form the Women's Missionary Society, Presbyterian
Church in Canada (WMS).

The Women's Missionary Society of the Methodist Church
originated in Hamilton, Ontario, in 1880. A Dominion Society
was formed the following year and the Manitoba branch in
Winnipeg was formed in 1885.

The Congregational Church, by far the smallest of the three
founding denominations in western Canada, organized the
Woman's Board of Missions nationally in 1885 and the Manitoba
auxiliary at Portage la Prairie in 1889.

A few holdings in the UCA-W collection relate to Union
Churches, members of various denominations (predominantly
Methodist and Presbyterian) who worshipped together because of
practical necessity if not always because of inclination.

    243

After union all these organizations amalgamated to form the Woman's Missionary Society of the United Church of Canada while continuing to use a variety of names locally (e.g., Ladies' Aid, Women's Guild). Most urban as well as many rural societies boasted several branches (usually at least one in the evening), which fostered various girls' clubs and children's groups, such as Mission Band, Explorers and Canadian Girls in Training (CGIT).

In 1950 the WMS officially became the Woman's Association (WA), and in 1962, in response to a re-examination of the work of women in the Church, it changed its name again to United Church Women (UCW).

The Manitoba and Northwest Ontario Conference, United Church of Canada, Archives in Winnipeg holds the records of these various organizations and of the old founding societies. There is an abundance of material, most of it organized by congregational charges, for those interested in pursuing this area of women's studies.

A. Congregational

1193. UNITED CHURCH OF CANADA. CONGREGATIONAL UNION OF CANADA. CENTRAL CONGREGATIONAL CHURCH OF WINNIPEG (1879-1939)
      Papers, 1879-1939. Finding aid.
      22".   PAM (MG7 G1)

      Ladies Aid Society, 1915-19; membership registers, 1879-1939; minute books, 1884-1928; financial records; miscellaneous papers including a request (resolution) in 1920 for increased representation on the Church Board.

1194. THE UNITED CHURCH OF CANADA. CONGREGATIONAL UNION OF CANADA. CANADA CONGREGATIONAL WOMEN'S BOARD OF MISSIONS (1890-1925)
      (a) Annual reports, 1890-1925.
      4".   UCA-W

      (b) Summary of the Women's Board of Missions.   UCA-W

1195. UNITED CHURCH OF CANADA. CONGREGATIONAL UNION OF CANADA. CRESCENT CONGREGATIONAL CHURCH
      Records of the women's associations, 1919- .
      Located at the Crescent-Fort Rouge United Church, N.E. Wardlaw and and Nassau N., Winnipeg, Manitoba.

B. Methodist

1196. UNITED CHURCH OF CANADA. METHODIST. BRANDON FIRST
      METHODIST CHURCH
            Film, 1918, b/w.
            16 mm (3"). Brandon Historical Society. 62
            Clement Drive, Brandon, Manitoba, R7B 0X2.

            Scenes of a Sunday school picnic hosted by the
            Brandon First Methodist Church.

1197. UNITED CHURCH OF CANADA. METHODIST. DEACONESS HOME
            Essay.
            3 pp.   UCA-W (Vertical file)

            Essay and photograph of Deaconess Home and the
            women involved.

1198. UNITED CHURCH OF CANADA. METHODIST. DEACONESS ORDER
            Papers, 1912-22.
            3".   UCA-W

            Annual Report of Deaconess Society of the Methodist
            Church, 1912-13; reports of each provincial
            conference, Manitoba, including photos of
            deaconess, deaconess home, projects, deaconess
            appointments, deaconess board of management, report
            of board, statistics, camp expenses, treasurer's
            statement, donors to Fresh Air Fund, and report of
            Deaconess Aid Society; the Deaconess Yearbook,
            1921-22; Treasurer's Book of Deaconess Board of
            Management, 1906-22; list of deaconesses for
            1908-22.

1199. UNITED CHURCH OF CANADA. METHODIST. KING EDWARD ST.
      METHODIST CHURCH
            Church records, 1908-   .
            Located at St. James United Church, Winnipeg.

            Includes women's auxiliary records, 1910-26.

1200. UNITED CHURCH OF CANADA. METHODIST. NINGA METHODIST
      CHURCH
            Minutes.   BCA (MG7 F1)

            Minutes of the Women's Auxiliary.

1201. UNITED CHURCH OF CANADA. METHODIST. WOMAN'S
      MISSIONARY SOCIETY
            Annual reports, 1899-1926.

      245

Original and printed.   UCA-W

Annual reports; financial reports.

C. Presbyterian

1202. UNITED CHURCH OF CANADA. PRESBYTERIAN. ANISHINABE
FELLOWSHIP
          Operating files.
          Located at 266 Ellen Street, Winnipeg, R3A 1A7.

          A mission of the Church designed to serve the
          native (Indian) population of Winnipeg.

1203. UNITED CHURCH OF CANADA. PRESBYTERIAN. ANDREW BAIRD
PAPERS
          Correspondence, 1889-1900. Finding aid.
          140 letters.   UCA-W

          Much information on the Women's Foreign Missionary
          Society with relevant references to such
          women-related topics as domestic work on missions,
          school curricula, finances, attitudes toward women
          missionaries, and women teachers, mistreatment of
          women, marriage of missionaries, child labour or
          missions, widow's fund, missions in the Northwest,
          and many more.

1204. UNITED CHURCH OF CANADA. PRESBYTERIAN. KILDONAN
PRESBYTERIAN CHURCH REGISTER
          Church records, 1851-1932.
          7 books.   PAM (MG7 C6 M35)

          Baptism, burial and other vital statistics records.

1205. UNITED CHURCH OF CANADA. PRESBYTERIAN. LITTLE
BRITAIN PREBYTERIAN CHURCH
          Minutes, 1863-1965.   PAM (MG7 C10)

          Ladies Aid minute book.

1206. UNITED CHURCH OF CANADA. PRESBYTERIAN MCCREARY
          Missionary activities, 1903. PAM (MG9 A39)

          Discussed by Dorothy B. Wilson.

246

1207. UNITED CHURCH OF CANADA. PRESBYTERIAN. NORWOOD
PRESBYTERIAN
  Church records, 1904-25.
  Located at the Norwood United Church.

  Include Ladies Aid minutes and records.

1208. UNITED CHURCH OF CANADA. PRESBYTERIAN. RIVERS
PRESBYTERIAN CHURCH
  See the J.E. Mitchell papers (PAM) for a concert
  programme.

1209. UNITED CHURCH OF CANADA. PRESBYTERIAN. ROBERTSON
MEMORIAL CHURCH
  Church records.   UCA-W

  Annual reports; financial records; minutes;
  historical items including biographies of those
  involved in Robertson House, a program of Robertson
  Memorial Church (see vertical file for a 2-page
  history.)

1210. UNITED CHURCH OF CANADA. PRESBYTERIAN. RURAL SURVEY
  Survey, 1914.   UCA-W

  A survey of farms owned and rented in the Swan
  River, Manitoba, area by the Presbyterian and
  Methodist churches.

1211. UNITED CHURCH OF CANADA. PRESBYTERIAN. ST. ANDREW'S
PRESBYTERIAN CHURCH
  Selected materials.   UCA-W

  Minutes of the Deaconess Aid Society, 1911-27;
  report book, 1912.

1212. UNITED CHURCH OF CANADA. PRESBYTERIAN. SPRINGFIELD
PRESBYTERIAN CHURCH
  Church records, 1880-1925.
  Located at Transcona Memorial United Church.

  Minutes of the Women's Auxiliary; church records.

1213. UNITED CHURCH OF CANADA. PRESBYTERIAN. WESTBOURNE
PRESBYTERIAN CHURCH
  Ladies Aid account book,
  1907-25.   PAM (MG7 C4)

1214. UNITED CHURCH OF CANADA.   PRESBYTERIAN.   UNION CHURCH,
      TREHERNE
            Minutes, 1923-31.   UCA-W

            Minutes of the meetings of the Union Church Ladies'
            Aid of Treherne.

1215. UNITED CHURCH OF CANADA.   PRESBYTERIAN.   WOMAN'S
      FOREIGN MISSIONARY SOCIETY
            Multiple volumes.   UCA-W

1216. UNITED CHURCH OF CANADA.   PRESBYTERIAN.   WOMEN'S HOME
      MISSIONARY SOCIETY
            Annual reports, 1905-14.   UCA-W

D. United Church of Canada.   Other

The records of the following churches, church-sponsored
societies or institutions, and "pastoral charges" (similar in
ecclesiastical government to the Roman Catholic "parish") are
in most cases in the custody of the local church of origin or
at the United Church Archives at the University of Winnipeg
(UCA-W).   In the case of the latter, records such as minute
books, birth, marriage and baptismal registers, financial
ledgers and account books, proceedings of auxiliary and
woman's societies and other official materials are presently
being reorganized into a new record group series tentatively
denominated the Pastoral Charge Collection (PCC).   A second
grouping, composed of secondary information on the church or
pastoral charge, such as newsclippings, short histories, and
other collected data, is referred to as the vertical file.
This study will mention the vertical file only in passing (see
"United Church of Canada. Archives" below).

1217. UNITED CHURCH OF CANADA.   ALEXANDER PASTORAL CHARGE
            Records and history.   UCA-W (PCC)

            Alexander Presbyterian/United, 1919; Ladies Aid,
            1913; "Historical Review 1881-1962." Charge
            includes Alexander, Kemnay and Roseland, Manitoba.

1218. UNITED CHURCH OF CANADA.   ALL PEOPLE'S (STELLA)
      MISSION
            Papers, 1922-1923 and
            1959-1971.   UCA (Box B)

            Deaconess work, 1922-73; correspondence;
            Mothers' Club correspondence on the Kindergarten; UCW/WMS

      248

miscellaneous papers.

1219. UNITED CHURCH OF CANADA. ARCHIVES (THE UNIVERSITY OF
WINNIPEG)

UCA-W

As described in the preface to this section, the
Archives has developed a "vertical file" of
resource material on various United Churches and
charges in the provinces. Included are
newsclippings, souvenirs, historical compilations,
snapshots and other unofficial but informative
secondary material on the following churches or
charges (year indicates date of founding).

Arrow River, Augustine Presbyterian/United
(Winnipeg), 1892, Balmoral Methodist and Victoria
Presbyterian, Basswood-Fairmount, Belmond-Hilton,
Beulah, Birtle, Brandon Trinity, Cardale, 1975,
Carman, Chumah, 1883, Current River, Decker, 1917,
Deer Lodge (Winnipeg), 1934, Eastland, 1884,
Elkhorn, Emo-Devlin-LaVallee, 1980, God's Lake
Narrows, 1894, Gordon (Winnipeg), Graysville, 1912,
Gregg, 1895, Grey Street (Winnipeg), 1946, Harrow,
1916, John Black Memorial, 1914, Kildonan
Presbyterian, 1851, King Memorial (Winnipeg),
Kirkfield Park, (Winnipeg) 1981, Knox United
(Winnipeg), 1868, Maclean Mission (Winnipeg), 1928,
McCreary, 1905, Marney, Meadowwood (Winnipeg),
1981, Melgrund, Miniota, Minniaska, 1966, Moore
Park, 1914, Morden-Knox, 1911, Neepawa Methodist,
1881, Nesbitt, 1892, Newdale, Norwood (Winnipeg),
Oak River, 1880, Oxford (Winnipeg), 1981,
Palmerston, 1910, Pettapiece, Pilot Mound, 1981,
Rapid City, 1909, Regent's Park (Winnipeg), 1908,
Reston, 1950, Riverview (Winnipeg), 1907, Robertson
Memorial (Winnipeg), Roblin, 1916, Rosedale
(Winnipeg), 1922, St. Andrews-Elgin Ave.
(Winnipeg), 1881, St. Andrews (River Heights,
Winnipeg), St. Giles (Winnipeg), 1884, St. John's
(Winnipeg), 1926, St. Paul's (Winnipeg), 1901, St.
Stephen's Broadway (Winnipeg), 1895, St. Vital
(Winnipeg), 1948, Silver Heights (Winnipeg), Souris
Elgin, Sperling, 1884, Strathclair, 1873, Sturgeon
Creek (Winnipeg), 1893, United Church Women
Presbyterian, Wawanesa, 1896, Westminster
(Winnipeg), 1892, Young United (Winnipeg), Zion
(Winnipeg), 1874.

1220. UNITED CHURCH OF CANADA. ATLANTIC-GARDEN CITY
(WINNIPEG)
Records, 1926.   UCA-W (PCC)

249

1221. UNITED CHURCH OF CANADA. AUGUSTINE
PRESBYTERIAN/UNITED CHURCH
Church records, 1892.   UCA-W (PCC)

1222. UNITED CHURCH OF CANADA. AUSTIN-SIDNEY-EDRANS
PASTORAL CHARGE
Church records, 1895-1913.   UCA-W (PCC)

Records of the following constituted churches:
Sidney Methodist, 1901; Austin Methodist/United,
1895; Arizona Mission Presbyterian, 1890; Austin
Presbyterian/ United, 1907; Edrans
Methodist/United, 1913. The Austin-Sidney records
also include Arizona, Austin, Castle Point, Deer
Range, Edrans, Ellwood, Elkpark, Emmeline,
Fairdale, Forestville, Helston, Melbourne,
Melville, Orangeville, Pleasant Point, Sidney,
Sight Hill, Springbrook, Valley Stream.

1223. UNITED CHURCH OF CANADA. BEAUSEJOUR PASTORAL CHARGE
Church records.   UCA-W (PCC)

Beausejour Presbyterian/United, 1906;
Beausejour-Tyndall, St. Owen's Presbyterian, 1891.
Alma, Baldur, Belmont.

1224. UNITED CHURCH OF CANADA. BELMONT-BALDUR PASTORAL
CHARGE
Church records.   UCA-W (PCC)

Records of the Alma Presbyterian Church of Belmont, 1906;
of the Greenway Methodist Church of Baldur, 1884; of the
Greenway Presbyterian Church of Baldur, Manitoba, 1909.
Also records of Alma, Baldur, Belmont,
Craigilea, Dry River, Glenora, Greenway, Maringhurst,
Roseberry, Tisdale.

1225. UNITED CHURCH OF CANADA. BOISSEVAIN PASTORAL CHARGE
Church records.   UCA-W (Vertical file)

Records of the following churches:
Boissevain Methodist, 1887; St. Paul's United, 1925;
Ninga Methodist/United, 1899; Whitewater Presbyterian,
1898. Items from the following charges or
preaching points: Lyonshall United, Rowland, Wood Lake,
Wassawa, Max Lake, Mannerman Mission, Desford, Wakopa,
West Lake, Hazeldean.

1226. UNITED CHURCH OF CANADA. BOWSMAN/MINITONAS/BIRCH
RIVER PASTORAL CHARGE
Church records, 1901-29.   UCA-W (PCC)

250

Bowsman River, 1929; Minitonas Methodist, 1901;
Minitonas Presbyterian, 1902.

1227. UNITED CHURCH OF CANADA.   BRANDON CENTRAL PASTORAL
CHARGE
Church records, 1883-1925.   UCA-W (PCC)

First Church Methodist, 1883; Brandon Methodist,
1892; St. Paul's Presbyterian, 1883; St. Paul's
United, 1925; First Presbyterian, 1884; Assiniboine
Mission (Methodist); Central United; First Church
Methodist/United; Kemnay Presbyterian/United;
Little Souris.

1228. UNITED CHURCH OF CANADA.   BRANDON-KNOX PASTORAL CHARGE
Records.   UCA-W (PCC)

Victoria Avenue, Methodist, 1909; Brandon Woman's
Presbyterial and WFMS, 1893.

1229. UNITED CHURCH OF CANADA.   CARBERRY PASTORAL CHARGE
Church Records.   UCA-W (PCC)

Carberry Methodist, 1884; Summerville WMS, 1910;
High Bluff-Oakland, 1934; Wellwood, 1894; also
churches in Bates, Brigden, Carberry, Century,
Eastland, Freemont, Mariposa, Petrel, Summerville,
Wellwood.

1230. UNITED CHURCH OF CANADA.   CARROLL PASTORAL CHARGE
Church records, 1907.   UCA-W (PCC)

Carroll Presbyterian (Carroll, Nesbitt, Berbank)

1231. UNITED CHURCH OF CANADA.   CHURCH HOME FOR GIRLS
Records, 1945-76.   UCA-W (PCC)

Records of the MacMillan House Project.

1232. UNITED CHURCH OF CANADA.   CRYSTAL CITY PASTORAL CHARGE
Church records, 1884-1922.   UCA-W (PCC)

Rosebud, 1917; Clearwater, 1922; Crystal City
Methodist, 1884; Crystal City Presbyterian, 1891;
Crystal City; Darlingford; Immanuel; Opawaka;
Thornhill; Zion.

1233. UNITED CHURCH OF CANADA. DARLINGFORD PASTORAL CHARGE
Church records. UCA-W (PCC)

Calvin Presbyterian, 1919; Darlingford Methodist,
1898; Barclay; Calf Mountain; Darlingford;
McFadden; Opawaka; Thornhill.

1234. UNITED CHURCH OF CANADA. DELORAINE PASTORAL CHARGE
Church records. UCA-W (PCC)

Deloraine Methodist, 1897; Deloraine Presbyterian,
1902; Deloraine-Hazeldean, 1925.

1235. UNITED CHURCH OF CANADA. DUGALD PASTORAL CHARGE
Church records. UCA-W (PCC)

Millbrook, Clearspring, Caledonea, Point du Chêne
Presbyterian, 1880; Dugald (Plympton) Methodist,
1884; Dugald (Plympton) Presbyterian, 1880; and
items from Bird's Hill P.O., Caledonea,
Clearsprings, Dugald, Dundee, Hazelridge,
Millbrook, Oakbank, Pineridge, Plimpton, Prairie
Grove P.O., Point du Chêne, Queens Valley,
Richland, Ridgewood, Rosewood, Rossmere, St.
Anne's, St. Boniface East, Sunnyside.

1236. UNITED CHURCH OF CANADA. FELLOWSHIP OF PROFESSIONAL
WOMEN
Papers, 1936-80.
5". UCA-W (PCC)

Reports of regular meetings (monthly) of Women's
Union and of annual meetings, 1946-75; annual
financial reports of Women's Union, 1936-77; list
of representatives of WA groups to Women's Union
and nominating committee slates, 1948-78; minutes
of monthly regular meetings and executive meetings
of Fellowship of Professional Women, 1949-72;
membership lists, 1950-51 and miscellaneous
correspondence; Winnipeg membership list, 1964-75;
membership and active members lists, 1949; Reports
of National conferences, miscellaneous
correspondence, National Executive Minutes; minutes
of regular monthly and executive meetings, 1954-75;
national and local constitutions; list of members,
1979-80 of Association of Professional Church
Workers (note name change).

1237. UNITED CHURCH OF CANADA. FISHER RIVER
METHODIST/UNITED CHURCH
Church records, 1894. UCA-W (PCC)

1238. UNITED CHURCH OF CANADA. GLENBORO PASTORAL CHARGE
      Church records.   UCA-W (PCC)

      Glenboro Presbyterian, 1887; Glenboro Methodist,
      1895; Glenboro (Stockton) Methodist, 1892; Glenboro
      United, 1934; also items from Glenboro, Hilton,
      Stockton, Treesbank.

1239. UNITED CHURCH OF CANADA. GORDON-KING MEMORIAL UNITED
      CHURCH
      Operating files. Church Records, 1903-80.
      Located at 127 Cobourg Avenue, Winnipeg, Manitoba,
      R2L 0H4.

      "Book of Memories" (a detailed history with
      photographs and clippings); women's group
      materials; church records.

1240. UNITED CHURCH OF CANADA. GREENWOOD METHODIST
      Church records, 1915.   UCA-W (PCC)

1241. UNITED CHURCH OF CANADA. GRISWOLD PASTORAL CHARGE
      Church records.   UCA-W (PCC)

      Griswold Presbyterian, 1894; items from Griswold,
      Huntington and Monteith, Manitoba.

1242. UNITED CHURCH OF CANADA. HAMIOTA PASTORAL CHARGE
      Church records.   UCA-W (PCC)

      Chumah; Hamiota; Oakner; Scotia; Hamiota-Scotia,
      1882.

1243. UNITED CHURCH OF CANADA. HARTNEY-LAUDER PASTORAL
      CHARGE
      Church records.   UCA-W (PCC)

      Hartney Methodist, 1919; Lauder Methodist, 1913;
      Lauder Presbyterian, 1911; Melgund Methodist, 1896.

1244. UNITED CHURCH OF CANADA. HIGH BLUFF OAKLAND PASTORAL
      CHARGE
      Church records.   UCA-W (PCC)

      High Bluff Presbyterian, 1908; East Prospect
      Presbyterian, 1890; Prospect Presbyterian, 1899;
      Oakland, 1937; Murray United (Oakland), 1962;
      histories, anniversary celebrations, guest books;
      High Bluff Union, 1924-26; High Bluff United, 1925;

253

High Bluff, Portage Creek, Prospect Presbyterian
(one record book), 1873; Assiniboine; East
Prospect; Flee Island; High Bluff; Jackson;
Oakland; Poplar Point; Portage Creek; Prospect;
Setters.

1245. UNITED CHURCH OF CANADA. HARSTONE MEMORIAL CHURCH,
WINNIPEG, MANITOBA

Church records, 1946-   .   UCA-W (PCC)

1246. UNITED CHURCH OF CANADA. HOME STREET, WINNIPEG,
MANITOBA
Anniversary publications.   UCA-W (PCC)

"Golden Jubilee: Home Street United Church,
1906-1956"; "Diamond Jubilee, Home Street United,
1906-76."

1247. UNITED CHURCH OF CANADA. HUNGARIAN UNITED CHURCH
Church records, 1906- (Hungarian).
Located at 732 Ellice Avenue, Winnipeg, Manitoba,
R3G 0B4.

Church records and those of the Woman's Auxiliary,
1934.

1248. UNITED CHURCH OF CANADA. JUSTICE PASTORAL CHARGE
Church records, 1934.   UCA-W (PCC)

Justice, Moore Park, Creford, Minnedosa, Manitoba.

1249. UNITED CHURCH OF CANADA. KILDONAN METHODIST/UNITED
CHURCH
Church records, 1924.   UCA-W (PCC)

1250. UNITED CHURCH OF CANADA. KILLARNEY UNITED CHURCH
Church records and registers (1890-1967).
Located at 432 Williams, Killarney, Manitoba, R0K
1G0.

Records and registers, 1890-   ; Presbyterian and
Methodist records and registers till union;
Killarney Methodist WMS, minutes, 1918-25;
Presbyterian Church WMS, newsclippings, minutes,
1911-25; Minutes of First Presbyterian WMS also
contain letter on unification of Erskine WMS and
First United Church WMS, questionnaires, letters
and documents on church union, and lists of

opposers and a petition to Advisory Committee; UCW
Annual Reports, 1926- ; names and addresses of
foster children supported by congregation, 1965-77.

1251. UNITED CHURCH OF CANADA. KNOX UNITED CHURCH
(WINNIPEG)
Church records and registers, 1881-   .
Located at 400 Edmonton Street, Winnipeg, Manitoba,
R3B 2M2.

Baptismal, marriage and burial registers;
photographs; minutes of the Geneviève Irwin
Missionary Auxiliary, 1916; WA, 1897; Langside
Circle, 1933.

1252. UNITED CHURCH OF CANADA. LENA UNITED CHURCH
Church records.
Located largely in the Killarney United Church, 432
Williams St., Killarney, Manitoba, ROK 1GO.

Marriage records; WMS minutes, 1920-78; quarterly
reports; financial records; correspondence.

1253. UNITED CHURCH OF CANADA. LITTLE BRITAIN PASTORAL
CHARGE
Church records, 1872- .   UCA-W (PCC)

Little Britain Presbyterian, 1872; Little Britain,
Selkirk, Cloverdale, 1884; Bird's Hill, 1895;
Cloverdale; East Selkirk; Gonor; Highfield;
Highland; Little Britain; Parkdale Station; St.
Andrews; Selkirk; West Selkirk.

1254. UNITED CHURCH OF CANADA. MANITOBA CONFERENCE UNITED
CHURCH WOMEN
Papers, 1958-78.   PAM (MG7 H2)

Minutes and reports, 1962-78; constitution, 1962;
programmes, publications and clippings, 1958-74.

1255. UNITED CHURCH OF CANADA. DEACONESS BOARD AND SOCIETY
METHODIST/UNITED CHURCH
Papers, 1923-37.   UCA-W (PCC)

Minutes, 1923-37; cash books, 1922-37; Minutes of
Manitoba Methodist Deaconess Board, 1923-37 list of
Board and finance committee members, 1923-26.

255

1256. UNITED CHURCH OF CANADA. MANITOU PASTORAL CHARGE
          Church records, 1880- .   UCA-W (PCC)

          Manitou Methodist, 1880; Manitou United, 1925.

1257. UNITED CHURCH OF CANADA. MELITA PASTORAL CHARGE
          Church records, 1884- .   UCA-W (PCC)

          Melita Presbyterian (Napinka, Princess, Otter),
          1897; Antlers Mission, Methodist, 1884; Melita
          Methodist, 1908; Antlers Mission; Broomhill;
          Chertfield; Elma; Maple Grove; Melita; Napinka;
          Princess; Otter; West Brenda.

1258. UNITED CHURCH OF CANADA. MORRIS-ALTONA PASTORAL
      CHARGE
          Church records.   UCA-W (PCC)

          Gretna Presbyterian, 1918; Morris, Silver Plains,
          Union Point Presbyterian, 1879; Morris Methodist,
          1883.

1259. UNITED CHURCH OF CANADA. MURILLO-KAKABEKA FALLS
      PASTORAL CHARGE
          Church records.   UCA-W (PCC)

          Murillo Ladies Aid, 1924; St. Andrew's
          Presbyterian, 1913.

1260. UNITED CHURCH OF CANADA. NAKINA PASTORAL CHARGE
          Church records, 1924.   UCA-W (PCC)

1261. UNITED CHURCH OF CANADA. NEEPAWA UNITED CHURCH
          Church records, 1926-71.   UCA-W (PCC)

          Ladies' Aid Report, 1926; Women's Missionary
          Society Report, 1926; The Cradle Roll, run by
          United Church women, 1935- ; Women's Missionary
          Society; United Church Women became the Women's
          Association, 1947; Red Cross work; hospital work;
          United Church Women, 1961 - U.C. Women combination
          of 4 pages, i.e. (1) Women's Missionary Society;
          (2) United Church Guild; (3) Evening Auxiliary; (4)
          Women's Auxiliary; Evening Auxiliary; United Church
          Guild, 1948-71.

1262. UNITED CHURCH OF CANADA. NINETTE, MANITOBA
          Church records, 1935.   UCA-W (PCC)

1263. UNITED CHURCH OF CANADA. NIVERVILLE, MANITOBA
Church records, 1885- .   UCA-W (PCC)

1264. UNITED CHURCH OF CANADA. NORTHEND WOMEN'S COUNCIL
Papers, 1916-18.   UCA-W

Minute book, 1916-17; minutes of 1916 annual
meeting and the weekly meetings of the Council and
report of 1918 annual meeting (loose pages);
roll/attendance record; financial reports.

1265. UNITED CHURCH OF CANADA. NORTHWEST-INTERLAKE PASTORAL
CHARGE
Church records.   UCA-W (PCC)

Gypsumville, 1933; Grahamdale, 1954; lists of
names, Northwest-Interlake (Ashern) Home missions
record book, 1946; Grahamdale; Gypsumville; New
Scotland; Spearhill; Steeprock; Woodale.

1266. UNITED CHURCH OF CANADA. OAKLAKE, MANITOBA
Church records.   UCA-W (PCC)

Oak Lake Presbyterian, 1904; Oak Lake Union Church,
1922.

1267. UNITED CHURCH OF CANADA. OAKVILLE/ELM CREEK PASTORAL
CHARGE
Church records, 1913- .   UCA-W (PCC)

Oakville/Elm Creek Methodist Church; Bellecourt;
Bethel; Elm River; Mill Creek; Oakville; Plumes;
S.L. Reserve; Willowood; Willow Range.

1268. UNITED CHURCH OF CANADA. OXFORD HOUSE METHODIST
CHURCH
Church records, 1894- .   UCA-W (PCC)

1269. UNITED CHURCH OF CANADA. PLUMAS-LAKESHORE PASTORAL
CHARGE
Church Records.   UCA-W (PCC)

Glenella, 1933; Plumas, 1928; Langruth, 1923;
Langruth Mission, 1923; Glenella, Grocklland,
Goodlands, Bellhampton, 1906; Glenella Mission,
1906; Mekiwin, Berten Village, Knox, Golden Stream,
1913; Plumas Presbyterian, 1902; Glenella, Oakleaf,
Molesworth, Purpleridge, Glenallen, 1911; Langruth
Methodist, 1918; Alonsa; Amaranth Presbyterian;

257

Bellhampton; Berton Village; Campertown; Gladstone;
Glenallen Mission; Glenlea Presbyterian/United;
Goodlands; Helston; Keyes; Knox; Langruth
Presbyterian/United; Mekiwin; Oakleaf; Ogilvie
Presbyterian/United; Plumas Presbyterian/United/
Purpleridge; Rockland. Bellhampton

1270. UNITED CHURCH OF CANADA. POPLAR RIVER, MANITOBA
       Church records, 1895- .   UCA-W (PCC)

1271. UNITED CHURCH OF CANADA. PORTAGE LA PRAIRIE/TRINITY
      UNITED CHURCH PASTORAL CHARGE
       Church records.   UCA-W (PCC)

       Knox Presbyterian, 1884; Grace Methodist, 1884;
       Trinity United, 1941; Burnside United, 1947; Knox
       and Grace United, 1935.

1272. UNITED CHURCH OF CANADA. PRESBYTERY CORRESPONDENCE
       Correspondence, 1935-75.
       Located at 120 Maryland Street, Winnipeg, Manitoba,
       R3G 1L1.

       Correspondence with the following Manitoba Indian
       communities: Birdtail, Cross Lake, Indian Springs,
       Nelson House, Indian Schools, Norway House, Oxford
       House, South Indian Lake, Deer Lake, God's Lake,
       Indian Lake, Pikawgikum, Red South Lake, Sandy
       Lake, Long Plain, Berens River, Fisher River,
       Little Grand Rapids, Poplar River, Roseau River.

1273. UNITED CHURCH OF CANADA. RIVERS PASTORAL CHARGE
       Church records.   UCA-W (PCC)

       Robertson Church, Shanks (Presbyterian), 1898;
       Robertson Church, Pettapiece, 1909; Rivers
       Presbyterian (Shanks, Oak River, Rivers,
       Pettapiece), 1890; Rivers Methodist (Daly circuit,
       Bradwardine circuit, 1904); Rivers, Knox
       Presbyterian, 1916; Aetna; Ancrum; Bradwardine;
       Dayl; Hunters; Moline; Oak River; Pettapiece;
       Rivers; Rosefille; Shanks; Spring Valley;
       Tarlbolton; Westwood; Wheatlands.

1274. UNITED CHURCH OF CANADA. ROBERTSON MEMORIAL UNITED
      CHURCH
       Minutes, 1921-72.   UCA-W (PCC)

       Minutes of the Ladies Friendly Society.

1275. UNITED CHURCH OF CANADA.   ROLAND PASTORAL CHARGE
      Church records.   UCA-W (PCC)

         Roland Methodist/United Church, 1896; Pomeroy;
         Roland.

1276. UNITED CHURCH OF CANADA.   ROSSENDALE PASTORAL CHARGE
      Church records.   UCA-W (PCC)

         Rossendale Presbyterian/United; Burnside Circuit;
         Burnside; Bagot; Fox; Loveville; Image Hil;
         Hartford; Elmwood; Southend; Ellsmith; Edwin;
         Lowenham; Rosehill; Ladysmith; Currie; "50th
         Anniversary of Rossendale United Church."

1277. UNITED CHURCH OF CANADA.   ROSSBURN PASTORAL CHARGE
      Church records.   UCA-W (PCC)

         Rossburn Presbyterian/United, 1907; Rossburn
         Methodist/United, 1891; Angusville; Argyle; Boyle;
         Ranchvale; Rossburn; Silverton; Valley; Vista;
         Culross; Shoal Lake; Kelloe; St. Mary's; Seeburn;
         Perth; Glenelmo; Birdtail Crossing; Oakburn.

1278. UNITED CHURCH OF CANADA.   ROWLAND UNITED CHURCH
      Marriage registers, to 1976.
      Located in the Killarney United Church, 432
      Williams St., Killarney, Manitoba, ROK 1GO.

1279. UNITED CHURCH OF CANADA.   RUSSELL-INGLIS PASTORAL
      CHARGE
         Unpublished history, 1975. By Beatrice Craig.
         Typescript.   PAM (MG9 A102)

         "As It Happened: Russell-Inglis Pastoral Charge,
         1880-1975," with information on Angusville United
         Church, Asessippi-Inglis United Church, Dropmore,
         Castleavery, Grainsby, Rochedale, Miniska,
         Shellmouth and Silverton United Churches, and their
         women's activities.

1280. UNITED CHURCH OF CANADA.   RUSSELL-INGLIS PASTORAL
      CHARGE
         Church records.   UCA-W (PCC)

         Russell Presbyterian/United, 1909; Russell
         Methodist (1884); Angusville; Binscarth; Millwood;
         Miniska; Russell; Shellmouth; Shell River; Silver
         Creek; Silberton; Union.

1281. UNITED CHURCH OF CANADA.   ROWLAND UNITED CHURCH
        Church records.   UCA-W (PCC)

1282. UNITED CHURCH OF CANADA.   ST. ANDREW'S PLACE UNITED
      CHURCH
        Deaconess records, 1911-23.
        Available in the Church and at UCA-W (PCC).

1283. UNITED CHURCH OF CANADA.   ST. PAUL'S UNITED CHURCH,
      MORDEN, MANITOBA
        Church records, 1972-74.   SCRLM (Vertical
                                        files)

        Annual reports, 1972-74; brief typed church
        history; 1976 Parish committee members.

1284. UNITED CHURCH OF CANADA.   SHAUGHNESSY HEIGHTS
        Church records, 1950- .   UCA-W (PCC)

1285. UNITED CHURCH OF CANADA.   SHOAL LAKE PASTORAL CHARGE
        Church records.   UCA-W (PCC)

        Shoal Lake Methodist/United, 1889; Shoal Lake
        Presbyterian/United, 1890; Shoal Lake, McConnell,
        Silver Creek, 1911; Shoal Lake, Oakburn, 1918;
        Kelloe.

1286. UNITED CHURCH OF CANADA.   SOLSGRITH
        Church records, 1926- .   UCA-W (PCC)

1287. UNITED CHURCH OF CANADA.   SOURIS-ELGIN PASTORAL CHARGE
        Church records.   UCA-W (PCC)

        "The Story of St. Paul's: Seventy-Fifth
        Anniversary," n.d.; photo of 1914 WMS picnic;
        Souris-Elgin, Presbyterian and Methodist, 1896;
        Souris-Elgin, Knox Presbyterian, 1919; Bedford;
        Deleau; Elgin; Fairfax; Forbes; Lily; Monteith;
        Millerway; Regent; Souris.

1288. UNITED CHURCH OF CANADA.   SOUTHWEST-INTERLAKE PASTORAL
      CHARGE
        Church records.   UCA-W (PCC)

        Eriksdale, 1927; Clarkleigh, 1892; Chalway;
        Clarkleigh; Eriksdale; Helendale; Lily Bay; Lundar;
        Mary Hill; Oak Point; Parkview; Posen; Seamo.

1289. UNITED CHURCH OF CANADA. SPARLING AND ROBERTSON FRESH
      AIR CAMPS
            Operating files, 1920-36.
            Located at Sparling United Church, 1609 Elgin
            Avenue, Winnipeg, R3E 1C4

            Photographs of camp activities, 1920-27; minute
            book (board), 1936-75; correspondence, 1920.

1290. UNITED CHURCH OF CANADA. STARBUCK PRESBYTERIAN/UNITED
      CHURCH
            Church records, 1906.   UCA-W (PCC)

1291. UNITED CHURCH OF CANADA. SWAN LAKE PASTORAL CHARGE
            Church records, 1899.   UCA-W (PCC)

            Swan Lake Indian Reserve, 1899; Indian Springs;
            Beaconsfield; Somerset.

1292. UNITED CHURCH OF CANADA. TEULON PASTORAL CHARGE
            Church records, 1882- .   UCA-W (PCC)

            Teulon Methodist (Dundas, Woodroyd, Greeridge,
            Woodlands, Windsor, Brand), 1896; Teulon
            Presbyterian (Balmoral, Gunton), 1916; Teulon
            Presbyterian (Greenwood), 1882; Teulon Presbyterian
            (Dundas), 1887; Teulon Presbyterian (Komarno,
            Gunton, Pleasant Home, Sarto, Morris Lake), 1910;
            Argyle; Balmoral; Brant; Dundas; Greenridge;
            Greenwood; Gunton; Komarno; Norris Lake; Pleasant
            Home; Ridgeway; Sarto; Stonewall; Teulon; Victoria;
            Windsor; Woodlands; Woodroyd.

1293. UNITED CHURCH OF CANADA. TRANSCONA MEMORIAL
      (WINNIPEG) CHARGE
            Church records, 1883- .   UCA-W (PCC)

            Springfield Presbyterian, 1883; Yale Methodist,
            1910; Knox Presbyterian, 1920; WMS, 1919; Transcona
            Memorial First Methodist, 1923; Bird's Hill;
            Suthwyn.

1294. UNITED CHURCH OF CANADA. TREHERNE PASTORAL CHARGE
            Church records, 1889- .   UCA-W (PCC)

            Treherne (McCreary Methodist), 1900; Chalmers
            Presbyterian, 1907; Treherne (Rathwell
            Presbyterian), 1902; Treherne (Holland, Bethel,
            Treherne Methodist), 1889; Hatchetville, McCreary,
            Olive, Rathwell, Treherne.

      261

1295. UNITED CHURCH OF CANADA.   TRINITY (ST. BONIFACE)
PASTORAL CHARGE
        Church records, 1952- .   UCA-W (PCC)

1296. UNITED CHURCH OF CANADA.   VALLEY PASTORAL CHARGES
        Church records, 1876- .   UCA-W (PCC)

        Dominion City Methodist/United, 1910; Dominion City
        Presbyterian, 1916; Valley Charge, UCW, 1962;
        Valley Charge Newbridge, 1933; Emerson
        Presbyterian, 1976; Dominion City Presbyterian
        (Greenridge, Langside), 1885; Emerson Presbyterian
        (Roseau Crossing, Dominion City, Emmadale, Green
        Ridge, West Lynn), 1880; Emerson Methodist, 1890;
        Emerson; Emmadale; Greenridge; Ridgeville; Roseau
        Crossing; Stockport; West Lynn; Woodmore.

1297. UNITED CHURCH OF CANADA.   WAWANESA CHARGE
        Church records, 1896- .   UCA-W (PCC)

        Wawanesa Methodist, 1896; Beresford; Brandon Hills;
        Cornwallis; Dalton; Glen Souris; Hebron; Kemnay;
        Little Souris; Nesbit (see also Carrol records);
        Roseland; Rounthwaite; South Brandon; Two Rivers.

1298. UNITED CHURCH OF CANADA.   WESTMINSTER
PRESBYTERIAN/UNITED CHURCH
        Church records, 1894- .   UCA-W (PCC)

        Church registers, 1903-   ; Presbyterian Ladies
        Aid, 1894; Minutes, 1898.

1299. UNITED CHURCH OF CANADA.   MANITOBA PRESBYTERIAL
SOCIETY
        Papers, 1957-70.
        2 boxes.   UCA-W

        UCW (and WMS) Manitoba Conference, annual reports
        from 1957; personnel files; scrapbook, 1963-76;
        Reports, 1969-70; annual reports; miscellaneous
        reports, minutes, constitutions and by-laws.

1300. UNITED CHURCH OF CANADA.   WOMAN'S MISSIONARY SOCIETY
        Papers, 1885-1972.
        12 boxes.   UCA-W

        A wide assortment of annual reports, membership
        listings, minutes, programmes, reports,
        newsclippings, agendas, scrapbooks, histories,
        index files of the Woman's Missionary Society on

the national, provincial and local levels.
Substantial holdings from local Manitoba branches
of the Society represent the following
constituencies:
Birtle Presbyterial (minutes, agenda, 1926-   );
Brandon Woman's Presbyterial (programmes, reports,
newsclippings, delegate lists, 1893-   ); Carman
Presbyterial (annual reports, scrapbook, minutes,
financial records, 1954-71). Manitoba Conference
Branch (early history, minutes, scrapbook of
Selkirk Presbyterial, annual reports, index file,
cash book, 1885-1961); Minnedosa Presbyterial
(minutes, agenda, financial reports, 1907-   );
North District Presbyterial (formerly Selkirk
Women's Presbyterial); Winnipeg Presbyterial
(minute books, reports, annual meetings, clippings,
night school reports, operating records,
1889-1968).

1301. UNITED CHURCH OF CANADA.   ZION UNITED CHURCH
      (DARLINGFORD, MANITOBA)
          Church records, 1912-78.   PAM (MG7 H1)

          Women's Aid Association minute books and membership
          lists, 1912-19; 1944-45; Women's Missionary
          Society minute book, 1946-48; Membership lists;
          Mission band minute books, 1953-77.

Other Churches

1302. OTHER CHURCHES. MANITOBA BUDDHIST CHURCH
          Operating files. Church records.
          Located at 825 Winnipeg Avenue, Winnipeg, Manitoba,
          R3E OR5.

          Founded by Japanese displaced during World War II,
          the Church has two women's organizations. The
          Manitoba Bukyo Fujin Kai, or Buddhist Women's
          Association, organized 1947, is composed largely of
          older, Japanese-speaking women; the Maya club,
          involving younger, English-speaking women, has been
          active since 1958. Both groups provide service and
          upkeep for charity although the Maya Club also
          raises funds for charity through Oriental Bazaars,
          Folklorama and similar efforts.

1303. OTHER CHURCHES. CANADIAN COUNCIL OF CHRISTIANS AND
      JEWS
          Operating files. Restricted.

          263

Located at 110-388 Donald Street, Winnipeg,
Manitoba, R3B 2J4.

An active organization directed by Olga Fuga, the
Council seeks to promote understanding and
awareness among Manitoba's multicultural population
by human relations programmes, student exchanges,
dialogue, conciliation and education which includes
publication, translation of publications and
workshops. Workshop programmes: publications;
lists of scholarship awards (80% are girls); lists
of co-operating groups and individuals; minutes;
reports; financial records.

1304. OTHER CHURCHES. CENTRAL ALLIANCE
        Operating files. Restricted.
        Located at 132 Rouge, Assiniboia, Manitoba, R3K
        1J9.

        The main Winnipeg congregation of this denomination
        contains several large and active women's groups,
        reaching women both single and married,
        professional and non-professional.

1305. OTHER CHURCHES. FAIRBURN SUNDAY SCHOOL
        Selected materials.
        9 pp.   BCA (MG10 B10 and MG7
                                        Ni)

        Betty Anne Turner's memoirs of the Sunday School in
        the 1950s and 60s; manuscript on Fairburn School,
        describing concerts, dances, Fairburn Ladies' Group
        and Sunday School; list of Fairburn teachers,
        1888-1917.

1306. OTHER CHURCHES. FAIRFAX CHURCH
        Selected materials.   BCA (MG7 H6)

        Clippings; programme for 75th anniversary.

1307. OTHER CHURCHES. FLIN FLON, MANITOBA, CHURCHES
        Historical sketches and
        reports.   FFHS/FFPL

        From the following local churches:
        Baptist; Church of Jesus Christ of Latter-day
        Saints (Mormon); Jehovah's Witnesses; Lutheran
        Church; Northern Fellowship; Pentecostal;
        Presbyterian; St. Anne's Roman Catholic; St.
        Peter's Anglican; Salvation Army; Ukrainian
        Catholic; Ukrainian Greek Orthodox; United Church
        of Canada; United Pentecostal.

1308. OTHER CHURCHES, HUTTERITES. JACOB ALDNER
        Essay.
        0.75".   PAM (MG9 A36)

        Social life; customs; historical and religious
        background of this Hutterian sect in Europe.

1309. OTHER CHURCHES, HUTTERITES. WOMEN
        Unpublished paper, by Barbara Harms-Froese.
        1 item.   MHCA (Vertical file)

        "Women's Role in the Hutterite Society."

1310. OTHER CHURCHES. JAPANESE ALLIANCE CHURCH
        Operating files and Church records.
        Contact: Rev. N. Matsubara, 88 Bluewater, St.
        Boniface, Manitoba, R2J 2P8.

1311. OTHER CHURCHES. PENTECOSTAL ASSEMBLIES OF CANADA
        Operating files. Restricted.
        Contact: Ruth Johnstone, 3081 Ness Avenue,
        Winnipeg, Manitoba, R2Y 2G3.

        The women of the Pentecostal Assemblies organized
        into Women's Ministries on a national and district
        level in 1944, with a national director to
        co-ordinate all WM activities. Each of the seven
        Canadian districts is served by a director and
        sectional representatives, while every local group
        seeks to "involve every woman and to encourage each
        one in her ministry."

1312. OTHER CHURCHES. ERSKINE PRESBYTERIAN CHURCH
        Church records, 1900-83.
        Located in Erskine, Manitoba.

        Presbyterian marriage, baptism and burial records,
        1950-83; minute books, 1900-83; session records;
        annual congregational meetings; Women's Group
        minute books, 1944-46; communion records, 1958-83.

1313. OTHER CHURCHES. UNITARIAN CHURCH. ALL SOULS UNITARIAN
        Minute books (Icelandic).   PAM (MG7 K1)

        Organized in 1904 with Margret Benedictsson as
        first president. Ladies Aid minute books, 1904-43.

1314. OTHER CHURCHES. UNITARIAN CHURCH. FIRST UNITARIAN
        CHURCH
        Private journals.

        265

Contact: Prof. David Arnason, University of
Manitoba, Winnipeg.

1315. OTHER CHURCHES. UNITARIAN CHURCH. WESTERN CANADA
ALLIANCE OF UNITARIAN WOMEN
Operating files.
Located at 790 Banning Street, Winnipeg, Manitoba,
R3E 2H9.

Organized in 1926.

1316. OTHER CHURCHES. WINNIPEG CHINESE ALLIANCE CHURCH
Operating files, 1968-   (Cantonese).
Located at 261 Colony Street, Winnipeg, Manitoba,
R3C 1W4.

Records contain information on the women's groups.

1317. OTHER CHURCHES. WINNIPEG CHURCH FOR THE DEAF
Operating files.
Located at 285 Pembina Highway, Winnipeg, Manitoba,
R3L 2E1.

An ecumenical Protestant congregation which shares
the edifice with St. Françis de Sales Catholic
Church for the Deaf. Services are held on Sunday
mornings; Bible classes, a women's group, Sunday
school, marriage counselling, interpretive services
and religious services at the School for the Deaf ·
round out the programme. Church registers;
records.

1318. WOMEN'S INTER-CHURCH COUNCIL.
Papers, 1933-85. Finding aid.
3.0'.   PAM (P857-863)

Originally called the Inter-Board Committee of the
Women's Missionary Societies of Canada, but changed
to its present name in 1946, the Council is an
interdenominational organization administering all
matters relating the the World Day of Prayer (first
observed in 1918). It is also responsible for the
records and financial affairs of the Fellowship of
the Least Coin.

Minutes from 1933 to 1985; constitution and
by-laws; financial records, 1948-82;
correspondence, 1949-79; annual area and committee
reports, 1943-82; related materials such as
handbooks, brochures, newsletters and posters.

Art

1319. ANTIQUE ARTS CLUB OF WINNIPEG
       Papers, 1945-79.
       1."   PAM (MG10 C69)

       Founded in 1945 to foster an interest in antique
       arts and crafts. Minutes, 1951-79; financial
       records, 1946-70; lectures given by and to club
       members, 1951-70; clippings; correspondence;
       constitution; by-laws.

1320. BRANDON ALLIED ARTS COUNCIL
       Operating files.
       Located at 1036 Louise Avenue, Brandon, Manitoba,
       R7A 0Y1.

       Organized in 1959 to promote various art forms such
       as dance, pottery, painting, weaving, ballet and
       yoga. Minutes; reports; programmes;
       correspondence.

1321. BRANDON ART CLUB
       Minutes, 1925-70.   BUA

       Organized in 1907 to develop appreciation of art,
       especially at the public school level. Minutes of
       executive and membership meetings.

1322. CRAFTS GUILD OF MANITOBA, INC.
       Operating files.
       Located at 183 Kennedy Street, Winnipeg, Manitoba,
       R3C 1S6.

       Organized in 1928 to preserve and teach various
       forms of craftmaking. Brief history of the Guild;
       the original charter; minutes, 1934-   ; financial
       records; presidents' addresses 1935, handwritten
       notes on activities of Indian section n.d., British
       section, 1935, and French Canadian section;
       Winnipeg Women's Institute aims and affiliation,
       1934-35; annual reports of the Czecheslovakian and
       German groups, about 1935; Hungarian ladies, 1936;
       Ukrainian Handicraft Guild, 1936; Polish Group,
       1935-36; miscellaneous reports; financial records;
       clippings.

1323. MANITOBA SOCIETY OF ARTISTS
       Papers, 1903, 1925-83. Unprocessed.
       Originals, 2.0'.; and microfilm, 1 reel.
                           PAM

       Organized in 1902 and reorganized in 1925 with the
       objective of fostering the arts and maintaining a
       standard of work within the province recognized and
       respected across Canada.

       Minute books, 1925-72 and 1978-82; correspondence
       relating to exhibitions, membership and Society
       activities; various resource material on the
       Society as collected by Barbary Endres.

1324. SHEWCHUK, JEANETTE
       Interview.
       Contact: Professor Stella Hryniuk, St. Andrew's
       College, University of Manitoba, Winnipeg.

       Transcript of an interview with this artist of
       Ukrainian descent.

1325. SISSONS, LYNN (1889-)
       Papers. Available by appointment.
       In possession of creator.

       Artist. Founder and past president of the Winnipeg
       Sketch Club and president of the Manitoba Society
       of Artists. Photographs; paintings; watercolours;
       oils; pastels.

1326. TYCHOLLS, ANN
       Interview.
       Contact: Prof. Stella Hryniuk, St. Andrew's
       College, University of Manitoba, Winnipeg.
       Transcript of an interview with this Ukraine-born,
       Dauphin, Manitoba, writer.

1327. WOMEN'S ART ASSOCIATION OF CANADA, WINNIPEG BRANCH
       Papers, 1895-96.
       Several items.   PAM (MG10 C4)

       Founded in Toronto in 1891 and organized in
       Winnipeg in 1893 to "disseminate a knowledge of
       art" among women. Minute books, 1895-96;
       membership list; constitution and rules, 1895;
       annual report of the Association and its branches,
       1895; catalogue of first and second annual
       exhibitions, Winnipeg, 1895.

       268

1328. ROYAL WINNIPEG BALLET
          (a) Papers, 1940-77. Finding aid.
          43'.   PAM (MG10 G25)

          Founded in 1928 by Gwenneth Lloyd and Betty
          Hay-Farally (two dancers from England), the Royal
          Winnipeg Ballet is Canada's first professional
          dance company and the oldest continually operating
          ballet in North America. Correspondence, 1960-76;
          tour arrangements, 1966-76; season ticket campaign
          files, 1964-76; newspaper cuttings, 1940-76; issues
          of Ballet-hoo, 1969-76; financial records, 1956-73;
          briefs, 1956-72; triennial fund campaigns, 1968-73;
          publicity and promotion files, 1968-77; publicity
          tapes and photographs.

          (b) Operating files.
          Located at 289 Portage Avenue, Winnipeg, Manitoba,
          R3B 2B4.

          Biographical data, files on all dancers; souvenir
          books, 1942-83; videotaped files of ballets (in
          vault); magazine articles and clippings;
          photographs; biographical sketch (3 pages typed) of
          founding director, Gwenneth Lloyd.

          (c) Videotape recording,
          1977.   PAM (AV D4)

          "Ballet in the Park." The Royal Winnipeg Ballet at
          Assiniboine Park, Winnipeg, dancing "Whims of Love"
          and "Rodeo."

          (d) Richardson, Kathleen Margaret Papers, 1949-73.
          Finding aid.
          8.5'.   PAM (MG10 G28)

          President, 1957-71 Royal Winnipeg Ballet.
          Correspondence; reports; clippings.

1329. WINNIPEG'S CONTEMPORARY DANCERS
          Operating files. Restricted.
          Located at 444 River Avenue, Winnipeg, Manitoba,
          R3L 0C7.

          Founded in 1965 by Rachel Browne. Minutes;
          reports; financial records; lists of dancers;
          programme notes.

Letters

1330. BRADSHAW, THECLA
Literary papers. Partially restricted. Finding
aid.
4.0'.   PAM (P288-298)

Author, editor and poet. Toronto-born Winnipeg
writer interested in the North and its people.
Author of Mobiles (a book of poetry), co-author of
The Indian Child and Education and A Cree Life:
The Art of Allen Sapp, and former award-winning
editor of the Northern magazine.

Manuscripts of articles, television program scripts
and other writings; working files of the Northern
magazine, 1964-73; extensive research files on
Allan Sapp, the subject of her book, A Cree Life,
1968-78; correspondence, assignments, articles and
other materials related to her employment with the
Manitoba Dept. of Tourism, 1968-73; various
biographical and personal papers, 1953-80.

Restricted are correspondence with various authors,
looseleaf notebooks and diaries, and files of
unpublished poetry.

1331. CANADIAN AUTHORS ASSOCIATION, WINNIPEG BRANCH
Papers, 1922-81. Finding aid.
6.5'.   PAM (MG10 C12)

Minutes; reports; newsletters; membership records;
financial records; correspondence and papers;
newspaper clippings; miscellaneous files. Includes
an article by Nan Shipley ("Women Writers of
Manitoba") correspondence of Betty Dyck and Laura
Salvesson.

1332. CANADIAN WRITERS CLUB OF WINNIPEG
Papers, 1937-40.
93 pp.   PAM MG10 C13

Several prominent women were members of this Club,
including Lillian Beynon Thomas. Minutes; by-laws;
reports and correspondence.

1333. CARSON, ANNE
Literary papers.
1 box.   UMA (A82-18)

Poet, librarian. Writings and poems.

1334. GIBBONS, LILLIAN
          Correspondence.
          9 pp.   PAM (MG 9 A96)

          Author, writer and newspaper columnist.
          Correspondence relating to her articles.

1335. HAWTHORNE WOMEN'S CLUB
          Papers, 1923-84. Unprocessed.
          1.0'.   PAM (P882-883)

          Organized in 1923 by a group of women living on
          Hawthorne Avenue in East Kildonan in Winnipeg to
          foster the study of the arts, develop community
          spirit and to advance charitable work among the
          sick and the poor.

          Minute books, 1923-78; programmes and membership
          lists; reports of programme and Music Committees; a
          history, 1960; constitution; newspaper articles,
          1971-84.

1336. JOHNSON, EMILY PAULINE (1862-1913)
          Letter, 1906.
          1 item.   PAM MG A14

1337. KNAPP, MARTHA (1892-1972)

          Writings on her father, Klaas de Jong, Margaret
          Baker, and about Ashton, Manitoba.

1338. KNOX, OLIVE ELSIE
          Literary papers. (Processing incomplete)
          53 pp.   PAM (P 267)

          Born in Fort Stewart, Ontario, Olive Knox lived in
          the United States, Saskatchewan and Manitoba. She
          attended Normal School in Brandon and taught for
          several years before being married to Harold C.
          Knox, teacher and amateur historian. Between 1943
          and 1958 Knox published six popular historical
          books as well as numerous short stories and
          articles. Five short stories: "Fort Garry Post
          Offices," "Watching for the Post," "Letters from
          Fort Garry," "Stories Letters Tell (Re-Smuggling),"
          "The Sayer Trial in Letter (Re-Smuggling"; a radio
          script, "Petticoat Pioneers, with covering letter,
          about 1942; two drafts of pioneer reminiscences -
          Edrans and Gladstone; two typed copies of a letter
          written by Mrs. Isaac Casson in 1928.

1339. LENT, GENEVA D.
      Writings
      10". Typescript.   PAM (MG9 A65-1)

      Manitoba author and journalist.

1340. LIVESAY, DOROTHY (1909-   )
      Papers, 1913-84. Finding aid.
      About 30 boxes.   UMA (MSS 37)

      Poet, author, teacher. Articles on Livesay;
      bibliographies of her work; correspondence both
      personal and professional; interviews; diary notes
      on the 1930s; reports and newsletters; contracts;
      financial papers; drafts of writings; personal and
      literary correspondence with poets; legal papers
      (will, etc.); letters from her parents; diary,
      1927-29; collection of musical scores of her poems
      set to music; family anecdotes, autobiographical
      notes; collections of poems; much more. (See also
      UMA SC29 for a letter from Florence Randall
      Livesay.)

1341. LONGMAN, A.D.
      Papers.   PAM (MG10 C48)

      Materials and programmes of the Poetry Society of
      Winnipeg.

1342. MCLEOD, MARGARET ARNETT (1878-1966)
      (a) Papers Finding aid.
      16 boxes.   PAM (MG9 A76)

      Author, historian. Correspondence; source
      material; drafts of published articles; scrapbooks.

      (b) Papers. Finding aid.
      7 boxes.   UMA (MSS15)

      Correspondence; notes and drafts of manuscripts of
      her book <u>Letitia Hargrave Letters</u> photographs.

1343. ROBERTSON, HEATHER
      Literary manuscripts Unprocessed collection.
      About 3'.   UMA (PC/7 MSS/SC/48)
      Journalist, free-lance writer, author.

      Original drafts of literary manuscripts to her
      books: <u>Grass Roots</u>, 1960; <u>Salt of the Earth</u>, 1974
      <u>Willie</u> 1984
      and others.

1344. ROSE, WILLIAM JOHN
        Literary manuscript.
        1 folder.   UMA (MSS SC 24)

        Unpublished novel by "Wes Turner" entitled Helen of
        Wheatville: A Tale of Winnipeg.

1345. ROY, GABRIELLE
        (a) Scattered materials.   SBHSA (Box #24)

        Author. Early recollections of Manitoba
        (photocopies) and education; newsclipping files.

        (b) Biographical sketch.
        13 pp. Typescript.   HP DEP CW

        "Gabrielle Roy House, 375 rue Deschambault," by
        Sheila Grover.

1346. SHIPLEY, NAN
        (a) Papers, 1953-78. Finding aid.
        18 boxes.   UMA (MSS 21 and
                                     PC 21)

        Author. Manuscripts; articles; correspondence;
        lecture notes; radio series notes; television
        series notes; drafts of publications; original
        hand-written northern Manitoba Indian legends;
        maps; scrapbooks; photographs.

        (b) Papers, 1955-76.
        2.5".   PAM P 268

        Nan Shipley has written extensively on Western
        Canadian Indians and missionaries. Her work
        includes radio and television scripts, several
        hundred short stories and articles, and
        approximately twelve books, among them The James
        Evans Story and Wild Drums. Shipley's special
        interest lies in Indian life and culture, and in
        recognition of her contributions in this area she
        received the 1966 Golden Boy Award.

        Research notes and papers of her work on James
        Green Stewart, 1926-82, chief factor of the
        Hudson's Bay Company; correspondence with the
        Stewart family; genealogical tables; daily journal,
        1901, of Angus McKay, an employee of the Hudson's
        Bay Company.

1347. STOBIE, MARGARET R.
        (a) Papers and research file. Finding aid.
        2 boxes.   UMA (MSS 13)

Native Studies researcher, author, teacher.
Research notes; literary criticisms of Frederick
Philip Grove; correspondence; oral histories with
those connected with or knowledgeable about Grove.

(b) Oral interviews, 1965-78.
4 boxes, 50 reels.   UMA (TC 24)

Sound cassettes, tape reels and transcriptions of
Prof. Stobie's interviews and conversations with
several Manitoba Indians specifically relating to
the Scotch-Cree dialect, "Bungi."

1348. SYKES, EILEEN
       Literary papers.
       2 boxes.   UMA (A84-18, A84-38)

       Author of children's stories. Literary drafts;
       tapes; correspondence.

1349. WADDINGTON, MIRIAM
       Poem, 1978.
       1 folder. Typescript.   UMA(MSS SC 36)

       Poet. Manuscript of her poem, "Mr. Never" (later
       published).

1350. WINNIPEG POETRY SOCIETY
       Scattered materials, 1941-75.
       2".   PAM (MG10 C1)

       Souvenirs; poetry contest; poems.

1351. WINTER, MAE (d. 1983)
       Papers, 1974-84.
       4.5".   PAM (P330)

       Author, novelist, short-story writer.
       Correspondence on her articles and various
       writings; unpublished manuscripts including
       fiction, non-fiction, several children's stories,
       articles and a novel; printed and published copies
       of her writings, including the novel, The Luck of
       the Draw.

1352. ARKIN, NATHAN
      Papers, 1911-72.
      1'.   PAM (MG10 G26)

      Noted Winnipeg collector of Canadiana, theatre and
      music concert programmes. Programmes of concerts
      and recitals sponsored by the Winnipeg Music
      Teachers' Association; the Manitoba Music Teachers'
      Association; Winnipeg Orchestral Club; Winnipeg
      Philharmonic Society; Women's Musical Club; Eva
      Clare; Phyllis Livesay; newspaper clippings of some
      performances and performing artists.

1353. CHARLOFF, ETTA
      Scattered materials.   PAM (MG10 F3 and MG6
                                     D5)

      Clippings, 1951-78, of her musical career (14
      items); score of contata by her son, Aaron, "If I
      Forget Thee, O Jerusalem."

1354. ECKHARDT-GRAMATTE, SOPHIE CARMEN (1902-74)
      Papers, 1905-74.
      Microfilm, 10 reels.   PAM (M597-706)

      Musician, composer and acclaimed violinist and
      pianist. After a life of fame and success in
      Europe, she came to Canada with her husband, Dr.
      Ferdinand Eckhardt, in 1953, when he was appointed
      director of the Winnipeg Art Gallery.

      Chronological list of her compositions; a
      restricted edition of her "Selected Works"; sheet
      music; compositions.

1355. FETHERSTONHAUGH, MARGARET A.
      Papers.   PAM (MG14 C78)

      Programmes, 1926-74; clippings of the Women's
      Musical Club and of the Wednesday Morning
      Musicales.

1356. FESTIVAL MANITOBA
      Recorded music.
      1 phonograph (45 rpm).   PAM (AV C11)

      "Manitoba Cities, Manitoba Towns," and "Lord
      Selkirk Songs," original compositions by Allyson
      Taylor, songwriter.

275

1357. HAHN, LIZZIE
         Musical composition, 1899.   BCA (MG14 G107)

         Copy of her composition, "The Coon's Promenade."

1358. HUDSON'S BAY COMPANY CHOIR
         Recorded music, 1945.   Recorded by CKY.
         2 cassettes (30")   PAM (AV A10)

         Conducted by W.D. Thomson.

1359. IMPERIAL ACADEMY OF ARTS
         Concert programme, 1909.   UMA (MSS SC27)

         Program of a concert by the Faculty of the
         University of Manitoba signed by Caroline Thomas.

1360. JUNIOR MUSICAL CLUB OF WINNIPEG
         Papers, 1902-76.
         1'.   PAM (MG10 C53)

         Formed in 1901 by Miriam Baker, to instruct girls
         in vocal and instrumental music, music literature
         and the encouragement of public performance.
         Minutes; reports; membership lists.

1361. KOSHETZ, ALEXANDER AND TETIANA
         Papers (Ukrainian).
         Unprocessed.   UCECA

         Mr. Koshetz, director the official Ukrainian choir
         during the days of Ukrainian independence after the
         Revolution, eventually immigrated to Winnipeg where
         he continued his musical activities. Mrs. Koshetz,
         an activist in several Ukrainian organizations, was
         also prominent in the choir but in its business
         aspects.

1362. LONGMAN, MRS. A.D.
         Papers.   PAM (MG10 C48)

         Include programmes (1950s) of the Young Women's
         Musical Club Choir.

1363. MCFARLANE, RODERICK (1833-1920)
         Papers. Finding aid.   PAM (MG1 D16)

         Included is a letter, 1908, from Agnes Deans
         Cameron to MacFarlane concerning the history of a
         piano brought through Hudson Bay.

276

1364. MANITOBA REGISTERED MUSIC TEACHER'S ASSOCIATION
      Papers, 1919-81. Finding aid.
      4'.   PAM (MG10 G30)

      Founded in 1919 and incorporated in 1938 to promote
      the teaching of music, encourage annual
      conventions, provide summer course instruction and
      improve musical education generally. Minute books
      of both Winnipeg and provincial organizations;
      financial statements; scrapbooks; newsletters;
      programmes; contest regulations; directories; an
      autographed copy of Louise McDowell's Past &
      Present.

1365. MANITOBA SCHOOLS ORCHESTRA
      Recorded music, 1941-48. Recorded by CKY.
      9 discs (161").   PAM (AV A10 Tapes 6,
                                 7, 8, 9, 12, 17)

      Radio broadcasts of concerts conducted by Filmer
      Hubble and Ronald Gibson with such soloists as
      Esther Cohen, Elaine Wilson, Elsie Jensen and Moira
      Wilson.

1366. MEN'S MUSIC CLUB OF WINNIPEG
      Papers, 1915-80. Finding aid.
      7 boxes.   UMA (MSS 11)

      Membership records; constitution and by-laws;
      minutes; correspondence; publicity; history.

1367. MENNONITE CHILDREN'S CHOIR (OF WINNIPEG)
      Operating files.
      Contact: Mrs. Helen Litz, 20 Appleton Street, North
      Kildonan, Winnipeg, Manitoba, R2G 1K5.

      Founded and directed by Helen Litz. Membership
      lists; programmes; brochures; travel accounts.

1368. SOUTHERN MANITOBA MUSIC AND SPEECH ARTS FESTIVAL
      Selected materials, 1952-75. WRL

      Clippings; programmes; typed history of the 25th
      anniversary of this musical event based in Winkler,
      Manitoba.

1369. SWEET ADELINES
      Operating files.
      Contact: Transcona Regional History Museum, 141
      Regent Avenue West, Winnipeg, Manitoba, R3C 1R1.

      277

Three chapters of this world-wide women's
barbershop singers organized in: Winnipeg, 1956;
Assiniboine ,1973; and Park City-Transcona,
1980-83. Membership lists; music; annual reports;
minutes; publicity.

1370. SCHOOL CHOIRS
Recorded music, 1946-47.   Recorded by CKY.
3 discs (45").   PAM (AV A10)

Radio broadcasts of choirs from Lord Selkirk School
and the Robert H. Smith School.

1371. WEDNESDAY MORNING MUSICALE
Papers, 1933-85.   Accession Inventory.
1.0'.   PAM (P1014-1016)

Founded 1933 with Mrs. A.M. Campbell as president
to promote the study and enjoyment of good music by
providing financial support to young musicians,
sponsoring recitals, and by encouraging original
compositions by Manitoba composers.

Minutes and reports of executive and general
meetings, 1933-83; financial records relating
mainly to scholarships and bursaries, 1946-85;
correspondence regarding programmes and
scholarships, 1956-84; programmes and clippings,
1933-84; and related papers including membership
lists and clippings.

1372. WILLIAMSON, NORMAN J.
Collection of musical concert programmes, 1922-75.
2.5'.   PAM (MG10 G29)

Winnipeg concerts including those from the
Celebrity Concert Series, the Junior Musical Club
and others.

1373. WINNIPEG SYMPHONY ORCHESTRA, WOMEN'S COMMITTEE
Operating files.
Located at 555 Main Street, Winnipeg, Manitoba, R3B
103.

Organized in 1945 to assist the Winnipeg Symphony
Orchestra in fund-raising, organizing school
concerts, and other related ways. Minutes;
reports; financial records; records of activities;
membership lists.

1374. THE WOMEN'S MUSICAL CLUB
(a) Papers, 1905-74. Finding aid.
40". PAM (MG10 C7)

Organized in 1898 for the study, encouragement and advancement of music through concerts and scholarships. Correspondence; minute books; financial records.

(b) Constitutions and by-laws; annual reports, 1906-20. LEG LIB

Sport

1375. BRANDON LADIES BROOMBALL LEAGUE
Operating files.
Located in Brandon with the league executive.

Provides competitive recreation at city, provincial and national levels.

1376. CANADIAN AMATEUR SYNCHRONIZED SWIMMING ASSOCIATION, MANITOBA SECTION
Papers, 1950-79.
20". PAM (MG10 D25)

Minutes, 1959-79; correspondence and papers, 1963-78; financial records, 1950-73.

1377. CANADIAN LADIES GOLF ASSOCIATION, MANITOBA BRANCH
Papers, 1933-84. (Processing incomplete.)
3.5'. PAM

The Canadian Ladies Golf Association was founded in 1913 to establish, promote, conduct and regulate ladies amateur golf at the inter-provincial, national and international levels and to maintain rules and regulations of play and a system of handicapping and course rating. The Manitoba Branch was founded in 1922.

Tournament records including name of event, competitors, scores and handicaps, 1944-78; scrapbooks; minutes of annual and semiannual meetings; financial records including tournament receipts and disbursements, grants and statements; bulletins, reports and notices for the C.L.G.A. and M.L.G.A.; yearbooks; photograph albums.

279

1378. CURLING. BOISSEVAIN HEATHER CURLING CLUB
Selected materials, 1910, 1931, 1975. BCA (MG10 D3)

Minute books; clippings.

1379. CURLING. FLIN FLON, MANITOBA
Selected materials.   FFHS/FFPL

Bonspiel schedule, 1933; ladies' curling history; curling championships booklet, 1967; general history of local clubs.

1380. CURLING. OAK RIVER LADIES CURLING CLUB
Selected materials, 1926-32.
20 pp.   PAM (MG10 D27)

Minutes of annual and general meetings; personnel lists; receipts.

1381. CURLING AND SKATING RINK. NINGA, MANITOBA
Selected materials, 1928-70. BCA (MG10 D2)

Minute book; index of members; ledger; share certificates; letters patent; share books.

1382. FIGURE SKATING. BOISSEVAIN, MANITOBA
Selected materials, 1968-71. BCA (MG10 D7)

Three-minute books; Recorder supplement on 1961-77 skaters.

1383. MANITOBA SPORTS HALL OF FAME AND MUSEUM
Archives museum.
Located at 1700 Ellice Avenue, Winnipeg, Manitoba, R2H 0B1.

Organized in 1975. Collected data on men and women inductees including Judy Moss (swimmer and diver), Joan Whalley (curler), and Sylvia Burka-Loyell (speed skater).

1384. O'DOWDA, ERNEST P.
Papers, 1922-77.
Microfilm, 2 reels.   PAM (MG10 D21 M314 and M315)

Clippings and data on the Winnipeg Ramblers Girls Softball Team, 1923-33 and on the Winnipeg Senior Girls Softball League, 1927-72.

1385. PAN-AMERICAN GAMES (1967) SOCIETY
       (a) Papers, 1963-79.
       18'.   PAM (MG10 D12)

       The actual games were held in Winnipeg 22 July to 7
       August 1967. Correspondence; minute books;
       National Executive Council minutes; press releases;
       financial records; daily events; programmes;
       participation certificates.

       (b) Papers, 1963-71. Finding aid.
       9 boxes.   UMA (MSS 28)

       Administrative papers; committee minutes, reports,
       correspondence and press releases; contracts and
       agreements for construction of the Pan-Am Pool, the
       Velodrome and the University of Manitoba Track and
       Field Stadium; insurance policies; dissolution
       files.

1386. PEMBINA LADIES CURLING CLUB
       Papers, 1947-77.   PAM (MG10 D20)

       Minutes; by-laws; journals; membership rosters.

1387. THACKER, MARY ROSE
       Oral history,1940. Recorded by CKY.
       1 reel (15").   PAM (AV A10)

       Discussion of her career as a figure skater.

1388. THE PAS LADIES FASTBALL ASSOCIATION
       Operating files.
       Located at Box 2915, The Pas, Manitoba, R9A 1R6.

1389. THOMPSON FIGURE SKATING CLUB
       Operating files.
       Located at 226 Mystery Lake Road, Thompson,
       Manitoba, R8N 1S6.

       Granted full membership in the Canadian Figure
       Skating Association in 1967.

1390. WEN-DO
       Operating files.
       Located at 730 Alexander Avenue, Winnipeg,
       Manitoba, R3E 1H9.

       281

Organized in 1979 to teach women self-defense.
Newsletters; correspondence.

1391. WINNIPEG CANOE CLUB
        Papers, 1897-1978.
        2".   PAM (MG10 D23)

        Short history including formation of the Ladies'
        Aquatic Section in 1925; minutes; reports.

1392. WOMEN'S FIELD HOCKEY ASSOCIATION OF MANITOBA
        Operating files.
        Located at 1700 Ellice Avenue, Winnipeg, Manitoba,
        R2H 0B1.

        Minutes; reports; lists of members and executives;
        financial records; photographs; printed materials.

Theatre

1393. ACTORS SHOWCASE
        Operating files, 1951- .
        Located at 800 - 504 Main Street, or 89 Princess
        Street, Winnipeg, R3B 1K6.

        Minutes; records of past performances; press
        releases; lists of personnel; correspondence;
        scrapbooks of reviews; photographs.

1394. BENOIST, MARIUS
        Collection, 1917-75.   SBHSA (Box 2)

        Numerous opera and theatre programmes.

1395. "CARRIAGES AT 10:45: A HISTORY OF EARLY WINNIPEG
      THEATRES"
        Unpublished paper, 1976, by Dorothy Garbutt.
        31 pp. Typescript.   PAM (MG10 F2 Box F-J)

1396. LE CERCLE MOLIERE
        Papers.   A St-B (Drawer 27)

        Manitoba's leading French-speaking theatre group.
        Brochures; letter of Pauline Boutal; clippings;
        reports.

1397. CHILDREN'S THEATRE OF WINNIPEG
Papers, 1951-75.
4'.   PAM (MG10 G27)

In 1951 the Junior League of Winnipeg established a
committee to investigate the possibility of setting
up a Community Children's Theatre Board. The Board
assumed the title of the Children's Theatre of
Greater Winnipeg, and drafted a constitution. The
next year plays were selected, a library was formed
and plans were made for a drama festival. The
Children's Theatre not only staged its own
productions and workshops, but also collaborated
with the Royal Winnipeg Ballet, the Manitoba
Theatre Centre and other groups to bring
entertainment to children.

Minutes, 1957-75, of the Season Ticket and
Evaluation Committees; treasurer's reports;
correspondence, 1959-75, pertaining to ticket
sales, school sales, and the Canada Council;
scrapbooks, 1951-72 of clippings, minutes of
founding meetings, and historical sketches;
statistics and records J(1956-1965) of ticket
sales, school enrollments, productions, and other
information; printed material (annual reports,
board manuals, miscellany).

1398. COMMUNITY PLAYERS OF WINNIPEG
Scattered materials.   UMA (MSS SC 9)

Newsclippings, 1920s to 1930s.

1399. DANIELSON, MRS. HOMFRIDUR F.
Papers, 1936-76.
1'.   PAM (MG10 G24)

Actress, writer, producer, director, adjudicator,
associated with drama circles in Manitoba for over
50 years. Correspondence; papers relating to
training in speech and drama; clippings;
programmes.

1400. DRAMA. MENNONITE
Collected skits and drama (Low
German).   MHCA (Vertical file)

Written by Mennonite women, often about rural
Manitoba women both real and imaginary.

283

1401. DRAMA. WINKLER, MANITOBA
Resource file.   WRL

Articles and photographs on plays performed by the
Winkler Collegiate Institute or Garden Valley
Collegiate; also data on Low German drama performed
between 1953 and 1973.

1402. MANITOBA DRAMA LEAGUE
Papers, 1932-74. Finding aid.
4.5'.   PAM (MG10 G1)

Founded in 1932 by representatives of the United
Farm Women of Manitoba, the Rural Drama Committee
of the Winnipeg Little Theatre and others, "to aid
in the development of the Dramatic Arts in
Manitoba." Minutes of meetings; programmes;
publications; financial records; clippings;
trophies.

1403. MANITOBA THEATRE CENTRE
Papers, 1953-79. Finding aid.
34'.   PAM (MG10 G14)

Founded in 1958 by the merger of the Winnipeg
Little Theatre and Theatre 77. Correspondence and
papers, 1959-79; production files, 1957-75; house
programmes, 1953-79; souvenir programs, 1978;
clippings, 1959-79; photographs; posters; set
designs.

1404. "PAINTED LADIES" THEATRE COMPANY
Operating files, 1979-80.
Located at 730 Alexander Avenue, Winnipeg,
Manitoba, R3E 1H9.

Now defunct, the Company specialized in feminist
drama.

1405. PYPER, NANCY
Selected materials, 1922-71.
6 folders.   UMA (MSS SC 46)

Correspondence about the Winnipeg Theatre and Nancy
Pyper's role therein; programmes.

1406. SINCLAIR, EDITH (1883-1945)
Papers, 1922-44.
5".   PAM (MG10 G22)

Amateur theatre producer and drama critic.
Correspondence; theatre programmes; radio talks;
scripts and scores; material relating to the Drama
Department, Adult Education Committee of the
University of Manitoba; newspaper clippings.

1407. WINNIPEG LITTLE THEATRE
      Papers, 1924-36.
      6'.   PAM (MG10 G16)

      Scrapbooks of newspaper clippings; programmes;
      photographs; correspondence concerning Community
      Players of Winnipeg, Manitoba Drama League and the
      Winnipeg Little Theatre.

Women and Reform

1408. CANADIAN ADVISORY COUNCIL ON THE STATUS OF WOMEN
      Operating and resource files.
      Located at 600-269 Main Street, Winnipeg, Manitoba,
      R3C 1B2.

      A national council appointed to advise the Federal
      Government on matters pertaining to the status of
      women. Its unpublished position papers include
      "Recommedations on Women Returning to the
      Workforce," 1974; "Report on Sexual Assault in
      Canada," by Dianne Kinon; and "Problems of
      Immigrant Women in the Canadian Labour Force, a
      Summary," by Sheila M. Arnopoulos.

1409. CANADIAN UNION OF PUBLIC EMPLOYEES
      Papers, 1943-74.
      18'.   PAM (P21-76)

      The formation of the Civic Employees Federation,
      No. 4, in 1917 is Local 500's earliest antecedent.
      The following year the Federation joined firemen,
      teamsters, electrical, clerical, and waterworks
      employees in a major strike over wages, job
      reclassifications, and the Fowler amendment. With
      the defeat of the Winnipeg General Strike of 1919,
      however, city workers were compelled to sign
      "yellow dog" contracts prohibiting membership in
      trade unions. The Federation remained hampered by
      these restrictions until the mid-1920s. It
      subsequently emerged as the chief rival to the One
      Big Union in organizing civic employees, while the
      International Brotherhood of Electrical Workers,

285

independent locals, and "free service" workers accounted for the remainder. Rechristened the Federation of Civic Employees, the local and the OBU's civic membership were numerically equal by the early 1940s. A Labour Board decision in 1949, however, recognized the Federation as the sole bargaining agent for civic employees in Winnipeg and St. Boniface. These gains were consolidated with the formation of the Canadian Labour Congress in 1956.

For much of its early history, the Federation remained unaffiliated to a labour centre or national union. In 1946 it was an affiliate of the Trades and Labour Congress, but later jumped to the CCL in a jurisdictional dispute. It affiliated with the National Union of Public Service Employees in 1957 and became Local 500. NUPSE and NUPE merged to form CUPE in 1963.

Central Council attendance records, credit reports, correspondence, financial records and minutes; minutes of the Central Council Executive and various committees; Local 500; National Office files; Butterworth-Byers Papers, 1952-73; general files; affiliation files.

1410. CANADIAN UNION OF PUBLIC EMPLOYEES
        Operating files. Finding aid.
        Located at 400-770 Portage Avenue, Winnipeg,
        Manitoba, R3C 0G4.

        Proceedings of annual conventions; contract settlements, 1970-79; current agreements; research reports, 1966-77.

1411. COUNCIL OF WOMEN (WINNIPEG)
        (a) Papers, 1892-1978. Finding aid.
        8'.   PAM (MG10 C45)

        Minutes; correspondence; records; reports; scrapbooks; copies of publications; material on Women's Model Parliament of Manitoba.

        (b) Correspondence with Premier Greenway, from Mrs. Culver, 1889-97.   PAM (MG13 E3)

1412. FEDERATION DES FEMMES CANADIENNES FRANCAISES
        (a) Selected papers.   A St-B
        1 folder, 1941-49.

        Correspondence; brochures.

286

(b) Some letters.
1 box (in the C.M. Boswell
papers).   PAM (MG14 C4)

Correspondence with Mrs. C.M. Boswell on the
formation of the Society.

1413. HIND, E. CORA (1861-1942)
      Agricultural and commercial editor of the Manitoba
      Free Press, a champion of women's suffrage and a
      strong supporter of the Women's Christian
      Temperance Union, the Political Equality League,
      the Quill Club, and the Manitoba Equal Suffrage
      Club.

      (a) Papers, 1922-41.
      3 boxes.   UMA (MSS SC7)

      Diary; correspondence; telegrams; speeches;
      newspaper clippings.

      (b) Letters, 1934 and 1941.
      2 items.   PAM (MG14 C80)

      (c) Oral interviews, 1973.   PAM (AV A3)
      2 reels. Produced by Sheila Rabinovitch for CBC.

      "Between Ourselves - E. Cora Hind."

      (d) Scattered materials.

      (See PAM MG14 C80; MG10 A1; MG13 E1; MG10 C3; MG14
      B45)

1414. ICELANDIC WOMEN'S SUFFRAGE ASSOCIATION
      Minutes, 1909-16 (Icelandic). UMA (Icelandic
                                         Library)

      Organized by Margret Benedictsson.

1415. INTERNATIONAL LADIES GARMENT WORKERS UNION, LOCAL 286
      Papers, 1935-81.
      6'.   PAM (MG10 A32)

      The International Ladies Garment workers Union
      organized Local 216 for cloak workers working out
      agreements with several local manufacturers. Local
      237 was organized soon thereafter and in 1941 Local
      304 was chartered to represent outerwear and
      knitwear workers. In 1967 Local 319 was formed and
      in the late 1970s the four locals merged into Local
      286 as part of a general reorganization. Minutes,

287

1940-78; collective agreements, 1935-80; dues
books, 1954-81; Cherniak, Cherniak and Marantz
files, 1954-70 (this legal firm acted for the ILGWU
at one time); miscellaneous, 1934-81.

1416. LABOUR WOMEN'S GROUP OF GREATER WINNIPEG
      Oral history, 1961.
      1 reel.   PAM (MG10 F2 Box 11
                                     Tape 12)

      Formed in January 1930 for the purpose of
      organizing the Labour Women's Social and Economic
      Conference. Information gleaned from and interview
      between Lionel Orlikow and Mrs. James Aiken.

1417. MCCLUNG, NELLIE LETITIA (1873-1951)
      Politician, author, suffragette.

      (a) Letters, n.d.   UCA-W (Biography
                                    file)

      (b) Historical sketch.   DHM("Manitoba People
                                    File")

      Typescript, clippings.

1418. MANITOBA ACTION COMMITTEE ON THE STATUS OF WOMEN
      Papers, 1967-83.
      2'.   PAM (MG10 A32)

      The Manitoba Committee on the Status of Women was
      organized in 1967 in response to the call for
      briefs from the Federal Royal Commission on the
      Status of Women. In 1971, the group, then known as
      the Manitoba Volunteer Committee on the Status of
      Women with June Menzies chairing, formally
      re-organized as the Manitoba Action Committee on
      the Status of Women (MACSW). Its objectives were
      to inform Manitobans of the recommendations of the
      Royal Commission of the Status of Women, to set up
      educational programs explaining the background and
      implications of these recommendations, to evaluate
      and implement them, as well as to work with
      voluntary organizations throughout the province as
      a clearing house for information relevant to the
      status of women in Manitoba.

      Correspondence, 1970-82, from the office of the
      director; minutes; constitution; organizational
      reports and activities; briefs to various
      departments of government and progress reports;
      conferences and project materials; information from

288

and about several other women's organizations;
publicity and mailing lists.

Some of the unpublished reports and position papers
include: "Abortion" (a pro-abortion position);
"Appointments of Women to Boards, Committees and
Commisions"; "Day Care Needs in Society" (argues
for subsidized day care); "Housing Facilities for
Women in Winnipeg"; "Indian Rights for Indian
Women"; "Indian Women and the Law in Canada:
Citizens Minus"; "Women Who Work for Wages in
Manitoba."

1419. MANITOBA ACTION COMMITTEE ON THE STATUS OF WOMEN,
BRANDON BRANCH
   Operating files.
   Located at 100-113 10th St., Brandon, Manitoba, R7A
   4E7.

   Brandon Branch also serves Birtle, Dauphin,
   Minnedosa, Hamiota and Crystal City. Minutes;
   financial reports; newsletters; outreach projects;
   staff briefs; scrapbook; videotapes.

1420. NATIONAL COUNCIL OF WOMEN OF CANADA
   Papers, 1894-1978. Finding aid.
   2.5'.   PAM (MG10 C47)

   Founded in 1893 and incorporated by a Statute of
   Parliament in 1914 to better "the family and the
   state" and women's societies and associations.
   Yearbooks; newsletters; reports; minutes.

1421. NATIONAL COUNCIL OF WOMEN OF CANADA. PORTAGE LA PRAIRIE
BRANCH
   Papers, 1916-78.   PPPL

   Minutes; treasurer's book; scrapbook.

1422. POLITICAL EQUALITY LEAGUE
   Papers, 1912-14.
   1".   PAM (MG10 C30)

   Organized in 1912 by E. Cora Hind, Nellie McClung,
   Kenneth Haig and Lillian Beynon Thomas with other
   members of the Women's Press Club in Winnipeg, for
   the specific purpose of winning the franchise for
   Manitoba women which was granted in 1916. Minutes;
   petitions; constitutions, 1914.

1423. THOMAS, LILLIAN BEYNON (1874-1961)
        Papers, 1893-1961.
        5". PAM (MG9 A53)

        Author; advocate of equality for women. Articles;
        stories; reviews; correspondence; photographs.

1424. UNITED FOOD AND COMMERCIAL WORKERS UNION, LOCAL 111
        Papers, 1943-83.
        20'. PAM (P132-181)

        The origins of Local 111 lie in two organizations
        established in Winnipeg by the Congress of
        Industrial Organizations in the late 1930s and
        1940s. The smaller of the two was the
        International Fur and Leather Workers Union, whose
        original three Winnipeg locals represented workers
        in various arms of the important local fur and
        leather-processing industry. Soon after the 1955
        merger of the IFLWU with the Amalgamated Meat
        Cutters and Butcher Workmen (AFL), commercial
        laundry workers and retail and wholesale meat
        cutters were also organized.

        The more important of the two precursors of Local
        111 was the United Packinghouse Workers of America,
        which established locals in 1943 in the Winnipeg
        plants of the "big three" - Burns, Canada Packers
        and Swift Canadian. Winnipeg was then the leading
        meat-packing centre for western Canada and the main
        source of processed meats for eastern markets.
        Smaller packers and other branches of the
        food-processing and storage industries were
        organized in the late 1940s and the following
        decade saw locals formed at several flour mills.
        This diversification was reflected in the name
        change in 1960 to the United Packinghouse, Food and
        Allied Workers.

        In 1968 the UPFAW merged with the AMCB and the
        Canadian district was called the Canadian Food and
        Allied Workers. In 1979 both the international and
        the Canadian district became known as the United
        Food and Commercial Workers Union. During the
        1970s the Union continued to extend its membership
        among workers in the food processing industry.
        Although the 1980 closure of the mechanized plants
        closer to the main sources of livestock supply,
        meat packing and food processing in general remains
        a significant employer in Manitoba.

        The formation of Local 111 in 1982 was the
        conclusion of a decade long consolidation movement
        among UFACW locals in the food processing and
        related industries in Manitoba.

        290

Minutes of the Manitoba Provincial Council and its
Education and Political Action Committee; minutes
of the Joint Board, 1946-77, and of the Joint Board
of the Amalgamated Meat Cutters and Butcher
Workmen; minutes, negotiation files, agreements and
grievances, and relevant labour records of the
following UFACW Locals; Local 91 (Fur Workers);
Local 175 (Fur Dressers and Dryers); Local 216
(Canada Packers); Local 219 (Swift Canadian); Local
224 (Burns and others); Local 228 (Small Meat
Packers and Abattoirs); Local 235 (Manitoba Cold
Storage); Local 255 (Brandon Packers); Local 369
(Laundry Workers); Local 405 (Manitoba Sugar);
Local 415 (Meat Cutters); Local 430 (Leather
Workers); Local 471 (Swift and Canada Packers,
Thunder Bay, Ontario); Local 520 (Ogilvie Flour
Mills); Local 534; Local 798; Local 1211 (Catelli
Food Products); International Representative files;
Business Agent/Manager files, 1948-81.

1425. VOICE OF WOMEN, MANITOBA BRANCH
      Papers, 1960-85

      1.5'.   PAM (P1017-1020)

      Organized in Canada in 1960 and the Manitoba
      chapter following year with the objective of
      stopping nuclear warfare. Sponsors peace rallies,
      demonstrations, vigils, knitting projects, letter
      campaigns, international exchanges of speakers and
      visitors in support of anti-nuclear war activities.

      Minutes of executive, committee, and general
      meetings as well as some conferences and council
      sessions, 1961-80; financial records, 1963-77;
      correspondence, 1961-82; printed materials
      including newsletters of both the national and
      local offices, submissions, scrap books and
      reports.

1426. WELLS, MYRTLE ANDERSON (b. 1903)
      Papers, 1960-84.
      0.5'.   PAM (P388-389)

      Along with her husband, Charles H. Wells, a
      life-long Manitoba peace activist and early member
      of the CCF/NDP party. As one of the founders and
      chief supporters of the Voice of Women (VOW) in
      Manitoba, she has contributed liberally of her time
      and means in anti-nuclear, anti-war campaigns and
      participated in peace marches, protests,
      fund-raising efforts and related activities.
      Proceeds from their store, Peace Boutique, were
      likewise donated to the cause.

Correspondence, 1962–84, relating to various peace
and disarmament movements and with such other
kindred associations as Women's International
League for Peace and Freedom, Operation Dismantle,
and Project Plowshares; reports, briefs, and
speeches, 1967–82, many of which pertain to human
rights and the status of women; various papers
pertaining to VOW including newsletters,
photographs, correspondence and scrapbooks.

1427. WINKLER, HOWARD W.
Papers, 1859–1971.
10'.   PAM (MG14 B44)

Manitoba politician. Collection includes letters,
1914, from his sister, Hazel Winkler, expressing
her views on the suffrage movement, Nellie McClung,
and other political activists of the time, and also
from Valentine Winkler.

1428. WINKLER, VALENTINE (1864–1920)
Papers, 1884–1920.
3.5'.   PAM (MG14 B45)

Businessman, politician and Minister of
Agriculture. Ledgers; account books; cash book;
letter book; journal of his visit to the Chicago
World's Fair, 1893; correspondence, 1898–1920;
references to suffrage for women.

1429. WINNIPEG WOMEN'S CULTURAL AND EDUCATIONAL CENTRE, INC.
Operating files.
Located at 730 Alexander Avenue, Winnipeg,
Manitoba, R3E 1H9.

Feminist Centre opened in 1979 as an amalgam of
several women's organizations including Brigit's
Books; Clothing Depot and Drop-in Centre; Resource
Library containing feminist material both in print
and on tapes and cassetes; Wen-Do, People on
Welfare (POW), Committee Against Violence Towards
Women; Lesbian Mother's Defense Fund; Painted
Ladies Theatre Co.; Artemis Reproductions; Women's
Line, Media Arts; Graphics; Ideas Co. (MAGIC) and
Women in Trades. Complete set of Harpies.
Correspondence; reports; minutes; financial
records.

A P P E N D I X

SELECTED PHOTOGRAPH COLLECTIONS

Note: While short references to photographs are scattered throughout this bibliography, the larger collections of historical photography are listed here.

1430. B'NAI B'RITH YOUTH ORGANIZATION
        Located at 2nd floor, 419 Graham Avenue, Winnipeg,
        Manitoba, R3C 0M3.

        Over 1,400 photographs.

1431. BOBERSKY, IVAN
                                    UCECA

        Approximately 10,000 glossy prints and negatives
        (almost half of them of Manitoba) documenting
        Ukrainian life.

1432. BRANDON GENERAL HOSPITAL
                                    BGHA

        Photographs from approximately 1883; newsclippings;
        historical sketches.

1433. BRANDON MENTAL HEALTH CENTRE
                                    BMHCA

        Photographs of staff, patients, living conditions,
        buildings.

1434. BRANDON UNIVERSITY PHOTOGRAPH COLLECTION
                                    BUA (R81-10)

        Finding aid.

1435. DARTNELL, VALERIE
        Located at 4T-716 Strathcona Avenue, Winnipeg,
        Manitoba, R3G 3E8.

1436. MANITOBA DEPARTMENT OF EDUCATION
                                    DEL

        Collection of photographs on various aspects of
        Manitoba history.

1437. MANITOBA DEPARTMENT OF EXECUTIVE COUNCIL INFORMATION
      SERVICES
        Located at 514-401 York Avenue, Winnipeg, Manitoba,
        R3C 0P8.

        Some 10,000 transparencies taken since 1970 on all
        aspects of Manitoba society.

1438. PROVINCIAL ARCHIVES OF MANITOBA, PHOTOGRAPHY DIVISION
        Tens of thousands of photographs, many well-indexed
        and on the history of Manitoba and the Northwest.

1439. RESTON AND DISTRICT HISTORICAL MUSEUM
        A substantial photograph collection housed here.

1440. TRANSCONA REGIONAL HISTORY MUSEUM
        Located at 141 Regent Avenue West, Transcona, R2C
        1R1.

        Over 1,000 photographs, postcards and greeting
        cards.

1441. UKRAINIAN CULTURAL AND EDUCATIONAL CENTRE ARCHIVES
        Photograph collections.   UCECA

        Dmytro Harapiati's professional photographs
        (wedding, family, children and other portraits)
        from Vorgue Studio; the personal family collection
        of Thomas and Olena Kobzey; the Olexander and
        Tetiana Koshitz Collection; Ukrainian Refugee Camp
        pictures; daily life pictures of Ukrainian society;
        2,000 to 3,000 postcards celebrating Christmas,
        Easter, and other special occasions.

1442. UNITED CHURCH OF CANADA
        Picture collection.   UCA-W

        Photographs, slides and lantern slides on:
        associations; buildings; camps; Indians; missions;
        outposts; personalities; schools; Winnipeg
        buildings.

1443. UNIVERSITY OF MANITOBA.   DEPARTMENT OF ARCHIVES AND
      SPECIAL COLLECTIONS
                                  UMA
          Several photograph collections of interest to
          women's history including those of Margaret
          Konantz, the University of Manitoba Information
          Office (pictures of people, places and events on
          campus since 1900), Heather Robertson, U. of M.
          Alumni Office, T. Glendenning Hamilton Collection
          of Psychic Phenomena (including meduims and seance
          participants), Margaret McLeod, H. Bruce Chown
          papers on RH negative blood studies in mothers and
          infants, Nan Shipley, and others.

          By far the single largest photograph collection is
          that created by the Winnipeg Tribune. There are
          600,000 to 750,000 prints and photos mainly
          concerned with Manitoba news, 1940-80.

1444. UNIVERSITY OF WINNIPEG.   RARE BOOK ROOM AND LIBRARY
          Photograph and archival collections. (1871-1984).
          Located at the University of Winnipeg Library, 515
          Portage Ave., Winnipeg, Manitoba, R3B 2E9.

          In addition to some 6,000 photographs, the
          University of Winnipeg Archives contain documents
          on the University and its founding colleges
          (Manitoba; Wesley; and United); University
          publications; staff and faculty files and papers.

1445. WESTERN CANADA PICTORIAL INDEX
                                  WCPI/U of W

          A selected assortment of approximately 15,000
          slides of Manitoba and Western Canada history
          produced from prints and negatives from private and
          public collections throughout the province.
          Available for viewing through its cabinet-display
          system.

1446. WINNIPEG FREE PRESS
          Located in the Winnipeg Free Press Library, 300
          Carlton Street, Winnipeg, R3B 2Z2. Access
          restricted.

          Over 1,000,000 negatives and glossy prints on
          Manitoba history over the last century.

299

303

307